THE SHIPHUNTERS

Another spout erupted just to our starboard, the spray glistening in the sun. We were running into their range now, but Robbie kept straight. Three more columns shot up in quick succession, one so close that I thought it must get number three, but he was still flying.

The ships were looming large now. It was time we were taking some sort of avoiding action. Immediately ahead, the sea began to break into little holes. We were running into the anti-aircraft stuff. In a second it was all around us, the sea boiling viciously.

I pulled away from the leader, kicking the rudderbar to put the aircraft in a series of violent skids.

Scarlet lines of tracer arced gracefully towards us, then, gathering speed, whipped by in a deadly dotted line.

I realised with a shock that the ships were not line astern. They were deployed in a V-formation with the tanker at the bottom, and we were flying into it . . .

THE SHIPHUNTERS

R. E. Gillman, DFC DFM

A STAR BOOK
published by
the Paperback Division of
W. H. ALLEN & Co. Ltd

A Star Book

Published in 1979
by the Paperback Division of
W. H. Allen & Co. Ltd.
A Howard and Wyndham Company
44 Hill Street, London W1X 8LB

First published in Great Britain by
John Murray (Publishers) Ltd 1976

Copyright © R. E. Gillman 1976

Printed in Great Britain by
Cox & Wyman Ltd, London, Reading and Fakenham

ISBN 0 426 18761 X

Contents

ILLUSTRATIONS

SOURCES

Commercial Aircraft Division, British Aircraft Corp., Filton, 1; Imperial War Museum, 2, 3, 5-14; K. C. Jordan drew the plan appearing as No. 4.

There is a plan of the Blenheim instrument layout at the foot of page 36.

Foreword

by Air Marshal Sir Ivor Broom
KCB CBE DSO DFC AFC

I FIRST MET Ron Gillman in Malta in November 1941. He arrived, as he thought, for a refuelling stop in his Blenheim aircraft en route to the Middle East – but he was to go no farther.

I was the only officer in No 107 Squadron, having just been commissioned after the squadron had lost all its officers. For a few weeks we were a squadron of sergeant pilots. The dynamic Air Officer Commanding, Air Vice-Marshal Hugh Pugh Lloyd, replaced his losses daily by 'intercepting' crews who theoretically were bound for the Middle East – and so Ron Gillman and his crew joined No 107 Squadron.

In 1941 it was vital to the success of the North African campaign to destroy enemy shipping carrying supplies to General Rommel from Italy via Tripoli. Two Blenheim squadrons daily flew low over the Mediterranean in search of these ships which were then attacked from a height of 50 ft. If no shipping was sighted, the Blenheims swept along the North African coastal road and attacked troop convoys, petrol lorries, coastal airfields and barracks which were supporting Rommel's campaign.

The story of the siege of Malta has been told elsewhere. Ron Gillman's story is of the Island on the attack and illustrates just one of the many reasons why it was besieged by enemy air and naval forces. Supplies to Rommel could never be assured whilst Malta remained as a springboard for attack. The shipping which escaped daylight attacks from Blenheims was sought out by Wellington bombers in various harbours by night. On several occasions aircraft took off as bombs fell on Luqa airfield and the quite magnificent ground crew hastily filled the bomb craters before the aircraft returned. This book is a story about flying – but none of it would have been possible without the tremendous support of all those ground crew who endured much hardship.

Ron Gillman's modesty prevents him from mentioning one point of detail. In December 1941 he received the immediate award of the Distinguished Flying Medal for a determined and successful mast-high attack on an enemy convoy. I know how well he deserved that award – I led the raid.

He has emphasised in the preface that this book is based entirely on his memory of two hectic months in that Blenheim squadron and he has used several fictitious names to avoid any possible distress to living relatives of those many young men who died. I can, however, vouch for the truth of this story which entirely captures the atmosphere among this rapidly diminishing band of sergeant pilots. It has reminded me vividly of many of the incidents which Ron Gillman describes.

IVOR BROOM

December 1975

Author's note

IT IS MORE than thirty years since I flew in low-level Blenheims, but the pictures still burn brightly in my mind. Perhaps this is because I was only twenty years old at the time, and ripe to be impressed with the realities of war. It is a personal story, but in setting it down, I was not moved by common vanity: there is a deeper reason which has lingered with me through all these years, the belief that one day the circumstances would be right for its telling.

The situation arrived unexpectedly a few months ago when the medical officer told me as gently as he could that my flying days were over and that the time had come for me to hang up my headset. I felt sadness but not rancour, for my life has been full and good, moving in the element which delights me and working among men who enjoy broader horizons than most; for me, this is the time to look back and to remember those who were not as fortunate as I.

Much of the action takes place from the tiny Mediterranean island of Malta involving an operation that was miniscule in relation to the total field of war, but for the young men involved it was their world, and for far too many of them that is where it ended.

Perhaps some of my colleagues may be embarrassed by my treatment of the story, when the convention among flying folk is to understate events, but I am anxious to get over if I can a true picture of what it was like for those caught up in the machine and from whom the power of choice was taken.

I have had to rely solely on memory as I failed to keep a diary at the time, so perhaps I may be forgiven for any errors and omissions there may be. I have merely attempted to describe the sequence of events as I recall them.

It would be inexcusable if I reopened wounds long healed by time, so I have changed the names of most of the persons involved, but to all my friends of that far-off time, both flying and ground crew, I offer this heartfelt tribute.

R.E.G.

CHAPTER ONE

Genesis

I SUPPOSE THAT in everyone's life, however disorganised they may be, there is a date, or a day, so deeply embedded in the memory it can never be erased. So it is with me. Mine was a Sunday, in the autumn, in the late 1930s.

As was customary, some student friends and I were strolling in a desultory fashion to the local pub, too engrossed in our discussions to notice much about us. There were four including me. One of us, Rob Walham was learning to fly with the RAF Volunteer Reserve and on alternate week-ends made his way to Gatwick where, as he put it, he 'wrestled with a Tiger Moth for two falls or a submission'.

I forget what subject had our attention at the time: probably politics. Like most students, we were left-wing to a man and ardently pacifist, appalled at what Hitler was doing in Europe and ashamed of Chamberlain with his slip of paper.

I do remember that the streets were quite empty of people and that a skittish wind chased the remains of the Saturday night rubbish in little dashes across the pavement, and swirled the dust into eddies in the pale autumn sunlight, but when I think back on our continual preoccupation with the events in Europe, I find it hard to understand why we were so unprepared for the events that followed.

Quite suddenly, in the middle of a sentence, Roy stopped walking. We turned in question, and then heard it too; the rising wail of an air-raid siren.

'God, not another flipping practice!' said Dicky.

'It's probably an alert for a Gatwick Tiger lost over London,' said Rob with a grin.

Practice air-raid warnings had become so common at that time, we took no further notice and returned to our discussions. When a policeman cycled past wearing a tin hat and blowing a whistle, this was still normal routine, but I remember being startled when a huge grey shape began to appear above the roofs of the shops near by.

It was, of course, a barrage balloon with its loose ears flapping in the breeze, reminiscent of a large grey elephant as it rose majestically into the sky. Then others appeared in the middle and further distance. With increasing height, more and more became visible until it seemed that the sky was filling with a massive herd to stand guard over the City. We all agreed that this was the most complete exercise we had seen so far.

We were now approaching our favourite pub. Although it was not yet opening time, the barman was in the doorway and he was gesticulating to us. There was something odd about the urgency of his manner and our pace quickened as we crossed the road.

'He's never been this pleased to see us before,' said Rob, but his voice was half serious.

'Come on you lot!' the barman shouted as we got within earshot. 'Get in here quick!'

Involuntarily we broke into a run and arrived at the door in some confusion. 'What's up?' we asked.

'What's up!' he said. 'The bloody war's started, that's what's up!'

The shock chilled me. On his directions, I stumbled down the steep ladder into the cellar. A number of people were already gathered there. I recognised one of the barmaids sitting on a crate with a baby in her arms. She was rocking gently to and fro and tears were running silently down her face. The publican was opening bottles with a brisk sense of purpose and passing them round. I sat on the edge of a rack feeling numb but relieved that I didn't have to talk.

Tubes from the huge wooden casks disappeared up through the ceiling, and I found myself wondering if the crude rafters would be able to support the weight of the masonry that would surely come tumbling down when the holocaust began. I looked at Rob. His face was very white. The realisation had come to him that flying for the Reserves was no longer a game. Tomorrow he and many like him would be in the First Division.

The barman had now taken the centre of the floor and was encouraging the assembly to follow him in a popular song of the day which he sang with more gusto than conviction. I noted an elderly woman, probably a relative of the publican, attempting with trembling fingers to get her gas mask out of the case. This sent another pang through me. I hadn't got mine; none of us had. Another thing: my parents were at home; they were elderly and without help. I felt caught out; angry at my own inadequacy. A feeling of bitterness was growing rapidly inside me at the thought of being forced into this position in the privacy of our own country.

The singing was now raucous and I was irritated by the thought that we couldn't hear what was going on overhead. Then the singing straggled away into silence. Everyone was listening; and I too heard the 'All clear'. The burden of distress relieved itself almost physically.

Throughout the night of 3 September 1939 I found sleep impossible, as did many other people I have no doubt. The reality of the situation was shocking. My convictions about the logic and practice of pacificism, which I had held so strongly and which I had followed with such youthful fervour, quite suddenly became suspect in the light of that day's events. I had always been impressed by the story of Mahatma Gandhi's followers lying down under the batons of the Indian Police until that worthy body became frustrated, and quoted the incident frequently in support of my arguments in favour of passive resistance; but what now? What to do when the bombs start falling? I couldn't really see myself lying down in the garden of my father's house to any good effect, neither did I relish the prospect of becoming a conscientious objector.

That night I turned traitor to my beliefs. In the morning I rose early, dressed myself with unusual care and made my way with a sense of purpose to the nearest recruiting office. The place was alive with confused activity and it was some time before I faced the sergeant in charge and told him of my decision. He didn't seem impressed. The Royal Air Force didn't need pilots, he explained; it was quite organised and ready for the task. However, if I really wanted to make quite sure that Great Britain would emerge triumphant from the conflict, I could do no better than to enlist as a fitter-airframe, or even a rigger. This was not my idea at all: it had never entered my head. I excused myself and regained the street a free man.

The sudden determination to become a pilot was all the more extraordinary as it had never occurred to me before. This doesn't mean to say that I wasn't crazy about flying: before becoming involved in serious study, many happy hours had been spent in the public enclosure at Croydon Aerodrome, head stuck through the railings to get a better view of the proceedings, or craning up to watch an aircraft side-slipping over the boundary fence with a fine swish of wings. More recently, I had listened with absorption to Rob Walham's story of his love affair with a Tiger Moth, but the idea of myself being at the controls of an aircraft was too outlandish to be seriously considered. I cannot really account for the sudden change of heart. Perhaps I felt instinctively that in the present emergency the authorities would take any material however unpromising and if I didn't make it now, then I never would.

Whatever the motivation, I decided to press on, discounting my first rebuff with the thought that the recruiting sergeant at Streatham had been, in all probability, a little suburban in his outlook anyway. I sought out recruiting offices in the more sophisticated areas such as Chelsea, Kensington, and even Kingsway, but it was five expeditions and as many months later that I found myself signing the form on which were such vital statistics as my father's Christian names and occupation, any identifying marks on my body and whether I had a history of haemorrhoids.

The Air Ministry had now realised that it would need more pilots than the gallant few, but the war machine was gathering pace slowly, and it was not until the summer of 1940 that my call-up papers arrived together with a travel warrant to Babbacombe and detailed instructions as to what I should bring with me for my life in the Royal Air Force. On the same day, I learned that Rob Walham had been killed in a flying accident.

I don't suppose that my goodbye was very different to many others that were taking place at that time, my father looking clearly proud though rather ill at ease, and mother finding it difficult to talk, not least because she had a handkerchief pressed tightly against her mouth. Many such groups were crowding the platform, and I was relieved when a shrill blast on the guard's whistle brought an answering toot from the engine and I felt the train begin to move under me and gather speed past a flurry of waving hands. I remained at the window until they looked like little pink flags fluttering in a distant breeze, then took my seat and slowly drifted into daydreams about the great new life that lay ahead.

On arrival at Babbacombe a sergeant with shiny brass buttons and a red face, recognising me as a recruit presumably by some God-given intuition, ordered me in a voice half-way between a shout and a woman's shriek to join a group of nervous young civilians each clutching an attaché case similar to mine, 'At the double!!' This was very different from the attitudes of the recruiting sergeants whom I had met so far; they had been courteous and extremely reasonable people, I thought. So had been the staff at Uxbridge, where I had spent two days taking the entrance examination and explaining to kindly officers why I wanted to join the Royal Air Force as a pilot. This man was clearly a very different animal; he didn't seem to have much idea at all.

He lined us up in threes and on the shout 'Quick march!' we moved off in some confusion. Periodically I did a little stagger as the case swung by the man behind caught me at the back of the knees. I looked round to protest, but he appeared to be quite unconscious of what he was doing, and anyway he was well over six feet tall. The local inhabitants appeared to view our progress with a mixture of resentment and alarm which was not difficult to understand. If we were the cream of British youth, then the future must have seemed far from certain.

I got the impression that Babbacombe didn't know what had hit it when the RAF set up an induction centre there. Respectable hotels with such names as Seaview, Silver Wings and Clifftops had been rudely commandeered, and stripped of their curtains, carpets and tablecloths. Bare trestle tables were crammed in the dining-rooms and more iron bedsteads filled the bedrooms than would ever have been approved by the local Chamber of Commerce. Indignity was heaped upon indignity as airmen clumped up and down the stairs in heavy boots, and steaming cauldrons of Irish stew were dragged across the floors from the kitchens and lifted on tables in front of lines of hungry airmen, each clutching his issue tin plate, knife, fork and spoon.

For me, the next fourteen days proved to be a period of traumatic adjustment. Behaviour which had been quite acceptable at home, and indeed had been condoned by kindly parents, was anathema apparently to the officers and NCOs RAF.

We were told to report on breakfast parade at 0730 hrs the first morning. I remember feeling particularly tired and reacted rather badly when a corporal burst open the door of the room in which eight of us had dreamed the night away shouting at the top of his voice, 'Wakey! Wakey! Rise and shine! On your feet you 'orrible lot! You're in the Air Force now!' I retreated farther under the blankets trying to hide from the growing racket as the other inmates milled around the single wash-basin. Eventually the noise dwindled away and I rose with dignity to complete my toilet alone. The hotel was surprisingly quiet as I made my way downstairs, and the sight that greeted me on emerging from the front door was unnerving. All of the men were lined up in the road and a sergeant was calling the roll. With a certain cunning I attached myself to one end of the line when attention was concentrated elsewhere and was gratified to have made it before they got to the G's. We were then told what had been arranged for the first day; it seemed an awful lot. I wasn't sure that I could get it all done. Besides, I was getting hungry and my attention was beginning to wander.

A corporal marched on to the road, stamped to attention, threw up a salute with such vigour that his arm bounced as if on springs, and handed a clipboard to the officer. This was scrutinised with some solemnity and then passed to the sergeant who read it, raised his head and shouted, 'AC2 Gillman!'

This was the second shock of the day. I staggered forward murmuring, 'Er yes; that's me. I'm Gillman—'

'Get back in the ranks!' shrieked the sergeant. 'And stand to attention!'

The officer made his way towards me. I was full of apprehension. Perhaps my mother had died, or Aunt Jane; she had been ill for years. The officer was speaking. 'Gillman, it has been reported to me that you failed to make up your bed this morning.' I blinked. He went on, 'I shall overlook it this time as you are new to the Service, but if it happens again, you will be put on a charge. Do you understand?'

I didn't but I said weakly, 'Yes.'

'Sir!' shouted the sergeant.

'Sir!' said I.

I found the incident very disturbing. It had never occurred to me to 'make up' the bed. I wouldn't know how. In the past it had always been something that just happened when I was out during the day. If there was to be so much drama over such a trivial thing, I trembled to think of my future in the RAF.

My fears were well founded. During that first day I was shouted at by a corporal for walking with my hands in my pockets, chastised for whistling in a moment of misguided cheerfulness, stopped by an officer for failing to salute and reprimanded by a warrant officer because I did salute him. My morale slid finally into the basement at the uniform stores when, having been told to hold out my arms, they were then loaded with a wild assortment of paraphernalia given with the compliments of a grateful government.

'Vests, woolly, airman for the use of.' 'Caps, forage.' 'Tunic, dress, other ranks.' 'Belt, webbing, ceremonial.' 'Socks, woollen, blue', and countless other goodies including a button stick and a housewife. This last item turned out to be a small cloth wallet containing a packet of needles, cotton, darning wool, spare buttons, etc. They really did seem to be expecting too much of a normal civilian, male, life for the enjoyment of.

Before lunch we were told to change into our uniforms. No tape-measure had been in evidence during the uniform parade; one was adjudged either small, normal, or big. The very personal idiosyncrasies of one's anatomy were of no account apparently. My tunic in coarse blue serge was excruciatingly tight across the shoulders but very full at the bottom, giving a flared skirt effect. Add to this a pair of narrow trousers and enormous boots to gain the final bizarre effect.

By bedtime, my morale had sunk to the lowest ebb, and the prospect of my ever being at the controls of an aeroplane seemed very remote indeed. I could sympathise with how the troops must have felt after Dunkirk.

But things did improve during our induction course, and at the end of two weeks, during our march to the station on our way to the Initial Training Wing, if we weren't a credit to the Guards, then at least we were walking in the same direction and at approximately the same speed.

In the military world, names can be very deceiving. When a Navy man at a shore station talks of his cabin, he means his room in the mess, and his bunk is a bed. During the train journey to

Aberystwyth, I looked forward eagerly to the prospect of getting close to an aircraft at the Initial Training Wing. When we arrived I was dismayed to find that there was no aerodrome, no aircraft and not even a control tower. We were billeted in hotels again and faced with the prospect of a four-month ground training course, but at least we were getting on to flying subjects such as navigation, radio, aerodynamics, aero engines, meteorology and aircraft recognition. Even drill sessions became pleasurable, and pride came with expertise. Some of the lecture halls were in the University and others scattered around the town, and we marched between appointments at a cracking pace, arms swinging, heads held high, the white flashes in our forage caps signifying that we were cadets, and our faces showing that we were proud of it.

The autumn arrived in a rush of gales that smashed the sea against the promenade and threw it high in the air, but nothing was allowed to interfere with the pre-ordained routine. With a fine disregard for the elements, our physical training instructor had us sweating in shorts and singlets performing routines normally reserved for prize-fighters; each session seemed like an assault course on our bodies and on our senses. At other times, we went on forced marches over the wind-swept hills and down into the shelter of the lush green valleys, singing in time with the rhythm of our marching feet popular songs of the day, or those from our fathers' war.

The average age of the course was around twenty to twenty-one, each young man a volunteer. In such an environment it wasn't possible to stay sluggish; the vitality stimulated by personal and corporate pride was quietly fostered. They did a good job, the officers and staff of the Initial Training Wing. In a few months they converted a motley bunch of civilians into a body of fit, keen, and alert young men nicely prepared for the tasks ahead. When a course moved on, I wonder if they stopped to consider that more than half of them would not live beyond another year. Probably not; there was hardly time for such thoughts.

By mid-November, the hurdle of the final examinations cleared, we found ourselves once more assembled in full kit and ready to march. It was midnight when we moved off towards the station, the officers and NCOs carrying shrouded lights at the front and rear of the column. The regular tramp of feet echoed through the sleeping town, and then the hitherto silent men began to hum the tune of The Men of Harlech, gently at first, and then with growing strength. Those who knew the words began to sing out, and voices swelled until, to a man, we were singing boldly. This was no time to leave a town in furtive stealth. We were marching to Armageddon!

Number 11 Elementary Flying Training School was based on the attractive grass airfield at Scone, near Perth. There was still a lot of groundwork to be covered, but the prospect of climbing into an aircraft was getting excitingly close. The year 1940 brought a hard winter, and by the time I was told to report to the hangar, the Sidlaw Hills and the Grampians had white shoulders set against the background sky of clearest blue. I was shivering partly with cold and partly with nervous anticipation as I struggled into the 'Sidcot, aircrew, for the use of,' and sat on the cold stone floor to pull on the fleece-lined boots. Some of the Tiger Moths on the tarmac had already started their engines, and their sharp crackle echoed in the hangar roof. I pulled on the cold leather helmet and slinging my parachute over my shoulder made my way outside.

The keen air was fanned into gusts by the whirling propellors and there was an exciting tang of high-octane exhaust fumes. I arrived at my aircraft at the same time as my instructor. He nodded curtly towards the rear cockpit and shouted above the din, 'Make sure your straps don't foul anything!'

Climbing on to the wing and then into the narrow cockpit was difficult with the cumbersome parachute pack hanging behind the knees, and the heavy flying suit, boots and gloves restricted all movements to a slow and clumsy pace.

The cockpit seemed even more confined as I slid down into the bucket seat and looked around for the safety harness. This consisted of two webbing straps that came over the shoulders and two from fittings on the floor. I had difficulty in finding the lower ones as they had slipped under the seat, and almost incapable of movement, I had to feel for them with groping fingers. Struggling and sweating, I finally got the quick-release pin through the lugs of all four and I looked up to see my instructor in the front seat impatiently banging the ear-pieces of his helmet. Clearly, he wanted me to plug in my speaking-tube.

It was then I discovered that the Gosport tubes of my own helmet were trapped under a welter of parachute straps and safety harness. There was nothing for it but to undo the harnesses and start again. The instructor craned his head round and I caught an impatient glare as he realised my predicament.

While still immersed in my struggles, I heard the shout, 'Switches off! Throttles closed! Suck in!' repeated from the fitter, who now swung the propellor with such force that the whole aircraft rocked. Then came the cry, 'Contact!' The aircraft rocked again, followed by a startling crack as the engine fired. The slipstream was vicious in the open cockpit and the goggles were whipped from my head to dangle and fret from the strap at the back of the helmet.

We were taxying by the time I had re-fastened the harnesses and plugged in the speaking tube, the tail skid scraping over the rutted frozen ground.

'I'm with you, Sir,' I shouted into the mouthpiece.

'About bloody time!' came a small but irate voice in return. 'Keep your hands and feet clear of the controls during the take-off.'

I was surprised to see that we were already in mid-field. He swung the machine sharply into wind. The note of the engine rose to a clattering roar as he opened the throttle. The icy slipstream snatched at my face making breathing difficult and I tried to crouch behind the tiny windscreen. In a matter of seconds, I felt the tail coming up. The wheels were still bumping and bouncing over the ruts. Then came the magic moment. I felt the dual-control column moving back gently between my knees. We were lifting. The wheels made two more bumps and then were silent. The white and green streaks of the frozen field were flashing by underneath, but receding.

I looked out past the wingtips to see that we were already rising above the hangar roofs and we seemed to be going more slowly. The earth was falling away and the horizons widening, revealing a distant landscape not seen before. Apart from the force of the slipstream, the aircraft seemed to hang almost stationary in the crystal air. I craned my head round and saw that the fir trees on the airfield boundary had lost their detail and looked like a bank of dark moss tinged with snow, while the hangars appeared as tiny black huts grouped around the postage-sized tarmac. To the north, the Grampians, so impressive from the ground, had now modestly subsided to show an even grander line of snow-capped beauties in the far distance.

I looked around in shivering wonder at the privileged view, conscious of a sense of escape from the tawdry details of earth.

I had never imagined it could be like this. The spell was cast and I knew it.

CHAPTER TWO

Raider in the dark

THAT FIRST TRIP was the only occasion during my time at Perth when I was able to sit back and enjoy the view. The war machine had eaten deeply into the reserves of aircrew during the autumn and the pressure was on the schools to keep the supply coming. The pattern of work was half a day in the classroom and half a day in the air striving to put into practice all the theory that we had so far absorbed, and the first week was the worst. In such a situation, there was no time for nursing. If a pupil had not demonstrated his aptitude in six hours flying, then the axe had to fall. His training was suspended and he was posted back to a pool where he could re-muster as a navigator or air gunner or accept his discharge. To young men dedicated to becoming pilots, none of the alternatives was acceptable, and this background added to the strain when one was grappling with a wayward machine in a hostile environment and not knowing half the time what was happening.

The Tiger Moth has no vices as such, but it is difficult to fly accurately and it is this feature which makes it such a good trainer. Its birdcage structure of struts and flying-wires induces drag and affects stability, so that to fly it accurately around the circuit demands good co-ordination of hand, foot and eye. But it was the landing which gave most trouble. Having a bicycle undercarriage and a tail-skid, it had to be set neatly on the ground on all three points simultaneously, otherwise it showed off. But the three-point landing is a bit more difficult than it looks; let me explain the technique for the benefit of those who have never tried it.

A descending approach is made to the airfield at a speed slightly in excess of the stall, that is, the speed at which all lift is lost and the aircraft goes out of control. Once the airfield boundary is crossed, the rate of descent is reduced in a smooth 'flare' which, if properly executed, results in the aircraft flying level fractionally above the ground. As the speed decays, so does the lift; but this must be resisted, for if the wheels touch when the tail is still in the air it will tend to swing down on impact, rotating the aircraft, increasing the angle of attack of the wings and their lift; so the machine takes-off again, but with the speed falling. The correct technique, having flared, is to keep the aircraft flying level fractionally above the ground by moving back the control column slowly, substituting angle of attack for speed, thus keeping the lift constant. This is continued until the machine attains its 'sitting' attitude just as it touches the ground. If the manoeuvre is rushed, then too much lift is generated and the air-craft climbs way or 'balloons'; leave it too late and the Tiger touches main wheels first and bounces. Remember too, that in a single-engined aeroplane of this kind, when the nose is high in the landing attitude, the pilot has no forward view; he must hang his head over the side and squint along the fuselage. Add to this the fact that on anything but the calmest day, gusts and windshears toss the aircraft about in a random fashion and quick reactions on the controls are needed to compensate.

The landings gave me a great deal of trouble initially; I just hadn't got the feel of the aircraft and my anxiety grew as I taxed the patience of my instructor and saw the number of hours 'dual' in my logbook approaching the fatal figure. After about five hours, I had mastered the take-off, circuit, and approach reasonably well, but control during the landing was variable. Time after time we bounced back into the air to a cry of 'I've got her!' from the small voice in the speaking-tube and the roar of the engine as he gave it full throttle, caught the bounce, and climbed away for yet another circuit.

Deeply worried by my own incompetence, I made my way to a quiet corner of the tarmac during a free period, so that I could watch the aircraft unobserved. The stream of Tigers coming into land was continuous and I was surprised to see how many of them were having my sort of trouble. The bounces and masterly recov-eries were spectacular, but never so much so as the odd pupil on a solo trip trying to land off a goodly bounce, dropping a wing on the way down and hitting the ground on one wheel with great force. But it was the good landings that I watched intently; there was something about the way the aircraft changed attitude just prior to settling that reminded me of a bird alighting. I must have got the feel for it as my first landing the next day was a real 'daisy-cutter'.

'Good Boy!' whooped the small voice. 'Do me another. Just like that!'

This I did, and another, and another; but the fourth! – I lost it completely. The instructor caught it with a touch of throttle, brought the aircraft waffling down into the grass again, and then, during the landing run, he kicked on rudder in a vicious turn towards the tarmac. This was obviously the end. I sat back helplessly, feeling the despair creeping up through my cold body.

Once on the tarmac, the instructor began to climb out, leaving the engine running. This was not unusual, for on occasions crews changed over without stopping the engine and then it was the rule that the pupil would remain in his place until another pilot had climbed into the other cockpit.

I sat slumped where I was. He was certainly taking his time about getting out. Then I realised he was fastening the safety harness to avoid it fouling the controls. He lifted and fastened the small door-flap of his cockpit and then turned to me, still standing on the wing. He pulled away the leather earflap of my helmet and shouted against the noise of the engine, 'OK, Bo. Off you go, and make it a good one!'

I just gaped at him, but he climbed off the wing and walked away. It took me several seconds for the implications to sink in. He intended me to go solo! I felt the control column banging my knees and I looked out to starboard to see the mechanic at the wingtip waggling the aileron, indicating that I should turn that way towards the field. I opened the throttle slowly, but the power wasn't enough to drag the tailskid over the concrete. More and more throttle now with the stick held back and the aircraft starting to shake; then it broke away and swung round the mechanic, who let the wingtip go as I rolled onto the grass.

It took me an unconscionable time to taxi to the leeward boundary and even longer before I had completed the elementary take-off drill and satisfied myself that there was an adequate gap in the stream of landing aircraft for me to get off. I turned the aircraft into wind, had a last look over my shoulder to see that I wasn't fouling anything on the approach, and then pushed the throttle slowly fully open.

The situation was irreversible now; whatever happened I had to go and, what was more, I had to get myself down again. I lifted the tail as it gathered speed, bumping and clattering over the hard ground. Not too high, or the propellor will touch the ground. Fifty miles an hour now. Check that swing with a push on the rudder-bar. Fifty-five. Ease the stick back – gently. At the lesser weight, the machine fairly leaped into the air. It was airborne, but the speed was too low! I flattened the climb and with agonising slowness the speed crept up to the sixty-five figure.

During the climb-out, the tension eased and I began to feel that wonderful sense of freedom again that had come to me on the first flight. There was no instructor in the cockpit in front of me; I had a clear view ahead. The aircraft felt light and responsive. It was my ship, modest though it was, and I, the master.

I turned onto the downwind leg and checked the circuit. Three aircraft were in a staggered climb-out, a number were manoeuvring across the field like hesitant insects, and there were two ahead of me. I followed them round leaving a fair spacing, and on the cross-wind leg, checked the airfield again. The point of throttle closure to start a glide approach is quite critical. I felt we were there; it was time to start on down.

On closing the throttle the roar and rattle of the engine subsided, to be replaced by the whistle of wind in the rigging-wires. The nose swung to the left as the propellor torque fell away and I corrected with the rudderbar, easing the nose down to maintain the approach speed while trimming out the stick load with the 'cheese-cutter', the crudely simple elevator trim. Of the two aircraft ahead of me, one was now on the ground, and the other approaching the airfield boundary. I intended going behind him and landing on his starboard side to give myself plenty of room.

My turn onto the final approach must have been pretty well judged, for I didn't have to touch the throttle again, neither was I too high over the hedge; now for the landing!

I leaned my head over the side, the slipstream fretting at my goggles. The ground was coming up to meet me now – but fast!

Don't overdo it! Christ, you've left it too late! Whip the stick back!

The late and rapid correction was overdone. The wheels didn't hit the ground, but the descent flattened rapidly and quickly reversed into a steep climb. We were ballooning! Fifty feet up and approaching the stall! I pushed the stick forward harshly, seeking the sanctuary of the ground. The nose pitched down, but this time I checked the descent earlier and we were flying level just above the ground.

The speed was down to fifty and the wind noise a low whistle. The engine ticked over hesitantly. Time was in suspension. Then she began to sink. Ease the stick back, slowly, smoothly, don't rush it, more, more – right back – and it worked, the wheels started making grinding noises and the tail touched almost immediately. Down in one piece although without polish.

I sagged with relief after those anxious moments and the warm glow started to come back. But I relaxed too soon! With the tail on the ground, the Tiger went into a swing to port and was heading straight for the aircraft which had landed ahead of me and which was now stationary. With urgency, I pushed on full right rudder, but it wasn't having effect. There are no wheel-brakes on a Tiger and the metal tailskid sliding over the frozen ground wasn't giving much drag. We weren't going to stop in time.

There was only one thing for it. I grabbed the throttle and thrust it forward. The engine coughed, then surged into life with a roar and the slipstream over the tail hit the offset rudder and swung the machine in a bouncing arc over the rutted ground. The other aircraft turned towards the tarmac and taxied away still with his back to me. He never saw what had happened, but I had little doubt that my instructor was watching somewhere over there by the line of parked aircraft.

I moved on to the tarmac at a snail's pace and waited until the mechanics had put the chocks in place before cutting the engine. As I fussed with my straps, I was conscious of a figure approaching the cockpit and knew it was my instructor. I really did not want to meet him just now, but he was smiling.

'Not the most polished arrival I've ever seen,' he said, 'but having ballooned you took the right corrective action and got away with it. You must watch that habit of relaxing once you've got the thing down. The landing's not finished until you've stopped rolling.' Considering he must have had a mild heart-attack when watching my antics, I couldn't help but admire his phlegmatic approach. I didn't feel quite such an ass, and his casual 'See you tomorrow' as he walked away made it seem that I did have a future.

Exuberance took me through the rest of the day, and in bed that night my mind went back over the past week as if I had just completed an era, which in a way I had. My morale had been deteriorating steadily. During the flying sessions to which I looked forward with such eagerness, I had become exasperated at my own incompetence and more deeply anxious as time went on, until that morning when we had taxied back to the tarmac and I was convinced that that was the end.

Looking back, I realise that I was sent solo at the psychological point. One more bad landing would have destroyed me, but he must have decided that I had just enough technique to survive. The finest judgement or a calculated risk? Whatever his reasons I shall be eternally grateful. His name was Sergeant Ansell, a fine example of that dedicated breed of outward-giving men who did a humdrum job with skill, patience and quiet devotion.

Many others were not so fortunate, for about a third of the course failed to make the grade; each day, friends and acquaintances were seen to be packing their kitbags and setting off alone on their way back to the pool.

For my own part, increasing confidence brought sheer enjoyment with each flight, some of which involved advanced dual instruction while others were for solo practice. The syllabus included cross-country flying, aerobatics, forced landings and precautionary landings into a small reserve field some distance from Scone. By now the snow was deep, and only the tops of the fencing posts marked the boundaries like dotted lines.

For my last solo trip of the course, I was sent off solo to practise aerobatics. Over the past three days, the school had been grounded by very low cloud, heavy snowflakes drifting down from a sullen overcast; but the weather now cleared, and by mid-morning pristine white cumulus clouds were sprouting actively in a blue and fertile sky.

I crouched behind the windscreen getting what protection I could from the bitter slipstream as the aircraft gained height, on course for a patch of clear sky some miles south of the airfield. It would take some twenty minutes to reach 5,000 ft, the rate of climb falling away at the greater height until one felt that the machine never would make the necessary altitude. The flying-wires were vibrating in a blur, and one could sense rather than see the fabric covering of the wings drumming.

By 5,000 ft I was numb with cold, but I put the aircraft into a vertical turn to see that nothing else was in my patch of sky or underneath me before I went into the first manoeuvre, which was to be a spin.

Levelling the wings, I closed the throttle, held the torque swing with my feet and kept the nose up. The lack of engine noise and slipstream was a blessed relief, and there was a period of gentle peace until the tension mounted as the needle of the airspeed indicator approached the stalling speed. The stick was now right back in my stomach, the nose high in front, and then she went. A slight shudder and the nose plummetted down, the controls no longer answering.

For a spin, full rudder is applied at this point. The aircraft yaws, the inside wing stalls first and the aircraft whips onto her back in a vicious arc, the nose falls farther and the spin tightens rapidly. Now in a vertical dive, the aircraft is rotating around its own axis; but rapidly. The 'G' forces press one hard down into the cockpit until one feels breathless. The whine of the tortured rigging rises alarmingly. Despite the sensations of noise and pressure, the aircraft appears to be stationary and the patchwork pattern of the earth spins in a swift rotary blur inducing a feeling of giddiness.

Full opposite rudder is required for recovery. The rate of spinning slows down and stops. We are now in a vertical dive, the nose pointing down at a saner, stationary world. During the pull-out, the wind noises subside as if in relief, the engine gives a nervous cough, picks up, and once again we are climbing back to height.

For a loop in a Tiger, one has to put the nose well down and dive at half throttle to pick up the necessary speed, then the stick is pulled back. Again, the unseen forces of gravity press the head into one's shoulders. As the nose comes above the horizon, full throttle is applied to keep it climbing, but the stick is kept coming back. Now vertical, the clouds are seen directly in front of the nose, and further rearward movement of the stick pulls the aircraft over on top of the pilot as it were, the wheels pointing at the clouds and his head underneath. As the horizon is seen coming up for the second time, the throttle is closed and the machine pulled out of the ensuing dive.

If the loop is accurately flown, one suffers no negative 'G' effects when the aircraft is inverted; the centrifugal force acts as a counter and one just becomes light on the seat, but a slow roll is very different, and if the safety harness is not tight the hapless pilot feels himself coming out of his seat as the machine rolls onto its back.

There is a wondrous sense of freedom when aerobating in a vast and empty sky. One becomes part of the machine and anything is possible. One can dive and wheel with the grace of a soaring bird, climb vertically and as speed is lost, cartwheel over the wingtip in a stall turn, or roll lazily onto the back and pull it through in the second half of a loop. One can change the pace by flicking into a spin then pulling out and climbing straight into the graceful contour of a loop again.

A fulsome ballet can be flown against the magnificent backdrop of the sky to a choreography of the lone pilot's choosing, but one needs to work for many hours at the routines until man and machine assume a common identity and the movements flow smoothly and without hesitation. I fully discovered these things some years later and in a machine more refined than the humble Tiger, but the first clumsy beginnings were put together at Perth and I developed a taste for it.

At the end of the second month in Scotland, I had forty-five hours in my log book, a ginormous hangover from an end-of-course party, and a railway warrant to South Cerney for the advanced flying training course. It was there that we hoped to gain our wings. At this time we were still Leading Aircraftmen, being paid the princely sum of seven shillings and sixpence a day while under flying training.

The aircraft at Cerney were Airspeed Oxfords, two-engined aeroplanes with a cabin that could accommodate six at a pinch; but they weren't too easy to land. I liked the look of them though, nicely proportioned and businesslike, and with them came new skills such as flight after engine failure, cross-country navigation, instrument-flying and night-flying.

It was during a night-flying session at the little satellite field of Windrush that I had my first encounter with the Enemy.

I was in the middle of a solo circuit and landing session, and having turned on to final approach and headed for the vague line of flares laid out on the airfield, I switched on the landing-light in the port wing. Immediately, I saw the large black shape of an aircraft shoot underneath me going in the opposite direction. Even in that brief glimpse, I identified the wing root fillets of the Heinkel III.

I had no radio on board, and I doubted if the duty pilot knew of the intruder, otherwise the flares would have been doused by now. It was vital that I get down and sound the alarm.

I landed well down the flarepath, turned off to the left, and switched off the landing-light which was flooding the huts and the aircraft dispersal area. But nothing happened. The light stayed on. I tried working the double-ganged switch a number of times, but I had no further control over that powerful beam of light.

The cage over the ignition switches operated an electrical master switch. I decided to cut both the engines and kill the circuits. The engines chattered to a stop; there was an eerie silence, but the beam still pointed at the dispersal huts. Any moment now, Jerry was going to return, and I was his closest ally.

In some excitement, I scrambled from the aircraft, ran round to the front of the wing, and stood with my back to the light port. This effectively blanked the rays but my back began to overheat – badly. The desperate situation merited drastic action.

I fled back into the aircraft again, wrenched the escape axe from its stowage and within seconds was wreaking havoc with the recalcitrant light. It exploded with a violence which dazzled me, and I threw down the axe and started running desperately along the flarepath towards the marshalling post. By the flickering light of the gooseneck flares, I could see that the grass was long and tufted, and although the physical training during the past year had put me in peak condition, I was heaving for breath by the time I reached the end and the Flight Lieutenant in charge challenged me from the darkness.

'What the hell were you doing out there?' he demanded irritably.

'There's – a – Jerry – in the circuit!'

'Nonsense, man! There's not even an amber warning on!'

'I saw him, Sir!' I insisted. 'It was a Heinkel one-one-one.'

'How the devil do you think you could identify on a night as . . .

But his voice trailed away as a large aircraft came streaking above the flarepath towards us with both headlights blazing. In the next second, red flashes broke out under the nose, and stabbing red dashes flew towards us.

We threw ourselves flat in the grass. I remember covering my head rather stupidly with my hands. The noise of the aircraft and the guns was shattering, and the bullets ricocheted off the walls of the nissen huts and whistled past like fireworks.

In the middle of all the racket, I heard the Flight Lieutenant's voice, very close and quite clear. 'I think you're right, Gillman. It must have been a Heinkel.'

We learned subsequently that the intruder had dropped his bombs the other side of Gloucester on his way in, fortunately for us, otherwise I might never have heard the Flight Lieutenant's vindication.

The pace at the Advanced Flying Training School was certainly brisk, involving as it did a flying programme that ran seven days a week and kept us at work until late in the evenings; but in two months, with flying hours approaching the three figure mark, we found ourselves lining up for the big moment – the wings parade.

Then came the postings to the Operational Training Units and it seemed to us that most of them were deliberately perverse, for those who wanted to go on bombers were posted to fighter OTUs, and others itching to get on to fighters found themselves on the way to a bomber establishment. I was more fortunate. I had always fancied low-level daylight bombing, so my transfer to the Blenheim Operational Training Unit at Upwood suited me well.

CHAPTER THREE

A matter of style

I ARRIVED at 17 OTU in the last week of May. The hedgerows had come alive and the air smelt mild and sweet after the long hard winter. There seemed to be an air of operational urgency as I checked in at the guardroom of RAF Station Upwood, and when the orderly addressed me as 'sergeant' with a certain deference, the feeling began to grow within me that I had arrived. My period of uncertain probation was over. I had been admitted to the Force as a sergeant pilot and providing I could bring my new-found skills to mastering an operational aircraft, within weeks I should be joining that unique band of airmen known collectively as a squadron.

It was late afternoon by the time I had unpacked my kit in the room allocated to me. This was another status symbol, a room of my own. Admittedly it was in a wooden hut on the edge of the airfield whereas the permanent staff were housed in the sergeants' mess, but the privacy seemed to add dignity to my situation, and putting on my forage cap at a jaunty angle, I checked my appearance in the dressing-table mirror before setting off on a tour of inspection.

Marching briskly between the line of huts I made my way towards the perimeter track and there I came upon my first Blenheim. Even in its drab camouflage pattern of khaki and green paint there was a sleek look about it. The engines were Bristol Mercurys, large radial engines driving three-bladed propellors. They seemed altogether too big for the aircraft, but therein lay the power. From the domed turret half-way along the machine's back, two Browning machine-guns pointed skywards, and a tray under the glazed nose showed where four other guns were mounted when the aircraft was undertaking its night-fighter role, for this was the Mark I Blenheim – the short-nosed version. The type had an odd background, for it was designed initially as a civil transport under the sponsorship of Lord Rothermere way back in 1934 Being of all-metal construction and having a retractable under-carriage, it was well ahead of its time, and its range of 1,000 miles and cruising speed of 240 mph attracted the military authorities – which was obviously the sponsor's intention. The design was adopted by the Air Ministry, modified for its fighter-bomber role and put into production.

In its original form, the aircraft had been a low-wing monoplane, its narrow tube-like fuselage accommodating eight people; but in the military version the wing had been raised so that the mainspars came through the body behind the cockpit, forming what was known as the bomb well. It was necessary to clamber over these to get through to the back of the aircraft, the only other access being a hatch in the top of the fuselage forward of the gun-turret.

Although the airfield was generally very active at this time, no one seemed to be bothering with this particular aeroplane, so I took it upon myself to climb up the footholds in the side of the fuselage, gained access to the catwalk on the top of the wing, and made my way forward until I could look down through the perspex hatch into the cockpit. It appeared very functional, and although the instrument panel was somewhat similar to the twin-engined Oxford that I had been flying at the advanced training school, there were other significant additions such as the gun-firing button on the yoke of the control column, a bomb-fusing panel above the throttles, hydraulic selectors and controls for the two-speed pro-pellors. No one seemed to be taking any notice of my intrusion, so I carefully slid back the hatch, climbed over the edge and slipped down into the pilot's seat.

I was conscious of that strange ether-like smell that all military aircraft exude, and which sets the nerves tingling for some strange reason. There were no concessions to comfort, and the metal frames and riveted stringers were left bare and angular. This was obviously the aircraft on which I would subsequently make my acquaintance with the type, for in front of the right-hand seat was a set of dual controls, but no instrument panel. The instructor's view would be straight out through the perspex panels in the nose and for instrument references, he would have to look across at the trainee's panel.

I took hold of the control yoke somewhat tentatively and pulled the control column back. It was heavy and a distant clunking came from the back of the aircraft as the elevators moved. Looking out, I found a ring-and-bead gunsight directly in my line of vision and looking past it, I realised that the pilot was higher off the ground in this type than in the Oxford. I found myself wondering how I would get on trying to land this particular animal.

My train of thought was broken by the arrival of a tractor to which three ground crew were clinging. I started to climb out rather sheepishly and one of the airmen called up to me: 'We didn't know you were there, sarge. We've just come over to tow it to dispersal – or would you rather taxi it?'

'No, carry on,' I said with what authority I could muster. 'I'm just off to the mess anyway.' I slid to the ground and hurried off to cover my confusion.

The sergeants' mess was of the solid brick pre-war variety, large and very comfortable by comparison with the airmen's messes that I had only known so far. Among its largely aircrew population, there were many with pristine new wings and sergeant's chevrons like myself, but others' insignia had suffered a little more weathering which marked them out as staff pilots or instructors. I had long since become accustomed to the importance which was attached by all ranks to 'getting some in'. This referred to one's length of service or time overseas or duty on a squadron. Pre-war regular airmen particularly seemed to take an inordinate pride in the time they had spent in the ranks and made no secret of their disdain for volunteer reservists recently joined. Although this was not quite so marked among aircrew, there was always an instinctive respect for the experienced squadron man.

I wandered into the bar, ordered myself a drink and took stock of the scene around me. For the first time, I saw numbers of observers wearing their distinctive half brevets. They were the navigator/bomb-aimers, and others with AG in the circle of their half wings were wireless-operator/air-gunners. Noisy groups were beginning to crowd the bar and I felt rather on the edge of things. Then a familiar face appeared. It was Dave Penrose, the only other fellow from South Cerney to be posted onto Blenheims. He was a cheerful soul with an unruly lock of dark hair that invariably fell over one eye. He, too, was pleased to find someone he knew, and thus fortified with friendship and a supply of ale our diffidence waned and we were eventually absorbed into one of the talkative groups.

The conversations were mainly centred around the day's flying with ribald accounts of 'hairy' landings and practice bombing runs that had nearly annihilated a neighbouring village, and I warmed to their apparently facetious approach to the task in hand. For me it was less intimidating than the rather intense periods at the elementary and advanced training schools during which we had struggled to demonstrate our competence for the award of the coveted wings.

During the weeks that followed my original impression was confirmed, for we were treated as qualified pilots converting to another type of aircraft rather than as inept pupils; it was the sort of environment which fostered self-confidence.

The first week was taken up entirely by ground school during which we were introduced to the mysteries of the Claudel Hobson carburettor, variable-pitch propellors and the Browning machine-gun among other things; but the second week, the flying began and I found myself once more strapping myself into a strange aircraft alongside an instructor whom I had met but an hour before. He was a young pilot officer named Wand with a pleasant encouraging manner, and apart from demonstrating certain manoeuvres he never touched the controls while I was flying, but talked me out of mistakes and into good habits in a calm clear voice. At the speed with which things can go wrong when an inexperienced tyro is trying to emulate the master, this takes a good deal of nerve and self-restraint, but it does have a really beneficial effect on the trainee. There is nothing worse than seeing out of the corner of one's eye the instructor's hands twitching at the controls, or having control of the machine taken away before one has had a chance to identify and correct an error of judgement. I think that I was very fortunate in the instructors allocated to me during the early stages of my flying career. Had it not been for their expertise and encouragement, I feel that my limited talent might not have survived the test.

During the first flight and after demonstrating an impeccable circuit and landing, PO Wand handed the aircraft over to me to taxi back to the holding point. Initially, I found myself over-correcting with the power causing the plane to swerve from side to side, for much smaller throttle movements than had been required on the Oxford called up an immediate response from these engines. Once this had been allowed for, I found it easier to taxi than the smaller short-coupled machine.

At the holding point, we went through the pre-take-off drills using the manemonic HTMPFFG – where H stood for hydraulic selector down, T – trimming tabs neutral, M – mixture normal, P – propeller pitch fine, F – fuel, check contents and cocks, F – flaps 20° down, and G – gills closed on the engine cowlings.

A continuous stream of aircraft were landing and taking off and ten minutes elapsed before it was clear for me to turn onto the runway. With the brakes on, I pulled right back on the control column as instructed and opened up the throttles to half power. The noise of the engines and the propellers thrashing within a few inches of the cockpit windows set my chest vibrating and the air-craft began to dance on the hydraulic springing of the under-carriage, then I released the wheel-brakes with a hiss of escaping air and we surged forward. I pushed the throttles farther forward to attain +5 inches of boost and countered the crosswind swing with left rudder. The acceleration seemed laboured at first, then as I pushed the control column forward to lift the tail, she seemed to gather up her skirts and go.

I kept the aircraft straight along the centre of the runway, flicking my eyes repeatedly to the instrument panel to check pro-gress and as the needle of the airspeed indicator moved towards the 90-mph mark, I heard PO Wand say quietly – 'OK, now let's fly!'

A gentle backward pressure on the control column brought a clean response from the aircraft. It lifted smoothly. The hammer-ing of the wheels on the runway lessened and stopped, though I could still feel some vibration as they continued to spin. I dropped my right hand from the control column and groped for the under-carriage selector. It was protected under a hinged metal flap to avoid inadvertent retraction and one had to prize up the flap with the fingers while feeling for the selector. As a result of a certain lack of foresight at the design-office stage, this flap had a very sharp edge and Blenheim pilots could always be identified by the graze marks on their wrists.

The undercarriage came up slowly and tucked into the bottom

of the engine nacelles. The power could be eased back to a more bearable level and the speed settled at around 130 mph. I found the Mark I Blenheim delightfully stable in all axes with surprisingly crisp response to control movements in what to me, at that stage in my experience, was a heavy aeroplane.

The visibility from the cockpit was excellent all round, which was just as well, for the circuit was crowded with a continuous procession of aircraft. I started to follow the man in front at a range of about half a mile but during the turn gained a little height. 'Let's get back to a thousand feet,' said the quiet voice beside me. 'No hurry. In your own time. Not critical, but good practice.'

The flat Lincolnshire countryside could be seen laid out in neat squares as we turned onto the downwind leg. To the left, the airfield with its hangars, buildings and workshops stood out aggressively from what was otherwise a rural landscape. The air was smooth and the visibility good – a great day to be flying aeroplanes!

I turned on to base leg and carried out the pre-landing drills, lowering the undercarriage and flaps and resetting the propellors to fine pitch. I felt I was a bit too close to the aircraft in front, but I didn't know what to do about it as my speed was already down to the minimum of 85 mph. I found myself tensing up as I turned on to final approach and this made me over-control a little. 'Settle down,' said the quiet voice. 'Forget about the aircraft in front. You're a crack low so put on a little power; just a gnat's whisker, that's right; now keep the speed on the button with the control column.'

The boundary fence seemed to be coming up awfully fast, and as we flashed over the top, I banged the throttles closed harshly and pulled on the control column. The aircraft responded readily and the descent was checked.

'We've flared a little high,' said my mentor. 'Wait until she starts to sink – now – and resist it. Hold it off! Hold it off! Come on, stick right back,' and at that moment, the wheels began to rumble and we settled on the ground with dignity. 'I like it!' he said, raising his voice. 'I like it! Let's do another!'

Under such tutelage, even I had to make steady progress, and four flying hours later, after we had covered stalling, engine failure on take-off and engine-out landings, I found myself countersigning the authorisation book for my first solo.

It went off smoothly and without incident. The following day, the instructor was back in the right-hand seat again, but this time to teach me the art of close formation-flying. This excited me. The three aircraft took off from the runway in a Vee-formation, the leader keeping to the centre and the wing men running along the edges. There was barely twenty feet between our wingtip and the leader's tailplane. I had never been so close to another machine in flight before. The leader lifted off slightly before us and I glimpsed his belly momentarily as Wand eased us up into position. We turned and wheeled out of the circuit without the slightest change in our position relative to the others apart from the fact that we were above and looking down the wings of the other two in the turn. Such was the perfection it might have been the images of the aircraft frozen in position on a sheet of moving glass.

In level flight at 2,000 ft, we eased out to two spans as did the the other wing man, and my guiding voice said quietly, 'Right! You have a go.'

I think that 'have a go' was a fair description. In such close proximity to another aircraft, and at such speed, the slightest movement of the controls brings about a rapid change in relative position, as I quickly discovered. With my new-found confidence, I decided that the whole thing looked so easy and I lowered my port wing to tuck in on the leader. Even as I started applying pressure to the control yoke I found our aircraft starting to close rapidly with the leader's tailplane. Alarmed, I wound on full opposite aileron. We rolled to starboard, the leader was now underneath our belly and I pulled up harshly to get clear.

'I have control,' said the unruffled voice. Wand levelled the wings and checked our position. The leader was now a quarter of a mile away and below us.

'You've got her,' he said. I replaced my hands on the control column, my heart still thumping. 'Let us try a little more finesse,' he went on. 'At this stage of the game, move in slowly and with caution. Take your time. Don't make beam attacks on the leader; it frightens him.'

I found myself grinning, but eased the nose down gently and went into the gentlest of turns towards the leader. In the lightly turbulent air he was rising and falling gently, dropping a wing momentarily and yawing slightly and continuously. No sooner had I established a reasonable station at two spans than I found myself sinking below or falling behind. Initially, I tended to over-control on the throttles and would suddenly be aware that I was over-taking the leader rapidly. A large power reduction was necessary to avoid shooting past and the nose would drop. A loss of only ten feet, which would in normal flight be considered negligible, set us down so that the leader's belly was above us, his propellor discs shimmering and puffs of exhaust smoke spurting past the side window of the cockpit.

'You're getting right underneath him,' said Wand, a note of no more than academic interest creeping into his voice. 'This is uncomfortable. Ease away to starboard; that's right. Now pull up gently and roll the wings level – good! If you fall behind again, just give it a touch of throttle and wait for it to have effect, mean-while keeping station with the ailerons and elevator. As you start to gain ground, make a small power reduction early. Now relax! You're much too tense.' And so it went on, an unhurried flow of quietly delivered advice that filtered into the brain and was trans-lated into control movements.

By the end of an hour, my station keeping was becoming accurate and stable, even on the inside and outside of turns, but I had lost all sense of time and direction and was surprised when Wand said, 'OK, the airfield's ahead. I have control. We'll do a low fly-past.'

I relinquished the controls gratefully and found that my leg was trembling after being so tensed on the rudderbar. I felt quite exhausted. We swept over the field low and fast in fine style, our wing tucked in behind the leader's and barely ten feet from the tailplane.

The accent was placed on close formation flying at the opera-tional training unit for a very good reason. When being attacked by enemy fighters, the best defence would lie in a tight-knit formation so that the air gunners could bring their concentrated firepower on the attackers. A pilot who could not hold station under the rather wild conditions of a running fight would become a straggler to be picked off at will.

I worked hard at it for the next few trips and was becoming intrigued with a feeling of skill; even so, it came as something of a surprise when told that my next solo formation session would be in a Mark IV long-nosed Blenheim. There was no means of giving dual instructions in these machines, and they were slightly different. The nose had been extended forward of the original cockpit to house a navigator and his bomb-sight, and this had not improved the longitudinal stability. The aircraft had larger engines than the earlier mark, but it was also heavier and thus it was a little sluggish and less responsive to the controls.

I spent an hour in the cockpit with an instructor, being shown the differences in the ancillary controls and advised of the take-off and approach speeds, power settings, flap settings and the like, and then was dispatched to keep a rendezvous with two other trainees also having their first ride in a Mark IV. However, the result wasn't as traumatic as I'd expected, and it made a good topic for some hilarity over a few beers in the mess that evening.

For our instruction in night-flying we reverted to the short-nosed machines, and being on the second detail I waited in the dispersal hut while P/O Wand took up another pupil.

The lights were kept turned well down so as not to degrade our night vision, and we sat in the semi-darkness talking idly. I noted, rather than consciously heard, the phone ring in the flight-sergeant's office next door. Almost immediately his bulk appeared in the doorway: 'Hey! Up chaps! There's a red warning on – two-six! let's get that bloody flarepath doused!'

We ran out of the hut and scrambled into the little Hillman truck, which set off at a crazy pace over the rough ground. We shouted a warning to the duty pilot as we swung round the marshalling post and then set course along the line of flares, one man dropping off at every third gooseneck to deal with the three in his vicinity.

In a little over five minutes, the airfield was in total darkness, the van returning at a more cautious pace to pick up the flarepath party. Back at the marshalling post we learned that there were two aircraft airborne, and both of them after making an approach and seeing the flarepath extinguished had put out their own navigation lights and presumably deployed to the north of the field where they would hold until the intruder had left the area.

'What happens if the alert goes on until they are running out of fuel?' asked one of our party.

'Then they have a problem,' said the duty pilot. 'We daren't relight the flarepath and expose the whole station.' The situation was made more difficult by the fact that the Mark I's carried no radio, so it was not possible to advise them to divert or even to help them find another field.

After half-an-hour, there had been no signs of enemy activity and we returned to the dispersal hut to wait for the 'All clear'; but the silence continued. I was just regaling the others with my story of how I had floodlit the airfield at Windrush during an alert when the noise of a distant but deep-throated explosion sent us dashing for the door. The flight-sergeant was already there. 'I saw an explosion over to the north,' he said. 'Must have been a bomb gone in.'

'But there hasn't been any anti-aircraft fire,' somebody countered.

'There's still a warning on,' he said. 'It sounded like a bomb to me.'

'I think I heard some firing, Flight,' put in one of the airmen. The Flight Sergeant shook his head slowly. 'I reckon it was a bomb. Look, there's a fire coming up now.'

We watched as a crimson glow developed behind the framework of some distant trees. Suddenly it blossomed and licked the base of a pall of smoke that hung over the area. In the general darkness of the night it looked particularly menacing. We stood there talking quietly among ourselves and eventually as the glow was waning the telephone rang in the flight-sergeant's office. We heard him shouting to be heard on the rather sub-standard field telephone: 'Roger! Any idea where the bomb went in?' He banged down the instrument and called out of the window, 'OK, the alert's over. Get those goosenecks burning!'

'Any idea where it was, Flight?' I asked, and he grunted a negative.

The flarepath party relit the wicks in the paraffin lamps and we watched as each one established itself out of the darkness. A green Very light shot up from the control-tower followed by the crack of the pistol, a sign to the holding aircraft that they could return. Shortly afterwards we heard the first Blenheim and then saw the twin red-and-green navigation lights describing an arc in the blackness of the velvet sky above us. He spelled out the letter of the day on his downward identification light and got an answering green from the Aldis lamp at the marshalling post. I could see the blue and crimson exhausts flickering under the wings.

I wondered if it were P/O Wand. I was feeling a tired reaction now, and realised glumly that he still had to finish off the other pupil before he could deal with me. It would be in the wee small hours before I could get airborne. With a rumble of muffled exhaust and a swish of air the Blenheim mated with the flarepath and slowed down. After taxying back, the machine stopped at the marshaller's post and held there for a considerable time. Probably they were waiting for the other machine to come in before continuing with their circuit-and-landing detail. This theory foundered when it started to taxi again, but this time towards the dispersal. An airman marshalled it in with two torches held at arm's length. The machine parked, its engines idling for a few minutes; then they were cut and the noise died to a muted rattle, then stopped. In the darkness we could hear a shouted exchange.

'God! Don't tell me he's put the thing US again!' said Sergeant King, the trainee on the other detail with Flying Officer Streeter as an instructor. 'He's so bloody fussy he put the aircraft unserviceable the other day just because the cover was broken on the Graviner!'

'You don't know for sure that it's him,' I said.

'I bet it is. I know him of old,' he answered somewhat morosely.

His hunch proved to be right as the group moved slowly towards the hut talking quietly. As they came within range, I heard the flight-sergeant say, 'Well, there's one way to find out, Sir; I'll ring Operations.'

They moved into the office and we stood listening by the open door as the flight-sergeant hand-cranked the field telephone. 'Hello!' he shouted. 'Is that Ops?'

'With a voice like that,' murmured Sergeant King, 'he doesn't need a bloody telephone; he could just as well shout out of the window and they'd hear him!'

I stiffened as the flight-sergeant went on, 'One of our aircraft is missing from the night-flying detail. Flying Officer Streeter thinks he saw a Jerry get him north of the airfield. Can you confirm?' There was total silence as the group of men inside and outside the hut waited. Eventually the flight-sergeant said more quietly, 'I see,' and replaced the telephone.

The implications sank in slowly. I looked to the north, but the glow was no longer visible. The fire that marked the end of Pilot Officer Wand had gone out. One part of my mind refused to believe that the calm and likeable young man was already dead.

'The bastards!' said Sergeant King slowly. 'Fancy shooting down an aircraft on a training detail!'

I felt a bitterness welling up from my stomach. He was, or had been, such a nice man, self-effacing and giving of his best to help a sprog like me. His machine had been unarmed; it seemed like murder.

'That Hun must be feeling pretty proud of himself, jumping a training aircraft in the dark,' King went on. 'He's probably hot-footing it for home now to claim his Iron Cross; great stuff!'

Flying Officer Streeter's voice cut out of the darkness, 'How d'you think he could tell it was a training aircraft, Sergeant King?' he said sharply. 'In any case we're all vulnerable; there are no such things as Queensberry Rules in wartime, so stop grizzling!' He dug me in the back, 'I'll take you next – get aboard!'

I hurriedly installed myself in the aircraft and sat waiting, feeling wretched and repressed in the confines of the dimly lit cockpit. I stared at the instrument panel, barely discernible in the muted light. Outside the night was dark and unspeakably hostile and all feeling of initiative had drained from me. The prospect of going through the motions of making the aircraft ready for flight and the effort of coping with an hour's detail appalled me.

Flying Officer Streeter soon put a stop to that. He clambered onto the wing in some haste and dropped heavily into the seat beside me. 'Have you completed the pre-starting drills?' he asked brusquely.

'No, Sir.'

'Then got on with it man. We haven't got all night!'

I went through the checks hesitantly, my thoughts muddled by the feeling of mutiny that was gathering inside me. Eventually, a disembodied hand outside the aircraft lit by a torch indicated that I was clear to start the starboard engine. Clumsily I lifted the spring-loaded cover and pressed the starter button. The lights dimmed as the starter motor forced the engine into a slow rotation. Suddenly it fired with a flash of orange flame that lit the cockpit momentarily, then it roared into life, the instrument panel dancing

with the vibration. The savage intrusion of noise and movement
jerked my mind back to the surface and I got on with starting the
other engine and completing the pre-taxi checks more briskly; but
my heart still wasn't in it.

Streeter shouted down the speaking tube, 'Right, when you're
ready, taxi out.'

Two illuminated hands at a further distance indicated that the
chocks were away and I released the brakes, cautiously opened up
the throttles and moved off into the darkness. The ride over the
grass seemed rougher than ever, though the dimly lit marshalling
post didn't seem to be getting any nearer.

'Slow down!' he barked. 'Didn't they ever teach you at AFTS
that due to the lack of external references one tends to taxi faster at
night?'

They had, but I didn't think I had been moving particularly
fast. I slowed the machine down to a crawl.

The duty pilot focused the green Aldis lamp on us as we
approached. 'OK to line up for take-off, Sir?'

'Well of course it's OK,' he shouted. 'What the hell do you
think he gave us a green for? There's no one else in the circuit
anyway.'

I knew that only too well, and I felt a surge of anger that touched
the borders of mutiny. Opening up to half power on the brakes, I
released them with a jerk and thrust the throttles roughly forward.
The instrument panel became a blur as we pounded along the
runway and at 50 mph I pushed the stick forward. The tail came
up quickly; I over-corrected and the aircraft sea-sawed uncomfortably. Out of the corner of my eye I was conscious of him
squirming in his seat. At ninety I pulled back the control again
harshly and the aircraft fairly leapt into the air. 'For Christ's sake!'
he protested. 'What are you trying to do, stall it on take-off?'

The wild leap into the darkness had frightened me too, and I got
a grip on myself. I looked up from the instruments as I groped for
the undercarriage selector, but the flarepath was now behind us
and we were enveloped in a black featureless gloom with no
indication whatever as to where the earth finished and the sky
began. 'Watch your heading,' he said, somewhat anxiously, and I
looked back at the instrument panel to see with some surprise that
we were in a marked turn to port. Concentrating on the artificial

horizon and the airspeed indicator, I rolled the wings level and with the aid of the elevator trim adjusted the speed to precisely one hundred and thirty.

'Watch your height!' he cried testily. 'We're going through a thousand feet. A thousand feet, that's what you want in the circuit!'

I was beginning to sweat but I eased the nose down obediently and pulled off a little power, gently and smoothly as I had been taught to do. Taught by Pilot Officer Wand. 'Now what about turning downwind?' interrupted Flying Officer Streeter testily. 'We'll be over the bloody Wash if you don't do something about it.' The Wash was a hundred miles away and his sarcasm nearly stung me to a reply. Instead I went into a carefully modulated turn to port and then craned my head round to look out of the window for the flarepath. A reflection of one of the cockpit lights on the perspex fooled me for a moment, then I realised that outside the blackness was total; there were no lights to be seen. His voice jerked my attention back into the cockpit: 'Watch your height man! Don't sit there staring out of the window! Haven't you been told, at night you look in and glance out!'

I glued my attention to the instrument panel and eased the aircraft round on to the downwind heading. When it was straight and level again, I looked briefly out of the side window, but we were floating in an inky blackness. There was no flarepath to be seen; maybe they had had to dowse it again. I looked back in time to check an incipient roll to port and looked out again somewhat anxiously. I was just about to look back into the cockpit when something caught my eye and I did a double take. There was the flarepath, minute and in the distance, not at all where I expected it to be. I started a turn towards it. 'Where are you going now?' shouted the irate voice. 'You were on the downwind heading; what are you turning for?'

'We're very wide, Sir,' I said. 'I'm turning in towards it.'

'If you hadn't made a cock of the turn after climb-out you'd be in a proper position,' he said. 'What about the undercarriage? Come on, get it down, and the flaps – what about the flaps?'

By the time we had turned onto the final approach, my mind was about as clear as a Mulligan stew. My reactions were now becoming late and harsh, resulting in over-corrections from one situation to another. The tiny avenue of twinkling flares seemed too narrow to contain the undercarriage as I weaved towards it.

In the last twenty feet when the flares came rushing towards us I felt Streeter pulling and pushing on the controls, seemingly opposing my every move. Between us we wrestled the machine on to the runway with a thud that vibrated the instrument panel into a blur. We taxied back to the marshalling post in silence. Safely on the ground, my upset thoughts were beginning to regroup. I felt that this man was going to destroy me. I had a longing to suggest that he release me from the rest of the detail, but this was unthinkable. He was talking excitedly about what should be done in the last twenty feet, but my mind wasn't listening.

This proved to be my salvation. From then on, I completely ignored his tirade and flew the aircraft in the series of slow, smooth manoeuvres that Pilot Officer Wand had shown me. Once or twice I felt the instructor's hands opposing me on the controls during landing but I opposed him, and the arrivals, although not polished, were acceptable. The last one was a beauty and his comment was, 'Well, that wasn't too bad, but why the hell couldn't you do that in the first place?'

The first grey streaks of dawn were gracing the eastern sky when I finally climbed slowly into bed, desperately tired and dispirited.

The following day, Dave Penrose and I were transferred to the gunnery and bombing flight. It would be all solo from now on.

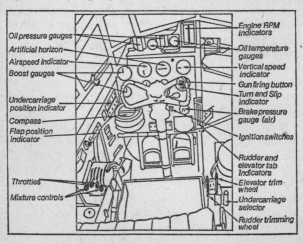

CHAPTER FOUR

Blenheim pilot

THE IMMEDIATE TASK now was to find a crew, and this seemed a delightfully haphazard affair though it worked on the principle that character compatibility was the most important issue for small groups of men who were to work, fly, and fight together. Different crews were rostered to fly with each other during the initial part of the course. It was rather like a mating season. Acquaintances were struck, or perhaps friendships, and eventually came the proposition thrown out casually between two mouthfuls of beer. 'How would you like to crew with me?'

I was fortunate in finding two stalwarts, Ron Weeks, a top scoring air gunner who played poker with a fierce intensity, and Benny Howlett, a quietly spoken Scot, as navigator. It was nothing less than an act of faith throwing in their lot with me, come whatever, for although my wings announced me as a qualified pilot, I had only eight hours on the type and but 110 hours overall. Thinking back on it, it is my opinion that those two were the bravest men in the last war; but we were certainly compatible. Weeky, as he soon became known, was an exuberant type and found endless pleasure in teasing the serious Scot. Benny took it well most of the time, but every so often his hackles would rise and then I would have to step in as a mediator. Life was never dull.

We now entered upon the crew training phase designed to sharpen our teeth for the warlike activities to come. This included bombing practice, gunnery sessions and general navigation.

Although the Blenheim had been used for mainly low-level attacks up to that point in the war, one also had to learn the technique of high-level bombing at heights of around 10,000 ft. In his nose compartment, the navigator had what would be thought now a crude piece of equipment, a course-setting bombsight. This had an ordinary magnetic compass as a base with two metal bars about a foot long sticking out ahead of it to which were attached 'drift' wires. Before running into the target, he set in the aircraft's speed, height and the assumed drift. When the target came into view through the perspex bomb-aiming panel, he gave the pilot course changing directions so that it appeared to travel straight between the drift wires from his point of view. When the image reached the ring sight, he pressed the button releasing the bomb load.

The equipment was not stabilised, so if the pilot rolled the aircraft, or the machine was subjected to turbulence, the wires swung either side of the target image. One's attempts at making a rock steady run could also be prejudiced by the fact that the aircraft was being shot at by ill-disposed people on the ground, and searchlights coming in gave one a certain feeling of exposure. It seemed to me that it would be little short of a miracle if one could hit the right city, let alone a particular building within it.

However, the low-level bombing technique was much more exciting and certainly more accurate. For our practice runs, we flew to the wreck of a ship that lay off the Norfolk coast, making the run-in at a matter of a few feet above the sea, letting the 6-lb practice bombs go when the hull loomed in front of us, and then pulling up over the superstructure. For this, the pilot dropped the bombs by means of a button on the control column. He had no bombsight of any kind, for the idea was to get so close to the vessel that the bombs couldn't miss it, but went into its side like torpedoes.

There is a saying among flying men that at 100 hours a pilot thinks he knows it all, at 1000 hours he's sure he does, and at 10,000 hours he is beginning to realise that he has a lot to learn. I was no exception to the rule and this was brought home to me during one of the low-level bombing practices.

Our results as charted by the bomb plotters on the coast had been quite creditable, but I determined that nothing but the top scoring position on the course would satisfy me. With each successive run, I got lower over the sea and left the pull-out later until I was missing the jagged tip of the vessel's broken mast literally by inches. The runs were made at full throttle giving about 260 mph; that's a lot of feet a second. On my final run, I went for the jackpot, left the pull-out until it seemed too late, and found that it was! We hit the top of the mast with a resounding crack and the aircraft went into a wild swing to port. Weeky let out a whoop of dismay from his turret as I regained control and went into a climb with my heart thumping.

The intercom crackled into life. 'That was a bit too bloody close!' he shouted.

'Is there any damage?'

'Not if you ignore three feet of wood sticking through the tailplane!'

I set course back to Upwood with a sinking heart. The Chief Flying Instructor wasn't going to like this. In an address at the beginning of the course he had warned us of his intention of 'coming down like a ton of bricks' on anyone who damaged a precious aircraft through carelessness. I shuddered to think what he was going to do about an incident that probably came under the heading of recklessness.

In the event, the dreaded interview was no worse than I had expected. The Wing Commander, in measured tones, described how I appeared to him as an individual, as a pilot and as a liability to the war effort in general. He discussed my prowess as an aviator and suggested that on this topic, his opinion and my own were obviously widely divergent. He went on to explain that over-confidence had killed more idiots than one could shake a stick at, and that with any luck this fate would overtake me, at which juncture he would become a happy man again. I couldn't believe my good fortune, when no punitive measures followed the interview. I have often heard it said that if you frighten yourself and live through it, you become a wiser man; the incident certainly had a salutary effect on me.

The operational training continued with air-to-air firing in which some unfortunate in a Miles Master towed at the end of a wire a silk drogue which we attacked with our machine-guns, I using the Browning 303 mounted in the wing, Benny the two guns under the nose, and Weeky blasted away from his turret. In other exercises, the Master, bereft of its impediment, made fighter attacks on us to give Weeky practice in giving me evasion instructions and in the use of his guns defensively, though now they were fitted with a camera, so the results could be analysed on the ground.

A number of cross-country flights gave the opportunity for

Benny to demonstrate his skill as a navigator and Weeky to under-
take his other role as a wireless operator. His receiver/transmitter
was a medium-frequency set, the range of which was enhanced by
dropping an aerial out through a hole in the floor. All communication was by Morse, and the hand-tuning somewhat critical, so not
surprisingly, the results were a bit unpredictable.

However, we really distinguished ourselves during our first
attempt at a radio-assisted letdown. This was called a 'Z Z' procedure in which contact was established with a radio-direction-
finding station whose job it was to provide a series of bearings taken
of the aircraft's transmissions. Firstly, the pilot flew directly to the
station until he got the 'overhead' signal, then he started letting
down, flying a 'teardrop' pattern with the aid of the bearings; if all
went well, he would break out of cloud in sight of the associated
airfield.

We were sent off to carry out a letdown at Watton, an airfield in
Norfolk, on a day when the cloud base was around 500 ft. We
climbed up into the murk and I settled down to fly the machine as
accurately as I could on instruments. To my surprise, Weeky soon
made contact with the D/F station and my earphones were filled
with the staccato squeaking of high-speed Morse. As each bearing
was read, I altered course until we were running towards the
station on the inbound heading. Sure enough, we eventually got
the 'overhead' signal and I started the stopwatch, went through the
pre-landing drills and began to descend. Things didn't go too well
from then on, for some of the bearings were corrupt, being twenty
or thirty degrees different from those which preceded them or even,
on occasions, coming out opposite as reciprocals. The altimeter
was winding through 1,500 ft as we turned back for the run-in to
the airfield. The bearings now became widely divergent according
to Weeky, and I found myself making large course corrections as
we entered the turbulence near cloudbase. At 700 ft we were still
in cloud and, I hoped, on the safe lane towards the airfield clear of
hills and other solid objects. Still the altimeter wound relentlessly
downward, and the tension mounted as we closed towards the
ground, the only visibility being what could be seen in the cockpit.
The instrument panel danced on its mountings, the Morse crackled
urgently and with each bearing that Weeky passed me his voice
rose another note or two.

At just under 500 ft, the cloudbase began to fragment and through the holes one had momentary glimpses of grey-green fields scudding past. Suddenly, we broke clear of the base, and there, miraculously, was a runway stretching before us! We were elated, particularly so as no other crew on the course had managed a successful 'Z Z' so far. Our instructions were not to land, so I opened the throttles and nosed up into the murk again. We used bearings from our home station to return to Upwood and then descended in a clear patch of sky and finished the journey underneath the overcast.

At debriefing we couldn't wait to tell of our success. 'And then,' said I, bringing my account to a dramatic conclusion, 'we broke cloud at just under 500 ft and there was the runway dead ahead of us!'

The Operations Officer looked at me sharply, 'Are you sure?'

I nodded my head vigorously, and turning to the crew for confirmation said, 'That's so, isn't it?'

They backed me up emphatically.

'That's interesting,' said the Operations man, screwing up his debriefing report and aiming it carefully into the wastepaper basket. 'Watton doesn't have a runway!'

It was high summer before we were ready for a squadron, and after an all too brief leave, we set out on our posting to 114 Squadron at West Raynham in Norfolk. The whole of the training course had been so intense that I had hardly noticed the passage of time and it came as a surprise to realise that it had, in fact, taken almost a year. Now it was behind me. I was about to become an operational pilot and I hoped that someone would be duly impressed.

In fact, we arrived at our new quarters in the middle of a blackout. Weasenham Hall, the great mansion that served as a mess for the Squadron, had suffered a power failure and we stumbled along darkened strange passageways in search of our rooms. Weeky was the first to find the bar and I a close second, but we were on our fourth pint before Benny appeared out of the gloom wearing a bemused expression and asking, 'How the devil will we ever find our way aroon this hoose?'

We reported to the Adjutant the next day and were mildly surprised to find that he was expecting us. Within minutes we found ourselves being interviewed by the Flight Commander. He was gangling tall and his eyes so deeply hooded that they seemed to glare at us from inside two small tunnels.

'All right, so you've finished training and you think you know it all! They all do! But remember, there are some very experienced men on this squadron. Take my advice, keep your traps shut and your eyes open. You're on a practice formation detail with me this afternoon together with another new crew. I want to see half a span and nothing more. We'll be doing some low-flying and I'm going to try to lose you. If I do, look out!'

That afternoon I sweated. Things went reasonably well until we got to the low-flying area, then he dived to hedge height and went immediately into a steep turn towards me. Naturally I was below him in the turn. From my peripheral vision I could see the ground flashing by my starboard wingtip, but I dare not take my eyes off the leader. I worked tensely at the controls and the throttles to keep in station and hoped to hell that he was allowing enough height for me to clear obstructions.

The other chap was above, silhouetted against the sky, and on several occasions he slipped in, dangerously close to the leader, and then swung away violently. During a turn in the other direction, when he was below, he became even more erratic. I felt sure he must come to grief. Then he went into a steep bank, obviously losing sight of the leader under his wing, but he had the sense to peel off. The radio crackled into life and the Flight Commander's high-pitched voice came over, 'Where the hell d'you think you're going, number three? Get back in formation!' and he rolled out of the turn so sharply that I was caught by surprise. I wrenched on full opposite aileron in desperation and my wingtip missed his mid-turret by inches.

I was seriously tensed up by this time and over-controlling in my efforts to keep station, but the real trouble came when we flashed over the coast and started to skim across the calm and featureless sea. It was almost impossible to judge one's height, but that was the leader's problem of course, as the wing men had to keep slightly above him at low level. Undoubtedly, we were desperately low, and Sergeant Hall, the other man, was coming back into station too fast. He overshot the leader and I could see puffs of smoke from his exhausts as he smartly throttled the engines right back. Slowly his speed fell away and he made another attempt to tuck in, but he was visibly over-controlling. Several times he dived beneath the leader and I held my breath as he snatched the nose up and leaped above him. Then he seemed to settle down in quite a good position, but to my horror, although he was stable in roll and yaw, he began to sink slowly and steadily beneath the leader.

Then he hit the water. A curtain of spray erupted. For a moment I felt sure he was lost, then he reappeared climbing sharply, but his propellor discs looked peculiar. They were shimmering and there were large blobs at the edges.

'What the hell do you think you're doing, number three! Return to Base! Return to Base!' The Flight Commander's voice had reached hysteria pitch. He turned to follow the unfortunate man and I swung out and followed at a distance.

'Steer two-eight-zero!' shouted the voice, and the aircraft obediently turned carefully to starboard. We found ourselves over-hauling him, and the Flight Commander flew on past ordering number three to follow. I throttled back and brought up the rear, my heart still pumping.

He got back to the airfield and landed successfully with six inches of his propellor blades bent back.

The incident was discussed in the mess that night, and I learned that Hall had been sent back to the Operational Training Unit for further dual; but I felt that part of the blame lay on the shoulders of the Flight Commander and said so.

'You've just arrived, haven't you?' demanded a dark and intense navigator with an Indian Campaign medal ribbon under his brevet. I nodded. 'Then I suggest you keep quiet until you know more about it. He's one of the finest operational pilots in the squadron.' My mind went back to the Flight Commander's interview – 'Keep your trap shut!' By sheer chance, I never flew with him again. When my crew and I found ourselves on the battle order for the first time, he was on leave, and I breathed a genuine sigh of relief.

The target was a reported convoy off Heligoland, four merchant-men escorted by three flak ships, and it was to be a full squadron effort. The briefing room was crowded and alive with activity, and amid the banter and in such good company, one felt more excited than fearful. Up till now, the ever-present concern had been clearing the next hurdle, getting through an exam, or passing a flight check. The hazard now was different: out there, some 200 miles away, was a convoy of ships steaming along the enemy coast-line. Undoubtedly it had seen the reconnaissance aircraft that had radioed its position and the crews would be alert, watching the northern horizon over which we must come. But we were all going in together; this thought gave one comfort and courage.

The briefing was somewhat rushed as the CO was anxious to get on the scene before the ships reached their next port of call, and as we hurried out to the trucks waiting to take us to the aircraft, Benny, overburdened with his navigation bag, parachute pack, helmet and gloves, was complaining that he hadn't had a chance to plot the return course.

'You'd better wait to see if we're coming back, first,' admonished Weeky.

'Aw be quiet, mon,' said Benny, 'there's many a true word spoken in jest!'

'Don't worry, Benny,' I said. 'You'll have plenty of time to catch up with yourself on the way out.'

Within twenty minutes the squadron was airborne and wheeling over the airfield as it closed up into formation. Being the junior crew, we were in the tail-end Charlie position, and the first two vics were already diving towards the coast when we turned on course in pursuit. The section leader I had to follow was a sandy-haired pilot officer who had introduced himself to me in the briefing-room as Adams, and any apprehension that remained after my last experience was soon allayed by his smooth flying and clear hand signals before he went into any turn. Maybe he was just nursing a new boy, but I appreciated it.

Over the sea, an easterly wind had brought up a short chop which made it relatively easy to judge one's height and I estimated that we were at about fifty foot initially, but as the target area was approached the leader began to ease down towards the water and the squadron dutifully followed until the wave tops were rippling by in a blur, very close.

It was a grey day with mediocre visibility, and after we had been running for about an hour and a quarter, the intercom started to hiss as someone switched on his microphone. I tensed and listened. Benny's voice came over hesitantly:

'Er, according to me, we should be in the target area aboot noo.'

'All right. They're not here, so let's go home,' cut in Weeky.

'We'll have to be pretty close to see them in this visibility,' I suggested.

'With any luck we've missed 'em,' said Weeky. 'Oh! Hang on . . .' and as he was speaking the leader lowered his port wing and went into a steepish turn. Both Weeky and I saw them together, dull grey shapes to our left, probably two miles away, but things were beginning to happen. Orange and scarlet flashes burst intermittently along the superstructure of the nearest ship.

'They've bloody seen us too!' shouted Weeky.

The formations in front were now in some disarray, the leader pulling into an even tighter turn while others were widening out and starting to take evasive action. Having seen the ships so late, we were coming in awkwardly. The leader was trying to get on a course parallel to the line of ships before turning to attack. Ideally, attacks should be made at right angles and in the middle of a ship so that if not sunk it will be immobilized by damage to the engine-room.

The whole formation was swinging wide, and being tail-end Charlie, I found myself desperately trying to hang on, like the victim at the end of a line of skaters. I couldn't get round any tighter, as the section leader inside me was beginning to cavort so violently that I had to sheer away. This was taking me onto the bows of the first ship at an acute angle.

It would be fatal to run the length of the ship. I had to get out and turn in again.

I rolled the port wing hard down and pulled her round in a steep turn just above the water. I had lost sight of the quarry now and my belly was exposed, but I was desperate to get round.

A hail of scarlet tracer was shooting past the nose and we were flying into it. I cranked the ailerons hard over the other way and as we rolled round, I realised with a shock that we were almost alongside the massive shape and level with the superstructure. The technique should be to come in at sea-level and at right angles, letting the bombs go like torpedoes and then climbing over the ship.

Cannon fire from the boat deck and fo'c'sle was coning in on us with vicious intensity. Both Benny's and Weeky's guns racketed as they fired indiscriminately. We were too close in, but I had to attack. It would be fatal to turn away.

In desperation, I wound on full bank and dived. The grey sea rushed up at a crazy rate. I heaved back on the control column and felt the aircraft shudder with the strain. The ship's side was a blank wall ahead of me.

I stabbed the bomb-release button and pulled the aircraft in a steep climb to clear the ship's side. But we weren't going to make it! She'd stall! The mast and derricks were coming towards us. Of course – the ship was moving at right angles!

With frantic strength, I twisted the control-column yoke hard over. The aircraft started to roll, but the boom of the derrick was dead in front of us. I pulled the turn tighter still and the boom with its huge block and tackle whipped under the nose. I ducked instinctively, but we were now over the sea again, miraculously, and I dived for it twisting and turning on the way down. Weeky was still firing back at the ship with a murderous racket.

Quite suddenly, the following tracer stopped. To the left I could see the sleek grey shapes of the other aircraft floating swiftly through the murk like a school of fish. I put the aircraft in a turn towards them.

'Christ! That was close,' said Benny.

'I thought we'd got that bloody crane,' said Weeky. 'It went under my turret.'

'You and me both,' I said fervently. My heart was still pounding.

'What's up?' demanded Benny. 'There's a hell of a lot of vibration.'

'I can't see any damage,' called Weeky. 'Oh! Hang on – er – yeh, there's some holes right over your bloody head, Ron, and some in the port wing just behind the cowling. Nothing serious though.'

Then I realised that the engines were still in boost override and I pulled the lever down so sharply that the engine note dropping and consequent deceleration brought cries of alarm from the crew. 'Sorry about that,' I said, 'but if I had left the plus-nine tit in, we wouldn't have made Great Yarmouth.'

'Glad you remembered,' said Weeky with a touch of irony.

Back in the briefing-room we learned that of the twelve aircraft two had been lost. I overheard the Wing Commander's navigator describing the anti-aircraft fire to the Intelligence Officer as 'just

moderate'. The CO was apologising to a group for the fact that
he had seen the ships too late to get into a good position, which
was why the result had been a shambles. When our turn came to be
de-briefed, Weeky claimed that the bombs must have gone into the
ship's side, but the Intelligence Officer looked sceptical; and when
I said that the ship we had attacked at the front of the convoy was
about 10,000 tons, he said that other estimates had put it at 2,000.

In the mess that evening, the crews were in an exuberant mood
like small boys released from detention. We, on the other hand
were noticeably quiet.

'Moderate anti-aircraft fire,' murmured Weeky, staring into his
pint pot.

The trip had had a chastening effect. To us, our first taste of
action had been dramatic. But the experienced boys had voted it
a relatively quiet one. The normal tour of operations was thirty
such trips, if one survived. If one survived. Our lives, up till now,
had always involved planning for the future. Suddenly, we couldn't
see it any more. Reality had taken its place, a reality which said, 'I'm
awfully sorry, but from here on there is an element of doubt. I
shouldn't make any plans if I were you. There's an awful lot to be
done.'

CHAPTER FIVE

The squadron spirit

OUR ENCOUNTER with the hawk-eyed flight commander on arrival at the squadron had had a depressing effect, and this was tinged with resentment that having completed our training and joined a fighting unit as a qualified crew, we had come up against treatment more humiliating than anything hitherto. But it soon became apparent that such a situation was not at all typical of squadron life. A few days later our tormentor was posted to a sister squadron. Subsequently he had what must have been one of the most meteoric rises in the RAF. Life in the low-level daylight bomber squadrons was hectic enough, but he hit the jackpot by being promoted from Flight Lieutenant through Squadron Leader to Wing Commander, being awarded the DSO and the DFC, and was killed all in a fortnight. Our new flight commander was a cheerful fellow with a warmth of personality which endeared him to his men.

Mess life was almost as hectic as the operational role in which we found ourselves, and rumour had it that there was a complete ward full of casualties at Halton Hospital, sustained in such games as chesterfield rugby, mounted combat, and bullfights. The pattern seemed to be that on return from a trip the mood at debriefing was either one of exhilaration or subdued by a sense of shock, and in the mess that evening, the talk initially would be of the operation as each man had seen it. But inevitably, the warming effect of alcohol loosened the unnatural strain and youthful exuberance rose again to the surface. To the onlooker some of the behaviour must have seemed inexcusably wild, but the authorities took a more understanding and tolerant view, realising that reaction had to come and be allowed to expend itself.

There was one great character in particular whose outbursts had an almost frantic quality. He was unusually old for operational crew being in his middle thirties, and the other unusual thing about him was that he had transferred from the Navy in order to serve as a navigator. His favourite party piece began when he climbed onto a chair, waved his pint aloft and giving his ginger moustache a couple of quick upward sweeps with his hand launched into a monologue which began – 'My sister's cat's. . . .' Each line would be shouted back by the audience, more loudly as the recital went on, and he would shout the loudest of all, his face changing colour and the veins on his neck bulging fit to burst. Inevitably his voice would degenerate into a croak after a while, necessitating a quick dip into the pint pot for lubrication and then a return to the fray even more loudly than before. Whether it was the strain of these performances or the effect of the operations on a man whom we considered to be of advancing years we never knew, but certainly on his return from a trip one day, he climbed out of the aircraft and dropped dead in the grass with cardiac failure.

His death dominated the conversation in the mess that night, overshadowing the loss of another two crews on the same trip. I suppose that it was the unnecessary waste that seemed galling. If man was lost in action, well, that was what it was all about, but to die after a safe return was difficult to accept.

I had another example a few days later. I shared a room with a young freckle-faced fellow from Hull. He was an open, honest youth and was deeply religious, but he would stay the course at a mess party, becoming as exuberant as the rest on an intake of orange juice. What really drew my admiration was the way that when the party was over and we returned to our room, he would kneel down beside his bed and say his prayers before wishing me goodnight and turning in.

One day, we were sent to attack a convoy off the Frisian Islands. There were two destroyers and four merchant ships which put up a stern fight. Only nine aircraft were deployed as the day before we had lost three and had a number damaged which were still being repaired.

The destroyers had manoeuvred into a position between us and the merchantmen we were out to get, their small-arms and anti-aircraft fire being the most intense we had met so far. The decks throughout their length sparkled with the flashes of the multiple cannon and the bass chorus of the bigger guns belched flame and smoke like a series of obscene eruptions. The sea before us was splattered with the impact of shrapnel and the sky was pock-marked with the black puffs of shellbursts.

I swung wide round the stern of the second destroyer, but those in the middle of the formation were committed to flying through the gap between them and it was in their numbers that the casualties occurred. Continuing an erratic zig-zagging turn, I got between the warship and the cargo vessel where the pressure eased a little as they couldn't fire at me without hitting each other. Rolling suddenly to port, I headed for the biggest ship, diving to the sea and releasing the bombs when its portholes were in a line above me. The aircraft leaped responsively with the release of the 1000-lb load and we cleared the ship easily, the hot air from the funnel giving us a bump as we went over the top.

On the run away, things hotted up. The ship opened fire with a pent-up fury, and Weeky's guns racketed in return. Suddenly they stopped and he let out a shout that sent a chill through my blood; but it was a whoop of excitement for a great spout of flame, debris and water had shot up from the ship and the firing immediately died away.

We were running now for the long grey line of the coast and I sheared away as the shore batteries opened up. Subsequently, we found two other squadron aircraft and flew home with them in company. But for my room mate it was a different story. Having survived the attack apparently, he was on course for the Norfolk coast and only a few miles out when he saw a formation of ships of the Royal Navy. The leading vessel challenged him by flashing the letters of the day, and according to another aircraft that was following, Johnny fired off the colours of the day in response and they were the correct ones. But nerves were a-jitter; a Blenheim looks rather like a Junkers 88, and the Navy opened fire and shot Johnny and his crew into the sea.

But life on the squadron was not all fire and fury. Between the sorties were arranged training days involving practice bombing and air firing, and for the less experienced pilots like myself, formation-flying. Under the urgency of war, our basic training had been cut to a minimum, but now every opportunity was taken to add the necessary polish. The atmosphere on these occasions was, of course, more relaxed; I think we even looked upon them as days out, and in the squadron bus that took us to where the aircraft were dispersed around the boundaries of the airfield, there was a great deal of good-natured banter.

The dispersals were in the form of concrete hard standings branching off from the outside of the perimeter track, sometimes even situated in what had been adjacent fields until they were requisitioned under the Emergency Regulations. By this means, the precious aircraft presented less of a target for the marauding enemy than if they had been concentrated in the hangar as was peace-time practice. Furthermore, it was possible to group them into Flights with their own ground crew in situ in charge of a flight sergeant fitter or rigger. Our particular man on 'A' Flight was Flight-Sergeant Dodds, a fellow as large in frame as he was in character, his background as a champion boxer of the RAF being indicated by a very broken nose. He was an 'ex-Brat', that is, he had entered the service as an apprentice at Halton at the age of fourteen or fifteen and worked his way up through the ranks before the war. Just as an ex-public-school boy has an air about him, so do those who originated from Halton have an identifiable stamp. It says a great deal for peacetime training that it breeds self reliance, a sense of discipline and authority. Promotion came slowly and was hard won in those days, and I could well understand that there was at times, a feeling of contention among the regular airmen at the rapid promotion of wartime aircrew from aircraftsmen 2nd class to senior NCOs in a little less than a year.

The flight-sergeant did not, as his title might indicate to a layman, have any authority over the aircrew, for they came directly under the flight commander. On the flying side there was another anomaly: although there were both NCO and officer pilots, commissioned ranks did not necessarily have superior authority in the air. Invariably, the more experienced squadron pilots would be detailed to lead the vics and flights, and it was not unusual for the leaders of formations to be sergeants or flight-sergeant pilots with officers flying subordinately in wing aircraft. This led inevitably to easier relationships on the ground, particularly in the 'family' atmosphere of a small flight, a situation which personnel in other services found difficult to understand sometimes.

Once established on a squadron, each crew was allocated its own aircraft which no one else was allowed to fly and each machine had its own fitter and rigger. As a result of this arrangement, both the aircrew and the ground crew took a deep pride in the performance of their particular aeroplane both on the ground and in the air and out of this came a strong team spirit. The ground crews on the Flights affected to disdain the soft working conditions of the mechanics in the hangars who were engaged on major repairs and overhauls, and certainly, in the vagaries of the English climate, they had at times to contend with some pretty rough conditions when servicing aircraft in the open; but their spirit was magnificent.

Our fitter was a former London bus driver, short, thickset and endowed with that incisive brand of cockney humour; his name was Bert. The rigger on the other hand was tall and awkward, a Yorkshireman who before the war had worked for the Gas Company engaged in emptying meters. Between them they had a fascinating collection of stories which usually came out when we were around the visiting NAAFI wagon enjoying a cup of char and a wad.

On one occasion, 'A' Flight was detailed to give a demonstration of formation-flying for a visiting posse of high-ranking air force officers from a South American republic, and we were enjoying our elevenses prior to take-off when a cavalcade of staff cars came swishing through the puddles and stopped near the flight hut. They disgorged a collection of the most immaculate airmen we had ever seen, resplendent in sky-blue uniforms and festooned with much gold braid.

Our group fell silent for a moment, the Bert said quietly, 'Cor look at that lot! Straight out of Drury Lane!'

Fred Coles, the rigger, had a few cutting remarks to make about the rows of medal ribbons that most of them displayed, recalling that that particular Country had not had a war for over 100 years and their air force had never seen a shot fired in anger.

We watched as they picked their way fastidiously over the mud towards the reception group which included the Squadron Commander, and Flight Lieutenant 'Dusty' Miller, our flight commander.

'What's the object of the exercise, Sarge?' asked Bert.

'I've no idea,' I said. 'There's a rumour that they want to buy some Blenheims, though I shouldn't think we had any to sell.'

'Maybe they're going to come in on our side,' mused Fred; 'though I'd hate to see those uniforms get dirty.'

There followed some speculation as to how they had acquired so many medals, and some of the suggestions bordered on the obscene.

'Well, come on, chaps,' said Flying Officer Bunny Hart who was to lead the formation, 'let's show 'em what it's like to be operational.'

Bert handed his tea mug up to the highly-coloured NAAFI girl. 'Save us a bit of doughnut for tonight, gorgeous,' he said.

'You'll be lucky!' she replied, eyelashes a-flutter. 'You get into line like the rest of 'em!'

'Why, you going to spread it around tonight then?' asked Fred. She picked up a mug and took aim, and he ducked round the side of the van.

On the way over to our aircraft Weeky asked, 'Have you fixed that twist-grip on the turret yet, Fred?'

'Yes, Sarge. Put a new one on last night and checked it out this morning while Bert was running the engines. Works a treat.'

'Incidentally, Skip,' cut in the fitter, 'there was a bit of a mag drop on the starboard engine, but I belted it and it seemed to clear itself.'

'You're going to be a bit unpopular with Flight if I have to drop out of this little show with a mag drop,' I warned.

'No, it'll be all right, Sarge,' he said cheerfully, 'it's number two mag. If you get more than a hundred rev drop when you switch it off during the engine check, belt it up to plus nine for a few seconds and then slam the throttle closed. That'll fix it.'

'He still thinks he's driving a London bus,' quipped Weeky.

'At least I don't try to fly an aircraft like one,' was his parting shot as we scrambled up to our crew positions.

The squadron aircraft were fitted with a small radio telephony set as well the wireless-operator/air-gunner's equipment, and this gave us speech communication over relatively short distances. It was called a TR9 and the transmit/receive switch was in the form of a lever which was not spring-loaded to the OFF position. This had caused something of a debacle a few days before when a pilot had left the switch in the transmit position inadvertently, and from then on, all the chat on the intercom was broadcast to a fascinated

community on the ground. It was monitored with particular
interest in the operations room where all transmissions were amplified by a loudspeaker, for the object of the conversation was the
red-haired WAAF plotter who worked there. The exchanges came
over clearly in such unselfconscious tones that the listeners felt
guilty of eavesdropping; temperatures certainly began to rise when
the air-gunner described her physical attractions in somewhat
picturesque language but when the navigator explained exactly
what he would like to do for her wellbeing if the opportunity arose,
the poor girl who had been standing as if fixed to the floor, her eyes
wide and mouth open, uttered a shriek and rushed from the room.
It wasn't until the pilot had tried to call the control tower on his
return to the circuit that he realised his mistake. As the crew's
light-hearted discussion had effectively jammed all the other transmissions to the control tower, the Squadron Commander was not
particularly amused and the errant pilot was asked to attend a
somewhat embarrassing interview.

From then on, we all became rather conscious of the little lever,
and on this occasion, I checked carefully that it was in the receive
position as I waited for the formation leader's instruction to start
engines.

A hissing noise in my earphones indicated the start of a transmission and a small and distant voice with a metallic ring to it
announced. 'This is red leader to red formation – start engines.'

I gave the thumbs-up signal to the fitter standing in front of the
aircraft and received the 'all clear' in return. The starboard engine
began to grind round slowly as did those of the other aircraft
around me, but although the others were bursting into life, mine
showed not the slightest inclination to do anything but rotate
under control of the starter motor. My temperature began to rise.
Perhaps the snag on this engine was rather more serious than the
cheerful fitter had diagnosed. If I didn't get going the balance of
the formation would be spoiled, and to my knowledge there was no
standby aircraft available.

Suddenly there was a loud crack, the engine spun over for
several revolutions and stopped. This activated Bert, who began
to run for the starboard side of the aircraft while snatching his
forage cap off his head. Undoubtedly the backfire had caused a fire
in the intake. The drill on these occasions was for the nearest

member of the ground crew to stuff his hat up the intake and douse the conflagration. The old hands could be readily identified by the colour of their hats, for they lost something of their pristine blueness in the operation. I couldn't see what was going on on the starboard side, but I hoped that our glamorous visitors would be suitably impressed by this rudimentary exercise.

Bert eventually appeared walking round to the front of the aircraft actively brushing his hat. He turned and stuck up his thumb again and I dutifully pressed the starter button. This time the engine fired in a swirl of blue smoke and we were in business.

The leading aircraft were by this time starting to move out onto the perimeter track, and I looked around for Pat Evans in 'D for Dog' as he was leading the second vic of three and I would be flying number two to him.

Eventually, after quite a bit of manoeuvring, the six aircraft were lined up into wind on the airfield in two vics of three, ours being to the right and slightly behind the leader's.

Bunny Hart's voice came through the earphones a little more clearly this time, 'Red leader to red formation take-off, take-off, Go!'

Obediently the engine noise of the aircraft rose to a crescendo and we all began to trundle forward over the grass, the leader using something less than full throttle to give his wing men a little power in hand to make up any ground temporarily lost. I concentrated on the front of my section leader's aircraft, juggling with the throttles and the rudder bar to keep station. It would be up to him to check when we had sufficient speed for lift off and to climb clear of obstructions, I would just have to follow. Running as we were, within a few feet of his side, it would be fatal to look away even for a second.

Beyond him, I was conscious of the first vic lifting and I began to 'gather' the control column as Pat Evans' wheels left the grass. We came off a second later and I eased the aircraft up until we were immediately behind the trailing edge of his wing again. His wheels began to disappear up into the engine nacelles and I changed my left hand from the throttles to the control-column yoke and slid my right hand down to fumble with the under-carriage selector and its murderous hinged flap.

We climbed steadily straight ahead into a sky washed blue by the rain, and at 1000 ft the leader's voice came through again—'Levelling off, turning left, turning left, Go!'

The formation rolled to port and wheeled in unison like a pack of sleek greyhounds in disciplined pursuit as we headed back towards the airfield. My concentration on the vic leader's aircraft was total and any movement in relation to him was minimal. I could see the back of his head as he watched the other vic to keep us in station, and in the clear morning air, the lines of rivets along the fuselage skinning were visible. On the wingroot fillet were painted the words NO STEP, and in the gun-turret the crewman sat motionless facing aft, his goggles and oxygen mask concealing the human features. Only the inevitable aircrew scarf, the end of which was flapping wildly in the slipstream, gave a clue to our cruising speed of 180 mph.

In the stable condition of straight and level flight, I took the opportunity to glance away for a second to check our position. We were approaching the upwind boundary of the airfield with the blocks of hangars on the right, and the dispersals on the far side. When I looked back, we had risen a few feet above the leader, and a slight forward pressure on the control column was needed to sink back to his level.

We flew on over the dispersal area, the faces of the spectators looking like pink dots as they watched our passage. The formation was tight and immaculate; not a man out of place to spoil the geometric pattern. I felt a glow of pride and pleasure at being part of such a team.

Once past the airfield, another wheeling turn brought us back on to the return heading, but this time, as we approached the dispersal, Bunny gave the order to change to a box formation.

Pat eased down slightly below the leading vic, I and his number three man sticking close, then he rolled slightly to the left and we slid in underneath the first vic and straightened up. A gentle acceleration now and we moved forward until their silhouettes completely filled the sky above us. The tailwheel of the number two aircraft was about ten feet above my cockpit canopy and rotating slowly the wrong way round in the slipstream. It was vital now to keep tucked in on Pat's aircraft, and equally essential that the two man should not sink below the leader, for I was just below him and only conscious of him out of my peripheral vision as I looked across at my vic leader.

Bunny Hart's measured tones came over the radio ordering a turn to starboard and I reacted to Pat's manoeuvre to keep the aircraft locked into that triangle of space between his wingtip and his tailplane; I wasn't really conscious that we were in a turn, for the relative positions of the six aircraft hadn't changed.

We ran up to the dispersal area in this box formation, and as we went over the top, the order came to revert to our original station. We slid out from underneath moving to the right and the sky overhead was bright and uncluttered again.

This time, the leader swung in a long slow turn that brought us on a run to one side of the airfield and then came the radio command, 'Change formation – echelon starboard – Go!'

Pat swung away from the leading vic while both number three men fell back, dropped below the leaders until clear of their slipstreams and then swung across to the right before pulling up into their new positions. I now had a wing man on my right, and Pat closed in on the number three man in the leading vic so that all six aircraft were strung out to the right of the leader and staggered back in echelon.

This is a more difficult formation, particularly for those near the end, for if the number two man makes a correction, number three will react slightly later with possibly a more exaggerated movement and this passes on like a ripple along the line of aircraft.

Eventually, we went into a long sweeping wheel to the left, those of us on the outside having to accelerate to keep in station and as we rolled out onto the run-in, comparatively large power reductions had to be made and the formation became a little untidy. We had just settled down in a neatly staggered line when the leader lowered his nose into a dive; obviously we were going to do a low run as a climax.

The engine noise began to increase as we gathered speed. The leader steepened the dive. We were hot-footing it for ground level now and little undulations were rippling the line of aircraft as we worked tensely to keep station. This was the finale, so it had to be good.

Although concentrating on Pat's wingtip, I was still conscious of the fact that we were getting extremely low. Fields, trees and hedgerows were flashing by in a green blurr. Then we whipped over the airfield boundary and the leader seemed to crouch down to almost grass height. I knew that the dispersal huts were ahead and beyond that there was a line of trees, but I daren't glance forward. We were streaming across the airfield now at God knows what speed. I could only cling tight to the next aircraft and trust the leader. The perimeter shot underneath like a whiplash, then a kaleidoscopic pattern of concrete, grass and scattered people. 'Break left! Break left! Go!' shouted the leader as he pulled up into a steep climbing turn. Number two followed, then three, four in swift succession. As I heaved on the control column I saw the green fingers of the trees reaching up to me as I looked forward for the first time. I pushed the throttles hard forward and followed the now straggling line of aircraft climbing to the left.

'Jeeesus Christ!' said Benny in a low voice. 'That was too close for comfort!'

'Those buggers down there thought so too!' shouted Weeky. 'They all threw themselves down!'

'We couldn't have been that low!' I protested.

'We bloody were!' said Weeky in some heat, and sure enough, events after we had landed proved him to be right.

The scene was somewhat confused as the six aircraft taxied back into the dispersal area, but I could see from the grin on Fred Cole's face as he marshalled me on the hard-standing that the groundcrew had enjoyed it anyway. I cut the engines, threw off my straps and reached up to slide back the canopy. I now realised how much I had been sweating and I needed some air.

Bert came scampering up the catwalk on the wing laughing excitedly, 'That was wizard, Skip!' he shouted down to me, 'but by Christ you were low!'

'Is that right?' I grinned appreciatively.

'Not half! We all took to the ground including the comic opera brigade. They're covered in mud and the CO's livid!'

The following morning, Bunny was told to report to the head-quarters block, but by this time the CO had received such a verbal battering from higher levels that his attitude to the affair was undergoing a change. Initially, he was mortified by the indignity which had been heaped on his guests and hinted darkly at a court martial to follow, but the over-reaction of the excitable South

Americans began to erode his sympathy, and when they not only threatened reactions from a diplomatic level but actually induced them, his anger began to swing in the opposite direction.

In the event, Bunny was given a formal reprimand and then invited to join the Old Man for a drink in the mess bar at lunchtime, indicating to the onlookers that although the exuberant young officer may have gone too far, the crime wasn't so heinous as to merit the dismissal of an excellent operational pilot.

Two days later the squadron was detailed to bomb an industrial complex near Bethune in the north of France, and we carried out one of the few high-level raids that the Blenheims had been involved in.

The formations of three squadrons flew over at 10,000 ft, weaving their way through the black puffs of ack-ack bursts that blossomed in our path, but the opposition seemed negligible compared with the holocausts we had met when attacking shipping at low level and we were surprised to lose an aircraft, and shocked to learn that the pilot was Bunny Hart.

A number of low-level attacks were made during the days that followed, mostly against shipping near the enemy coast, and although we still suffered an infestation of butterflies in our stomachs at briefing and during the run-in for the attack, the fact that we got through cross-fire virtually unscathed each time had given us a hardening of confidence and perhaps even a feeling of 'it won't happen to me'.

At the end of three weeks we had seen enough action to be considered veterans in an activity where the life expectancy was somewhat short; we were now accepted members of the squadron and were happy to be committed to it and grateful for the comradeship of the men around us. Because of this, our dismay was all the greater when in an interview with the Squadron Commander, I learned that my crew and I were to be posted to the Middle East.

He was sorry, he said, but there was nothing he could do about it. Squadrons in North Africa were getting desperately short and one crew from each UK-based Blenheim Station was being re-deployed. The names had been pulled out of a hat at Command Headquarters as this had seemed the fairest way.

We left the next day with a feeling of betrayal.

CHAPTER SIX

Birds of passage

SEVEN DAYS overseas posting leave ended with another part-ing from my family which was more harrowing than the first had been. Africa seemed a long way away in those days, and the war was going badly there. The British Army were already retreating towards Cairo and a number of desert airfields had been overrun and taken by the enemy. When Weeky, Benny and I met at Watton to collect a new aircraft, we were not a very cheerful group.

For the long journey south, overload fuel tanks had been stowed in the bomb-bay and a large ammunition box fitted in the naviga-tor's nose compartment to feed the Browning machine-guns mounted under the nose to protect the belly during the high-level cruise.

The trip to Gibraltar keeping well clear of the Iberian Peninsula would take the aircraft to the extreme limit of its range, so it was necessary to carry out an accurate consumption test at the sort of height we would be flying. After short low-level trips of about two to three hours, we found the business of cruising somewhat aim-lessly at 10,000 ft rather trying, and in an attempt to break down the boredom I suggested to Benny that he might like to try his hand at the controls.

Weeky, trapped in his mid-turret, reacted with some alarm to the suggestion, but Benny accepted readily; climbing out of my seat, I held the control column while he wriggled out of his nose compartment and into the pilot's position.

He reacted to my handling instructions with slow concentration and although his flying was far from accurate, it wasn't alarming either, and Weeky soon lost interest. When I thought that Benny had had enough, I nodded to him and he slipped out of the seat, pushed gently round me and crawled back into the nose com-partment.

Once back at the controls, I decided that the consumption test was over and that the quickest way down from that sort of height was to do a half roll, close the throttles and pull the aircraft through in a half loop. This I proceeded to do, with Benny holding on to his navigation table with some anxiety. But as the nose came down into the vertical dive and the engine note rose to an exceptional pitch, there was a loud report and a rush of air that lifted a flurry of papers, dust, and dirt that swirled around my head. I started easing out of the dive and called Weeky on the intercom to ask if he could see anything wrong; but he didn't reply.

Craning my head round to peer through the narrow gap of the bomb well, I saw to my horror Weeky's kicking legs disappearing through the escape hatch. I continued pulling through harshly so that the 'G' forces would stop him going all the way out, and when we were flying level again, I shouted his name with all force. To my relief, his white face appeared below the coaming and he was mouthing something at me angrily. I learned what it was after landing.

When I had resumed the control from Benny no word had been spoken, so that when the aircraft went into an aerobatic manoeuvre Weeky thought that the worthy navigator had lost control and without further discussion he decided to leave. He had been half-way out of the escape hatch before I realised the position. Had he succeeded in baling out, then the questions at the subsequent court of inquiry could have been embarrassing, for the Blenheim Mark IV was not scheduled as an aerobatic aircraft.

At the end of another week, the aircraft was cleared and ready for the journey and positioned to Portreath on the Cornish coast, where a number of other unfortunates were waiting for a following wind before setting off for Gibraltar. This influx of crews was more than the station could accommodate, and we found ourselves living in a colony of bell tents on the hillside. We felt like a group of convicts waiting to be deported.

Each morning we rose before dawn and stumbled in darkness to the briefing-room, where inevitably the meteorological officer told us that the weather was unsuitable for the trip. We needed a good following wind to make the 1000-mile hop, and even so there would be no fuel left for a diversion when we got there. Life in the mess was dull and dispiriting, for we were not accepted by the resident members and our morale was low at the prospect ahead of us; so at the end of the first week we decided to take a bus to the nearest town and live it up a little.

It wasn't a success. The locals seemed to resent our intrusion, and try as we might, the spirit of revelry refused to come. Demoralisation became total on realising that we had missed the last bus back to camp. It was only a few miles back to Portreath, but a somewhat officious Special Constable wearing a tin hat and full equipment insisted that we take a short cut over the hills which he described.

It was the blackest of nights but with a refreshing breeze, and after a while I found myself enjoying the walk, the tramp of our feet echoing on the quiet air. We came eventually to a fork in the road which hadn't featured in the policeman's itinerary and our dilemma was increased because all the signposts had been blacked out or removed so that they could not be of any assistance to German paratroops who might decide to drop in. After a brief conference we took a vote on the two alternatives and finally set off again. This was the first of many mistakes that night. We became utterly and completely lost. Not a house did we see, nor a soul did we meet. We were somewhere in a dark and deserted Cornwall and we couldn't find the way out. We just kept on walking as it seemed equally pointless to sit down.

Benny had been trying to keep us on course in relation to the stars, but the twists and turns in the road were frustrating him and Weeky's scepticism only aggravated the situation. We must have been wandering for about four hours, when we realised that we were running into a small village. For some reason, we started walking on tiptoe while looking round somewhat hopelessly for a sign of life. Then we heard muffled voices. They were coming from the tiny village hall, and they grew louder as we approached. We pushed through the blackout curtain and surprised four men sitting around a table. They were air-raid wardens on night duty and they immediately regarded us with the gravest suspicion. We were asked to produce our identity cards. These were taken to the light and scrutinised with care. We were then interrogated at some length until they were satisfied that we hadn't dropped in from Germany, and only then did they give us clear directions to Portreath, which they said was only two miles away.

When we finally trudged through the camp gates, a shouted

challenge from the sentry made us jump, and tired and weary as we were, the pantomime of 'being recognised' seemed long and irksome. But we were in for a second shock as we approached the group of tents on the hillside, for most of them had lights glowing within. Weeky lifted the flap of one of them and stuck his head inside.

'What's going on?' he demanded.

'Haven't you heard?' came an answering voice. 'They've got a favourable weather report. Briefing is in half an hour and we're off at dawn!'

I went through the briefing in something of a daze, appalled at the prospect of the critical flight ahead of me. There would be no radio aids available and nagivation would have to rely on accurate course keeping and dead-reckoning. Focke-Wulf Condors of the Luftwaffe were known to patrol the west coast of Spain continuously, and the supposedly neutral Spanish were intrinsically hostile. If we had the misfortune to come down in their territory we would surely finish up in a prison camp for the duration of the war. In the event of trouble, we were advised to make for Portugal.

In the watery light of dawn we found ourselves clambering into the aircraft which was overloaded with fuel and spare parts packed into the most unlikely cavities. We were to proceed separately at the economical height of 10,000 ft and at a speed of 140 mph to conserve fuel. 'Like bleeding sitting ducks!' as Weeky said. If we were jumped by the enemy and had to make a run for it, even if we got away the excess fuel used would make our chances of getting to that lonely rock just north of Africa very slim indeed. The estimated flight time was 7 hours 30 minutes; the maximum endurance with the fuel aboard – 8 hours.

Lumbering to the take-off point, I found myself number four in line and I watched dully as the first machine started to trundle along the runway, its exhaust flames glowing in the still grey light. His rate of acceleration seemed incredibly slow and the machine was half-way along the runway before the tail came up. Still it rolled on, disappearing into the dull light still solidly on the ground.

'Who's taking any bets?' said Weeky on the intercom. We continued to watch. We couldn't tell for sure, but it seemed that he must be approaching the end of the runway, and the runway ended at the edge of a cliff. We never knew if he got airborne; we just saw him disappear.

'Poor sod!' said Benny in awe.

I sat there waiting for the column of black smoke which must inevitably appear, but a green light was flickering impatiently from the control tower and the second aircraft was moving into position.

He, too, used all the concrete available during his take-off, but he appeared to get airborne and then sank out of sight below the level of the cliffs. His navigation lights had been on, and eventually we saw the white tail light like a faint rising star in the distance. The number three aircraft had by this time pulled off the taxi track and cut his engines; either he had gone chicken or had a snag.

I lined up on the runway in response to the flashing green light from the tower and opened up to full throttle against the brakes until the whole aircraft rattled and shook. I switched off each magneto in turn and checked the drop in engine speed. They were all within limits. Cylinder-head temperature, oil pressures and oil temperature needles quivered by the right figures. We were going to need every pound of thrust available. I released the parking brake with a hiss of escaping air and we were away, trundling over the rough concrete.

The rate of acceleration was noticeably below normal; the aircraft felt heavy and sluggish on the ground. I had to push hard on the control column to lift the tail and with only 200 yards to go, the wheels were still bumping solidly. It was too late to abandon the take-off now; we would go over the cliff for sure. The speed was hesitating around the eighty mark. It wasn't enough. The sharp end of the concrete was moving rapidly towards us. After that there were a few yards of grass visible and then – nothing. I eased back on the control column but there was no response. Then a firmer pull – with anxiety. It would be fatal to snatch it: she might get airborne but she would stall immediately. We bounced off the end of the runway onto the rough ground. I had no choice now. I was still heaving back on the control column when we shot over the chasm above the sea and started to sink. There was only one drastic thing to do, push the nose down to try and gain flying speed before we hit the water.

The restless grey-green mass was coming up towards us at a

startling rate. I held the nose down until it seemed almost too late and then with a smooth powerful pull on the control column flattened out just above the sea. The water was rushing past close underneath, but we were holding our own. The airspeed indicator showed an acceleration that was agonisingly slow and it was several minutes before we had sufficient speed to attempt a climb and a further ten before we gained 500 ft and could ease back on the power for the slow economical climb to our cruising height.

We decided subsequently that this must have been what happened to the first aircraft, for we had seen no wreckage. He was probably too far away from the airfield to be observed by the time he regained the cliff height.

The journey was uneventful though it went on for a long time, and as much of the route was covered with medium cloud I flew in it for protection, hidden in the all-embracing gloom from the hostile eyes of the Condor crews who we knew patrolled the area. Their primary task was submarine-hunting but they were not averse to taking any fish that was foolhardy enough to swim into their sights.

After four or five hours, the droning of the engines and the instruments dancing before my tired eyes began to have an hypnotic effect. I was finding it difficult to keep the instrument panel in focus and my reaction times to any excursion from the desired flight path were becoming so slow that I was shocked to find on one occasion we had drifted twenty degrees off course.

The aircraft was much lighter now that half of the fuel had been used, and I decided to climb above the overcast and clear of cloud. We broke through into dazzling sunshine at around 12,000 ft and I felt stimulated immediately. Flying by visual references was much less demanding and I held the aircraft just above the cloud level, racing over the silver tops. If we were jumped now, it would take only a moment to dive for cover.

When the time came according to Benny's reckoning for us to start the descent towards Gibraltar, I slowly throttled back the engines and slid down into the cloud again. This was the critical part. Our last known position was the cliffs of Cornwall seven hours ago. My instrument flying had not been all that accurate at times and there was an element of guesswork about the forecast winds for the middle part of the route.

The petrol gauges indicated that we had about thirty-five minutes of flight time left, if they were to be believed. When we eventually broke cloud, we needed to be in sight of Gibraltar; if we weren't, then that was bad news! At one time, I had to force the chilling thought aside that if we were a few miles farther east than we thought, we could, right now, be descending into the mountains of the Spanish mainland. The briefing officer had told us that the forecast cloudbase for the area around Gib was 3,000 ft for the time of our arrival. If that was so, we could dive into a granite peak while still in cloud. We wouldn't know what was coming to us; perhaps that was just as well.

I summoned all my concentration to keep the aircraft on a stable descent. My world was confined to the instrument panel twenty inches from my nose and the low drone of the engines outside the cockpit windows. There was no point in looking out for there was nothing to see. We were suspended in a colourless opaque world of unknown dimensions. There had certainly been much more cloud en route than was forecast. The man could also be wrong about the height of cloudbase. The needle of the altimeter moved inexorably around the dial, now passing 5,000 ft. The vertical speed indicator showed a descent of 500 ft/min. The airspeed a steady 180 mph.

A microphone hissed into life. 'What height are we now, Skipper?' asked Weeky in an anxious voice.

'Five thousand,' I said. Weeky's microphone continued to hiss and crackle. The altimeter wound down past 4,500.

'They were wrong about the cloud en route,' he went on. 'I hope they're bloody right about the base here!' I felt a flutter of irritation: he was reinforcing my own doubt.

'Keep a good lookout and if you see anything close, shout!'

'Too right!'

Benny's microphone crackled into life and we heard him fumbling with the mask as he pulled it to his mouth.

'I did allow a few degrees on the courses in case the wind had more west in it than they said. We should be just off the coast right now.' His confidence was good to hear.

Passing 3,000 ft we were still in cloud and the aircraft was beginning to jiggle. This could indicate that we were in the lee of the mountains. Why should the cloud become turbulent near its base if we were over the sea? I had a growing urge to turn onto a westerly heading in case we were inside the coast, but I hesitated to doubt the navigator's word. In any case, we couldn't afford to turn through ninety degrees; it would add precious distance to the track, particularly if Benny was right and we were already west of course.

The aircraft was beginning to bounce about markedly now, the instrument panel dancing on its spring mounting. My grip on the controls was tightening. Then they both cried out together.

I looked up in time to see through a rapidly passing hole in the cloudbase a grey indeterminate mass below; but well below. Then it was gone.

'Well, we're over the sea all right!' said Benny with some satisfaction.

'Yes, but which bit?' retorted Weeky. 'There's an awful lot of salt water in this part of the world!'

The fact that we were definitely clear of the coast relieved some of my tension. Now we had to worry about finding the objective, but quickly! I had never seen fuel gauges so low.

The cloudbase began to break up again and we had a glimpse farther ahead. It was definitely a seascape. I realised with a shock that we were passing 2,000 ft, then with dramatic suddenness we dived out of cloudbase. We were no longer confined, but the bluey-grey scene was still featureless and ahead the lightly mottled sea merged with the distant horizon.

'What's that over on the left?' cried Weeky.

I looked to the east and groped to find what his sharp eyes had seen.

'It could be land or a bit of low cloud,' he said. Then I made out a vague suggestion of a patch slightly more solid than the surroundings, but still nebulous. I was already turning the aircraft in that direction when Benny suggested that whatever it was we certainly needed to turn east anyway.

I levelled off at 1,000 ft and with each minute the outline ahead became clearer until without any further doubt we could identify it as the 1,500-ft peak of the Rock; but it was still some way off.

'How are we off for fuel, Skipper?' asked Weeky.

'We've got none left for mistakes,' I said. The fatigue of the last few hours had left me. We were on the last dash for the sanctuary of the airfield we had come 1,000 miles to find.

As we closed the land, the details emerged more clearly. On the right was the harbour and dockyard embracing many large ships. To the left was the wide sweep of the bay to Algeciras and in the farther distance the mountains of Spain merging into the cloudbase.

In between was the neck of land at the foot of the precipitous rise of the rock of Gibraltar itself. I could make out some buildings and a gaggle of parked aircraft to the left of which appeared to be the landing strip. Yes, it was! There was an aircraft just going in. I pulled back the throttles, trimmed the nose up as the speed fell, lowered some flap and the undercarriage and settled the aircraft into an approach.

The airfield was, in fact, merely a landing strip with a loose dirt surface within the confines of the racecourse. It was very short and terminated in the Mediterranean at the far end. We had been warned that if we hadn't touched down within the first third, then power should be applied and the aircraft overshot, but this meant making a complete circuit of the Rock to position for another approach. We hadn't enough fuel to do that. It must be right the first time.

I was coming in a bit low to ensure we touched down good and early. It looked good. Then I saw a bright red light winking at me from the side of the runway.

'What the bloody hell is that for,' I cried out in alarm, although I knew it meant, 'You are not clear to land!' I glanced at the fuel gauges. They were touching zero. What did they think they were doing?

Then Weeky shouted, 'Skipper! There's an aircraft above us!'

I looked up and saw the dark silhouette of another Blenheim just fifty feet above us. Instinctively, I rolled to starboard and slid out from underneath. He had his wheels down and was also going in to land. I was heading for the harbour area now.

The red Aldis light was flashing frantically, but the other aircraft kept on going. He probably couldn't afford to overshoot and neither could I!

I put the aircraft in a careful turn to port and slid behind the tail of the other machine. We were much too close and both going at approach speed. I couldn't go any slower and here we were down to 500 ft and turning at right angles to the runway. Common sense was saying, 'Throw it away! Overshoot and go round again!' But that was a blank cheque.

I had instinctively reduced the rate of descent and saw with a shock that the speed was falling. I grabbed the throttles and thrust them forward. We were heading for the Spanish border now. 'Whatever you do, keep close to the Rock,' the man had said. 'They have been known to fire at insurgents.'

I wound the ailerons into a clumsy turn to starboard. We were close to the airfield boundary now and had gone slightly above the other aircraft, which had gained some ground on us during our manoeuvres.

As we slid behind him again I made up my mind and heaved the aircraft around on to the runway heading but on his starboard side. I was overcontrolling with the rudder and we skidded and fishtailed horribly. We were high and fast. Just what I had set out not to do. I pulled back the throttles and thrust the nose down sharply. Weeky and Benny's microphones were still hissing but they said nothing.

As the threshold was crossed we were about a hundred yards behind the other Blenheim and a couple of spans to the right. Formation landings had been commonplace on the squadron, but this chap couldn't know that he was the leader! I hoped to hell he didn't swing to the right!

He was going down the middle of the strip and we were on the right-hand edge. I concentrated on the landing, made a good touchdown and went for the brakes. The aircraft began to slide on the loose dirt surface, but the gap between us was growing. We were OK.

'I reckon the duty pilot's going to want to see you,' said Benny as we taxied into the aircraft park, 'coming in against a red.'

'It could have been for either of us!' said Weeky sharply.

'I couldn't care less!' I cut in, my voice shaking a little. 'We've got down in one piece and that's the main thing.'

'Amen!' said Weeky.

CHAPTER SEVEN

On to Malta

IN THE EVENT, nothing was said at de-briefing and after we had been on the Rock for a few days we realised why. Dramas on the busy landing strip were an hourly occurrence and it really wasn't surprising, for like myself most of the pilots had about 200 hours total flight time in their logbooks, the trip out from England was made without any navigational assistance and the weather forecasts were of doubtful value. On arrival the fuel reserves were minimal and the airfield itself was small with watery hazards at either end.

We slept late the next morning, and it was almost noon before we made our bleary-eyed way to the ablutions. By this time, all the cloud had vanished and the air was sweet and mild like an English spring day. We stripped to the waist and refreshed ourselves at the makeshift line of taps and tin basins that had been set up in the open.

The sheer north face of the Rock loomed straight up from the edge of the airfield and the muffled explosions of quarrying were followed by the rattle of loose stones and shale that tumbled on to a vast heap at its base. We learned subsequently that the Rock itself was honeycombed with gun emplacements and ammunition stores, and that these were being extended continuously.

Returning to the barrack block, we plunged into the depths of our kitbags for the tropical uniforms which we were to wear for the first time, and although they were somewhat crumpled, the light khaki jackets and shorts with matching socks were smarter and more comfortable in this environment than the heavy blue serge. Marching in step to the mess, we felt uplifted after the depression of the past two weeks. We seemed to be entering a new phase which promised to be much more stimulating than we had thought in the closeness of the English countryside.

A few beers in the bar before lunch and then an excellent meal

buoyed our morale further, and by mid-afternoon we were marching into the town with another transit crew. The narrow streets
were alive with a press of people, while the cars and trucks – which
were not allowed to use their horns in wartime less they conflict
with an air raid warning – moved forward cautiously, the drivers
banging the doors with the flat of their hands to alert people in
front. After the austerity of ration-bound England, the range and
diversity of goods in the shops reminded us of peace, and to be
invited to buy chocolate without so much as a mention of a ration-
book gave us an odd feeling of guilt. The servicemen who crowded
the many giftshops were predominantly naval; they had seen it all
before, in other places, and were more than a match for the garru-
lous traders. Our interest in the goods was purely academic, and
as Weeky said when he was offered a pair of silk stockings to
'take home to his sweetheart' – 'We're going the wrong way,
mate!'

The food market which was housed in a square stone building
by the waterfront exuded a pleasantly ripe smell, and inside, the
stalls were dressed in tiers of washed fruit and vegetables. It was
much cleaner and more orderly than anything I had seen in
England.

We tired of window shopping eventually and made our way up
to the southern end of the town where the road began its climb out
of the busy complex, the houses thinning out as we climbed
Telegraph Hill towards the summit. The steepness of the road and
the heat of the afternoon sun combined to slow our pace, and when,
at around the half-way mark we came upon a convenient wall, we
sank down on it gratefully to rest our legs and admire the view.
From this height, the town was just a profusion of roofs scattered
down the hillside, with the naval base at the bottom. We could see
a number of capital ships dominated by the forbidding bulk of the
aircraft-carrier *Ark Royal*, and lying at anchor in the waters outside
the harbour were a group of merchantmen, smoke curling lazily from
their funnels as they waited for the next convoy to be assembled.

Inside the base itself, we were aware of a great deal of activity,
even at this range, for the rattle of rivet guns echoed against the
hillside, and the arcs of welding torches flickered incessantly as
they worked on urgent repairs. We knew that the convoys taking
vital supplies to Malta were being badly mauled as they ran the

gauntlet between Sicily and North Africa. To their crews, the
Rock must have seemed a haven of peace in a very hostile area.
We watched in silence for a while as the wakes of the launches and
liberty boats described a lacey pattern in the water.

'I've never been on a boat,' murmured Benny, after a while.

'Not any kind of boat?' Weeky asked.

'If I hadna' made aircrew I think I would have liked to join the
Navy,' he went on.

'I'm not sure which is the worst of two evils,' I put in; 'certainly
in wartime. We're all taking a bit of a battering particularly in this
part of the world.'

I looked to the south and tried to make out the contour of the
African coastline, which although only a few miles away was
obscured by the light haze. Things were going badly for the 8th
Army, and each day brought news of further retreats back along
the road to Cairo. Gibraltar seemed fairly secure at the moment,
but Malta was in the middle of it, surrounded by hostile territory.
The thought that tomorrow might see us on our way there,
reminded me that we had to report to operations at 1800 hrs to
check on the prospects.

In the event, we need not have hurried back, for we learned that
the weather farther east was not good, and that our departure
would be delayed until at least the day after tomorrow.

We went back into the town again that evening to live it up a
little, and were delighted to find the gaily-lit shops still doing
business and the bars crowded with servicemen bent on relieving
their tensions in a welter of beer and good humour. Naval ratings
predominated and they were clearly determined that such time as
they did have ashore was not to be wasted. As for ourselves, we felt
somewhat languid as the past forty-eight hours were catching up
with us and we rounded off the evening by making our way into a
bar that announced 'Cabaret' in large letters together with a picture
of a well-proportioned young lady wearing little more than a veil
of long dark hair.

'Rosy', in the flesh, was no less endearing than her picture, for
she undulated onto the little stage stripped to the waist apart from
two tassles that hung from suitable fittings that nature had provided on her superstructure. She was obviously a favourite with
the regular clientele for they whistled and stamped as she started

to jerk her body to the music causing the two appendages to go into rotation.

Benny chuckled appreciatively, 'Tha's the nicest little twin I've seen so far. I wonder what's her take-off speed!'

'Now, now!' admonished Weeky. 'That's not like you Benny! What would your mother say if she could hear you?' Benny continued to chuckle with satisfaction.

With a flashing smile, Rosy broke the rhythm of her body momentarily so that the left tassle stopped spinning and fell dormant while the other continued to rotate.

'Feather port!' shouted Weeky to general laughter.

In a further display of versatility, she restarted the port fan and stopped the starboard, and then, when both were spinning again, with a final contortion of her shapely body, she got them both going in opposite directions.

'I want to see you doing that, Benny, when we get back to camp,' said Weeky as we made our way out of the bar after the show. Benny just chuckled again. He seemed to be quietly relishing the experience.

The last section of the road to the airfield gates was completely dark, and we were making our way in the direction of what we thought was the entrance, when a voice near and loud shouted, 'Halt! Put your hands up!' We froze in our tracks and hastily complied.

Two figures closed with us, one holding a rifle ready to fire from the hip and the other flashing a torch in our faces. They gruffly demanded our identity cards, in a Scots accent. They seemed almost disappointed when we were able to produce them, and let us go with reluctance. The airstrip was guarded by a battalion of the Black Watch. Rumour had it that they were the only unit lifted off the beaches of Dunkirk which, instead of being returned home, were shipped straight down to Gibraltar for another overseas tour; the story went that they relieved their feelings by bumping off airmen who reacted the wrong way or too late when challenged.

In the morning we lay in late again as no one seemed to mind very much what the transit crews did, but at lunchtime we learned that a convoy of Wellington bombers was due in from the UK that afternoon, and that their arrival was a spectacle not to be missed. Accordingly, we made our way to the edge of the strip, found ourselves a perch on a bomb trolley, and settled down to await events.

There was quite an assortment of aircraft parked untidily, and beside our Blenheims were three Swordfish which we were told were used for weather reconnaisance, a Hudson in RAF markings, two Hurricanes looking rather lost, an assortment of training planes and several Wellington bombers in various states of disrepair. On the other side of the strip was a pile of wreckage in which were embedded identifiable objects such as a Hercules engine with the propellor blades twisted, the charred framework of a tailplane, and a mass of geodetic structure that once had been a Wellington.

At the western end of the strip, we saw a continuous procession of pedestrians and vehicles crossing by the only route to the Rock from the Spanish border. A high percentage of people who worked in Gibraltar were Spaniards with day permits, and we fell to discussing what must have been a major security problem. We were told quite seriously that all aircraft movements were monitored from the other side of the boundary with Spain, and certainly the number of successful interceptions by the enemy of our aircraft flying eastwards suggested that in many cases they had had prior information. It gave us an uncomfortable feeling to know that we would be the next crew to run that particular gauntlet. A gunner from the Royal Artillery had told us the previous evening that on one occasion an RAF machine in overflying the strip inadvertently strayed for a short distance across the border and had been promptly shot down by a Spanish machine-gun, which so outraged a Bofors gun team mounted high up in the Rock that they replied and wiped out the 'neutral' nest. However, the imparter of the information had obviously visited more than one bar before we met him, and we decided to treat the story with reservations.

There was quite a bit of ad hoc flying going on during the afternoon, and just before each take-off and landing, the flow of traffic across the strip was held up until the aircraft had passed. Later, the flow stopped completely, and shielding our eyes against the glare of the sun, we searched the sky to the west until we spotted a dark shape making a long low approach, and in the farther distance, another. Gradually, the details emerged until we could identify a Wellington, or 'Wimpy' as the type was known in deference to a cartoon character of the day, J. Wellington Wimpy.

We watched in silence its descent over the water, on what in the absence of wind was a steady approach. The machine looked very large crossing the shoreline in a nose-up attitude, indicating that the pilot was dragging it in at the minimum safe speed, for it was obviously going to take some stopping within the landing distance available. Approaching the Spanish Road, the throttles were closed and the main wheels touched almost immediately sending twin spurts of dust into the air; then the tail began to lift and the wheels slid for a short distance as the pilot over-braked anxiously. But the landing was well judged and as the machine trundled past us it was obvious that it would have no difficulty in stopping before the end of the strip.

But the second man did not make such a good job of his arrival. Even from where we were sitting, it was obvious that the pilot was overcontrolling somewhat excitedly. He left his landing flare too late, the wheels hit the ground and the machine bounced. The nose was pushed violently down again and on the second impact one could see the undercarriage legs shorten as the rams compressed. It was projected back into the air, this time even higher; the engines roared as the pilot either tried to catch the bounce and soften the next impact, or attempted to go round again. But he was too late: the great machine fell back as if exhausted of lift. The hydraulic shock absorbers shot it back into the air again just as he closed the throttles. The pilot was out of phase with events. In a last frantic effort he must have pulled the stick back, for the tail wheel hit first as he approached our position, the port wing dropped and the wheel that side hit hard, gave a short bounce, and as it passed us we saw the oleo leg on that side collapsing.

The wingtip and propellor hit the ground with a loud scraping sound sending up a shower of dust and debris. The drag swung the machine round in a cavorting arc. Hidden in the dust cloud momentarily, its bulk reappeared as it swung through 180° canted over helplessly. We watched fascinated as it continued to swing, slowed down and stopped diagonally across the strip.

Through the dust cloud that drifted slowly towards the frontier fence came the fire engines, ambulance and a convoy of tractors. We saw the crew men climbing out through the various hatches rather slowly as if dazed. The best thing we could do was to keep out of the way: there was no sign of fire. We saw one man clutching his head and being led stooping to the ambulance. As we watched, our attention was suddenly diverted by the roar of an aircraft's engines very close. We looked round to see another Wimpy a few feet above the runway pulling up into a climb. He cleared the wreck easily enough and went into a climbing turn over the sea.

'I hope the poor sod's got enough fuel for another circuit,' said Weeky fervently.

'Och yes!' put in Benny. 'They're no so pushed for range as we were, Weeky.'

However, the predicament of the other aircraft had sent the ground crew into a flurry of activity: chains were being fastened to the starboard undercarriage leg and to the twisted structure on the other side with a speed that could only have come from practice. But the Wellington was making another approach before the tractors could take up the slack.

'God! He got round the Rock quickly!' I said in some surprise.

'Mebbe it's another one,' suggested Benny.

'It must be He couldn't have got right around in that time!'

The tractors were now taking the strain, but the rear wheels of the nearest one were beginning to spin in the dust. The aircraft was coming lower on the approach. If he tried to land, it could only end in disaster. A number of men had climbed onto the tractor to put more weight on the rear wheels.

'Jesus! I wouldn't like to be in their position,' murmured Weeky fervently.

'He is going ta land!' shouted Benny, and sure enough, the other aircraft landed heavily just beyond the road. Immediately it began to slide as the brakes locked. It started to swerve, first one way then the other. Weeky scrambled up with a cry, 'I'm getting out of here!'

The aircraft came rumbling on; but fast! It had passed the point of no return. It was too late to get airborne again and he couldn't possibly stop in time. The crippled aircraft was being dragged now in short quivering jerks. It had barely moved ten feet as the other aircraft bore down on it.

It was now swerving heavily to port, but the impact was inevitable. The starboard wing hit the fin of the crippled aircraft and large fragments of the structure burst into the air.

As the landing aircraft disappeared behind the other, I saw its tail lifting and scrambled up on the bomb trolley to get a better look. It reappeared beyond the wreck sliding sideways, smoke and dust billowing from its wheels. The fire engines and ambulance were now setting off in pursuit.

Just before the impact, a number of men in the crash party had taken to their heels; now they rushed back and rejoined the efforts to drag the crippled aircraft clear. The engines on the other machine were still running, and in response to frantic signals from one of the ground crew it started to taxi clear, spiked jagged pieces of metal sticking out where the first twelve feet of its wing had been amputated. Another Wellington flew over the scene with flaps down but wheels up, obviously sizing up the situation. By the time another aircraft, or maybe it was the same one, was making an approach, the wreck had been dragged clear.

Three more machines landed that afternoon, not with polish, but safely, and the show was over.

The next morning, we were on our way. The weather forecast wasn't all that good, and Benny began to look worried on learning that we would be leading a vic of three, low-level, on the flight to Malta. It wasn't a pleasant prospect, for we had been briefed to keep radio silence and thus would not be able to get any bearings, and Malta was a very small piece of land to find after some seven hours flying over the sea, particularly in the sort of visibility that had been forecast for the second half of the route. Add to that the fact that we would be flying between enemy territory on both sides and it seemed to us a pretty rotten way to spend a Sunday.

The sun was already warm in the cockpit as I settled myself in, fastened the straps of the parachute and the safety harness and tested the intercom. The other two aircraft in the formation were parked behind me so I couldn't give hand signals to indicate 'start engines'; in the event, I got my own 'turning and burning' and Weeky confirmed that they had too. Bearing in mind that we had 1,000 miles of sea to cross at low level and with no friendly diversions available. I checked the performance of the engines with care before signalling to the ground crew to pull the chocks clear. As we moved out onto the strip, the antlike procession of commuters across it was broken, and a green light winked at us from the control-tower.

Although some of the spares we had brought out from the UK had been taken off, the aircraft was still heavily laden; with so much fuel on board it responded sluggishly to power changes. At briefing it had been decided that a formation take-off was not on, as each of us would need all the power we had to lift off before the end of the strip. So I went right to the beginning of it before turning into wind, and the other two aircraft stood off to one side to let me pass.

When a steady green from the tower indicated that I was cleared to go, I pulled the control column hard back and opened up the throttles to the take-off gate. The yoke was butting me in the stomach as the aircraft stood bouncing on its wheels. I put one arm right round the front of it to free my hand and reach out for the boost override lever on the instrument panel. I had in mind to open up to full power with the brakes still on to get the best possible take-off run. The aircraft racketed and shuddered as the boost override came in. The elevator buffet was so severe that it took all my strength to hold the control column back; the aircraft seemed to be fighting to get away.

Then I let it have its head by releasing the brakes: it surged forward and the motion smoothed out. When a pilot is anxious about the length of his take-off run, the acceleration always seems lower than usual and as the end of the runway approaches, sudden doubts cloud the judgement. It doesn't seem that there can be enough runway left to get to flying speed and yet, if the take-off is abandoned, could one possibly stop? Other aircraft have made it, but then some haven't. The machine is certainly overloaded and it is truly a miss and hit affair.

By 80 mph, the details of the boundary wall are clear in the sunshine, and the sea sparkles immediately behind it. We are committed. The airspeed indicator needle quivers uncertainly round the dial. It's eighty-five now. We really need ninety, but there is no more time. I start pulling back the control column. It feels heavy and although the aircraft's attitude is changing, it is not lifting. There's only one thing left now – pull, desperately. When it seems inevitable that the wheels must hit the wall, the aircraft sags into the sky, sluggish and unwilling. The wall flashes underneath, I am still pulling on the control column, but the aircraft skims over the water in a nose-up attitude and without gaining height. The speed is increasing very slowly, one mile an hour at a time. The aircraft is beginning to lift and I can ease the pressure on the control column and let the speed increase.

It took ten minutes to gain 400 ft in height and to accelerate to the economical cruising speed of 140 mph; then I turned onto the first course slightly north of east to take us between the Island of Alborah and the Spanish mainland.

'Any sign of the other two?' I asked Weeky on the intercom.

'Just about. Number two is half a mile behind and very wide, and I can just see number three in the distance.'

The idea was to fly in very loose formation most of the way to conserve fuel, and if we were jumped by fighters, I would call them into half a span and dive for the sea. This would give us the best protection, for when aircraft are attacking a formation from above, they like to be able to dive past and underneath as they break off, where the air gunners can't get at them. If the formation is flown just above the sea, a fighter will have to break off above and with his belly exposed to the air gunners. This deters him from pressing the attack home too close – or that is the theory.

I checked the instruments, and was relieved to see that the cylinder-head temperatures had now dropped below the 200°C mark. The oil pressures and temperatures were good and I trimmed back the power slightly to contain the speed at the agreed figure. The sky was quite without cloud and the visibility good; too damn good. To the left the coast of Spain ran away northeast towards Malaga before finally disappearing in the blue haze. The air was as smooth as ice, allowing for very accurate flying, and below, the sea undulated lazily in the sunshine. It was hard to believe the forecast which had indicated that the visibility during the second half of the trip would be around 800 yards.

We passed north of the Spanish Island of Alborah and Benny took a compass bearing on it to check the groundspeed.

'There's nae wind at all on this leg,' he announced after making a few calculations. 'Turn onto O-nine-O now, Skipper.'

We were running parallel to the coast of southern Spain, and its outline could just be discerned about thirty miles to the north. The engines droned on contentedly and Benny calculated that we would have about forty-five minutes reserve fuel on arrival in Malta; not that that would be of any use to us for a diversion, the nearest friendly territory being some 400 miles away, but at least we could take our time about landing, and in the visibility forecast that might be necessary. In our present position, there was little likelihood that we would be jumped by fighters; our cruising height of 400 ft meant that we would not be giving our position away over too wide an area and we could relax rather more than if we were skimming along at sea-level.

After about three hours, our estimated position was north of Algiers, the sky was going a bit yellow and light turbulence had developed. It looked as if the forecasters were going to be right in their assumption that in Malta the Gregale would be blowing, a hot southerly wind from the desert which brought with it a swirling dust haze.

By the time we were between the southern tip of Sardinia and Bizerta on the Tunisian coast, the visibility was down to less than a mile and the aircraft was bucketing about in the rough air. We had been flying for a little over five hours, and to conserve my energy I didn't fight the aircraft for accuracy, but let it undulate either side of the course, and when we lost fifty feet in a down-draught, I eased it back to cruising height slowly. The other two had closed up a little to keep me in sight, but they were still standing off at about four spans, so my loose flying was no embar-rassment to them.

Every so often, Benny's bottom would appear backed out of the nose compartment as he crouched over the bombsight to take a drift on the white caps that now laced a rising sea. We had about 10 degrees of port drift, indicating a wind from the south of about 30 knots, and it was getting rougher all the time. One blessing of the reduced visibility, though, was that it would give us some cover as we raced through the Sicilian Channel between Sicily and the Island of Pantelleria, for it was known that there were a number of fighter airfields on the mainland, and intelligence reports indicated that there were at least two squadrons on the tiny island.

On the other hand, we could miss Malta in the murk. It would be quite easy to do as we had had no accurate position check in the last seven hours and the wind had been changing continuously. We would have limited fuel reserves to go about and start a square search for it. I had already decided that if we had not seen Malta by five minutes after the estimated time, I would order Weeky to break radio silence and call for a bearing, on the assumption that we must be near enough the island to be able to home-in before the enemy could plot our position and dispatch their fighters. But there was an added problem according to the intelligence officer in Gib: the nasty habit that the Italian radio stations had of answering a call for a bearing, and giving one which would lead the unsuspecting aircraft straight to the anti-aircraft guns on the Sicilian coast. We were advised to interrogate any station that answered, with care.

Benny gave me a change of course to the southeast for the final run-in along the channel, and I eased the aircraft down until we were racing a few feet above the sea, with myself in mental over-drive. Even at this height the air was rough, and the other machines which had closed up now to about a span were having a tough time holding station.

The air was oppressively hot, and trickles of sweat ran down my neck as I worked at the controls trying to keep the aircraft as stable as possible to give the wing men a chance. At this height we were intimately aware of the roughness of the sea as we coursed swiftly over the wavetops, and our forward vision was down to about 1,000 yards. The sea appeared to be rushing at us out of the murk.

I couldn't imagine that fighters would be deployed in this sort of weather, but there was the danger that if we were not dead on track we could find ourselves running along the coast of Sicily on the one hand or right on to the hornet's nest of Pantelleria, if the courses that Benny had given me were in error. He kept trying to take further drifts, but at this height they were suspect.

We streamed on in this world of rough sea and encircling gloom, and as the tension mounted, the minutes ticked by with irritating slowness. The last hour seemed interminable.

Benny's microphone crackled into life, 'I estimate the northwest tip of the island at 1528.'

'Roger,' I acknowledged; then silence on the intercom as we tried to penetrate the gloom to see what lay ahead.

Just before the appointed time, I thought that the sky had lightened a little and began to wonder if we were already running in the lee of the island; then the visibility closed in again rather worse than before. In any case, there was too much sea running for us to be off a lee shore. The waves were mountainous and white spume was being whipped from the tops in the wind.

I kept checking the clock at the top of the instrument panel; the time was getting very near.

'I reckon we've got aboot fifty minutes' fuel left,' announced the navigator.

'OK, Benny,' I said a bit sharply. 'Now concentrate on keeping a good lookout.'

'Roger.'

The appointed time arrived. I half expected Malta to come speeding towards us out of the murk ahead. And there was another snag: the secondary island of Gozo at its northern tip had cliffs some 300 ft high. If we were slap on track I hoped I would see it in time to turn and take the formation clear.

The minutes ticked on but there was nothing around but the restless sea. I'd give it two more minutes, then call for a bearing.

Weeky's sharp eyes saw it first. About a mile to starboard, the sandstone bulk of Gozo sliding by, vaguely contoured in the haze; at least we assumed it was Gozo. It had to be, but there was one way of finding out and I hand-signalled a turn to the right to the wing men who had now closed up, at the same time lifting the nose and rising above the sea. The cliffs slid past us and there was sea again. That confirmed it was an island. Then a flatter coast came into view – probably Comino – and immediately beyond, more coastline. It was running northwest-southeast and must surely be Malta.

A small point of light was flashing at us from the top of a hill. I ordered Benny to fire the colours of the day from the Very pistol while I tapped out the code letters on the downward-identification light. The bark of the pistol was loud in such a confined space, and the cockpit filled with the reek of cordite. The small point of light stopped flashing. We had been challenged and identified correctly; all was well.

As we made our way along the coastline towards Valletta, the air became more turbulent and the formation was thrown about in some disarray. There seemed little point in arriving en masse at the airfield, so I broke R/T silence and ordered the wing men to disperse and proceed independently.

My first impression of Malta was of a rocky island made untidy by a haphazard scattering of angular buildings all of the same dull honeycomb colour, set in a patchwork of tiny stone-walled fields, the whole surrounded by a rugged coastline laced with foam. Ahead we could see the more densely populated area of Valletta itself, Sliema Creek, and the Grand Harbour packed with shipping.

I turned inland where the airfield at Luqa lay on high ground. The visibility was, in fact, better than we had thought now that we had identifiable objects to help us judge the range, but the wind was still very strong and blowing right across the runway. Certainly during the approach the turbulence became severe; the aircraft dropped and floundered in the downdraughts and I had to work hard on the controls to contain the fluctuating airspeed within a safe range.

The landing could only be described as an arrival, and after the heavy touchdown I had to give a bootful of rudder to stop us weather-cocking into wind. We snaked along the runway as I used some differential brake and it was only towards the end of the landing run when the speed had fallen that I managed to get things completely under control.

Weeky started to make some cutting remark just as the tower called me up with taxying instructions and I told him rather irritably to pipe down. I was feeling very tired now, somewhat angry with myself for the poor approach and landing, and generally depressed at the bleak scene around us. We taxied to the dispersal that the controller had indicated, where it was a blessed relief to cut the engines and have their racket die to a final chuckle; then silence, except for the soughing of the hot wind which rocked the aircraft and sent the dust scurrying between the rocks and stones that littered the area.

In the distance and below was the confusion of flat roofs punctuated by many church spires that was Valletta. To the north the ground rose again, barren and craggy, supporting a few small olive trees and prickly pears. There was no greenness, just a dull uniform ochre.

An open truck pulled up alongside, the driver getting out and leaning against the radiator waiting for us to disembark. He didn't seem very enthusiastic about anything. My body felt cramped and my legs ached after sitting for over seven hours in the same position, and I climbed up through the top hatch awkwardly and then sat there in the snatching wind to slowly re-establish my affinity with mother earth.

Benny was backing out of his nose compartment dragging the navigation bag behind him, and Weeky standing head and shoulder out of his own hatch by the turret was shouting against the wind. 'This looks a bright bloody place to nightstop. Why don't we go back to Gib?'

I shrugged in reply, and leaning down, heaved my parachute out of the bucket seat and slung it over onto the wing. Benny handed me up his chute and navigation bag, and then climbed up wearily after me.

We were unloading our kitbags from the rear hatch and the airman was still lounging against his vehicle watching without particular interest.

'Airman!' I shouted, suddenly angry. He pushed himself into an upright position and came sauntering towards us with his hands in his pockets.

'Get your hands out of your pockets!' I said sharply. 'And help us load this gear in the truck.'

'I'm supposed to be an MT driver . . .' he started to argue. I cut him short: 'You're also an aircraftman 2nd class. Now do as you're told!' He picked up a kitbag with obvious bad grace.

'I don't think I'm going to like this place,' observed Weeky quietly.

CHAPTER EIGHT

Tanker attack

WE WERE too tired to take an active interest in our surroundings that evening and sought an early bed in the transit mess; but it was a mistake, for soon after sunset the sirens wailed and the night sky erupted in a battle for conquest or survival. By the morning, our minds were still dusty with fatigue, and we made our listless way to the briefing-room hoping to be able to absorb the details of our next leg to North Africa.

The scene was one of confused activity; no one appeared to know anything about us or to be particularly interested, and we were sitting dully on a line of chairs waiting for events to overtake us when a sergeant approached and asked if we were the crews that had arrived the previous evening. We nodded and were led away through a maze of stone corridors to a door marked Adjutant, 107 Squadron. It was open and the flight-lieutenant inside bid us enter. I was cheered to find that he was a genial fellow as he checked our names against a list handed to him by the sergeant.

'Well chaps,' he said finally, 'I have a signal here from the Air Ministry, taking you out of transit and posting you to 107 Squadron here in Malta. Your wanderings are over!' he added brightly.

We looked at each other with dismay. Sensing our reactions he went on, 'Oh, it's not so bad. There's plenty of grub on the Island, and beer, and in any case squadron detachments here don't go on for very long.'

We knew why. Losses on Blenheim anti-shipping squadrons in Malta were higher even than those in the UK.

There followed an interview with a harassed-looking Wing Commander who bid us welcome, seemingly without enthusiasm, gave the Adjutant instructions for accommodating us, and ordered that we should come to the briefing-room at 0900 hrs the following morning.

The transport took us a short way down the hill from the airfield to a large sombre building known as the 'Poor House', because it had once been a workhouse. The tall Gothic windows were without glass and the lofty rooms were lined with iron bedsteads. Our morale was not lifted very much by an orderly who pointed to a building beyond a crumbling stone wall explaining that it was a leper colony and out of bounds. I dropped my kitbag in a corner, fell on the unmade bed and surrendered to a sleep without dreams.

On awakening, I decided that something must be done for the morale of the crew and harangued them into freshening up, putting on their best khaki tropicals and walking up to the mess for some food and drink. We met a number of crews who had been at Portreath or Gibraltar with us and accepted their condolences when they heard that we had been shanghaied to stay on Malta. The air raids started at dinner-time and apart from a concerted exercise directed at the Maltese waiters to stop them absconding, nobody appeared to take much notice. By the end of the evening, our morale was in better shape, and during a lull when the sky was quiet we marched down the hill singing lustily that popular song of the day:

> *I don't want to join the Air Force,*
> *I don't want to go to war!*
> *I'd sooner hang around Piccadilly Underground*
> *living on the earnings of a highborn lady ...*

That night I slept so deeply that I was genuinely surprised when told the next morning that a bomb had dropped close enough to make the plaster rain down from the ceiling. I even had some in my hair.

On arriving in the briefing-room as ordered, it was with relief that we found we were not on the battle order but merely pencilled in as reserves. We listened to the briefing and I looked around me at the faces of our new colleagues. There was something different about them. The freshness and enthusiasm of the squadron we had recently left was clearly missing. Some looked strained and jaded, and when briefing finished they broke up murmuring among themselves. There was no sense of excitement, only perhaps resignation.

We went out onto the airfield to watch them get away. The

wind had dropped and the visibility cleared to let the sun beat down on the sandstone which now seemed a brighter yellow and made one squint in the unaccustomed glare. Six aircraft took off in quick succession and in a couple of circuits of the airfield had formed up into two neat vics of three and then set course south, descending towards the sea until they were out of sight.

We hung around outside the operations room for some time, intrigued by the amount and variation of the flying activity that was going on. On the far side of the field sat a line of Wellingtons, the underside of their wings and bellies painted soot black for their night-bomber role, while the tops were camouflaged in a pattern of various shades of beige which must have made them as difficult to see as chameleons on a rock. Trains of bomb trolleys were being hauled by tractors in an almost continuous stream and the general bustle of vehicles and personnel around them indicated a maximum effort raid once darkness fell.

Each morning, the news was of a pounding that the Wimpys had given the enemy supply lines in North Africa the night before, for Rommel's front line was now approaching Benghazi, and in bloody and continuous fighting, the Eighth Army although contesting every yard of ground given, were being pushed relentlessly eastwards.

There were two Wellington squadrons based on Malta at this time, and on occasions, some were sent northwards to try and incapacitate the Italian airfields in Sicily and southern Italy. When they were successful, there followed a merciful period when the bombing of Malta lessened or even stopped for twenty-four hours, but the respite was never longer than that, for the enemy had large aircraft reserves on which they could call, and many airfields from which they could operate.

Malta on the other hand, had but three: Luqa, the bomber airfield, which was also used for transitting aircraft; Halfar, a Fleet Air Arm field on the top of the southern cliffs near Dingli about four miles from Luqa; and Tai Kali, the fighter field which nestled at the base of the hill on which stood the towns of Rabat and Mdina. This was equipped with Hurricanes, though we had heard a rumour when we were in Gib that the Ark Royal would be transporting a squadron of Spitfires to the Island on its next trip. Certainly, the fighter boys were in constant action, and their numbers were totally inadequate to try and stem the flow of German and Italian bombers that seemed to roam almost at will in the sky above Malta.

We watched rather wistfully as the two Blenheims which had flown from Gib with us two days before took off and joined company with three others before setting course eastwards to Cairo. For some reason, it seemed that being part of the Desert Air Force one would not be as exposed as we felt, left in this small and vital fortress in a totally hostile area, and certainly the casualty statistics appeared to justify such a feeling. However, life in the desert would have its drawbacks; at least we were going to be able to sleep in comfortable beds with a roof over our heads – providing it wasn't blown off in the night.

A gaggle of Hurricanes came streaming over the airfield with a smooth hum of Merlin engines, and when the leader turned sharply to starboard to interrogate a Maryland that had appeared over the coast, the others followed in swift pursuit. The Marylands were American aircraft that had been provided by the United States under the lease-lend agreement, and in Malta, their role was primarily as reconnaissence aircraft; but every plane approaching the Island was suspect as far as the fighter boys were concerned, and the leader made a dummy beam attack on the lone Maryland before breaking off, satisfied that it was a friend and not a foe. It occurred to me that we had not been molested on arrival due to the poor visibility, which was just as well, for in the heat of the moment a Blenheim looks rather like a Junkers 88.

We stood shading our eyes against the sun's glare. Joining the busy scene came a number of Wellingtons presumably from Gib on their way east, but there were no further dramas for the strip at Luqa was much longer than that at the foot of the Rock, and not surrounded by such daunting hazards. They landed without incident and were shepherded out to the dispersals among the olive trees to be refuelled and serviced for their onward trip the next day. We envied them.

'Sergeant Gillman?' An orderly was asking the question. I nodded. 'The adjutant said that you and your crew can stand down now,' he continued, 'but you will probably be on the battle order tomorrow.'

·   ·   ·   ·   ·

Next day our turn did come, along with every other man on the strength, for it was to be a maximum effort. In the briefing-room the buzz of conversation died away as the Wing Commander came through the door. I was surprised to see that he was lame and learned subsequently that his foot had been badly smashed in a crash-landing, but he had refused to stay in hospital long enough for a total repair. Because of his disability, he was not allowed to return to flying duties, and the bitterness he felt at finding himself the commanding officer of an operational squadron, who could only send his men aloft and await with anxiety for their return, came over during the briefing in his aggressive, almost callous approach.

The most vital task for the Blenheim Squadron in Malta was to stop the oil tankers from successfully running the gauntlet to North Africa. They were essential to Rommel's continued advance in the desert, he explained, and if the British and Allied armies continued to retreat at the present rate, then for us the war would be lost, in this theatre at any rate. For these reasons, the tankers sighted southeast of the Island had to be stopped, whatever the cost. If the whole Squadron were wiped out then this was a small price to pay when seen in relation to the total exercise.

The logic of the argument was clear and so was our own position in the matter. The realisation that at this point in time we had become expendable had a gut-dropping effect. It was difficult to concentrate on the details of the exercise. Apparently, two huge tankers had been sighted 140 miles to the southeast heading for Tripoli. They were escorted by a destroyer, four flak ships and two frigates, which gave one some idea as to the scale of importance that the enemy placed on that convoy getting through.

Benny's hands were shaking as he struggled to plot the ships' position and track on the chart provided and even the redoubtable Weeky was drawing on a cigarette with nervous puffs as he looked around the crew-room, his eyes alive with concern. Over the hubbub came the Wing Commander's voice exhorting us to 'get cracking, or the bloody ships will be in harbour before we get airborne!'

Outside, the light was cruel to the eyes, and the hard blue sky was burnished and swept clean of clouds. Although the ground-crew removed the cockpit covers only as they saw the transports turning into the dispersals, the atmosphere was that of a tropical hothouse as I slid down through the hatch and into my seat. I was wearing only a shirt beneath my lifejacket and parachute harness, but the sweat was dripping from the end of my nose as I went about the pre-flight checks. I heard the engines of a near-by aircraft stutter into life and looked out to see our own fitter standing with thumb raised awaiting my answering signal.

Despite Weeky's suggestion that I 'find a mag drop somewhere', both of our engines took life without hesitation and we were soon taxying out in a confusion of aircraft, bumping over the rough ground and sending up a series of duststorms with their slipstreams.

We took off in quick succession aiming to look for our position in the formation once we were airborne. Having just arrived on the Island we were, in the view of the CO, new boys, and as such relegated to the tail-end Charlie position again. Once airborne, we followed round in a slow climbing turn over the complex of roofs and spires that was Valletta, bumping and swerving in the hot morning air. There were ten aircraft on this sortie, all that were serviceable after the raid of the previous day, and the formation was to be two vics of three and one of four, we taking up the wing man position on the last vic.

Once over the coast, the leader rolled to starboard and immediately put his nose down in a long flat dive to the sea as if already scenting the prey, and the pack were using full throttle in untidy pursuit. It was ten minutes before some sort of order had been established and by this time the Island was well behind us as we raced over the sparkling sea.

The air was smoother here, and I tucked into a half span position on the number two man, the details of the aircraft's structure and the silhouettes of the pilot and air gunner standing out very clear.

The gunner was looking aft, unmoving, probably watching the low smudge of sandstone which was Malta receding; not a haven of security in such a war, but at least they were on our side. Soon it would disappear and we would be left alone in the centre of the vast encircling blue horizon, eating into the mileage of what was left of our future. Sombre thoughts for young men in their early twenties, and for the next three-quarters of an hour, half of my mind recalled memories of home which seemed so very far away, and of a young girl with light blue eyes and tumbling hair.

The run to the target area always seemed protracted until unworthy hopes began to germinate that perhaps the ships' position had been wrongly reported, that we wouldn't find them and could return to base and be allowed to live another day.

Then I realised that the leader was starting a turn to starboard. In a quick glimpse ahead I saw the reason. On the horizon, just a vague smudge of smoke. The formation was increasing speed now and crouching even lower, the sparkling diamonds of the sea shooting past underneath.

So incredible was the visibility in the Mediterranean at certain times that the first tangible things one saw were the tips of the masts, the bulk of the ships still being hidden behind the earth's curvature. Despite our speed on the run-in, it was some appreciable time before the funnels came into view still some twenty miles away, then the bulk increased as the superstructures were revealed and at ten miles the dark masses of the hulls materialised, solid and menacing.

If we could see them so clearly then surely they had sighted us, and the black puffs of smoke that suddenly appeared indicated that battle had been joined. Just as one waits for the sound of a distant explosion, an appreciable time elapses before the sea erupts in the vicinity as the big bricks go in. They were grouped to the right but they would soon compensate for that. The leader swung to starboard again, the formation following in a smooth turn, and sure enough, the next group dropped slightly to the left and ahead, but closer.

The leader now pulled up and went into evasive action following a violent and irregular cork-screwing path. The formation split open, each pilot starting to fly for his own salvation.

The escorting ships were now firing with vicious intensity. A snaking line of Bofors tracer whipped through our section and I saw debris fly off the aircraft on my left. He stopped gyrating as if shocked, then began a graceful turn to the left as if going back. He passed dangerously close behind his leader and continued to roll onto his back, until, incredibly, he was flying upside down just above the sea. Then the nose dropped and he was lost in a mountain of water.

All this had happened in a few seconds, in a kaleidoscopic series of pictures as I struggled with the controls, my mind a confusion of desperate thoughts.

I was now wide of the formation and being singled out for attention by the flak ship at the extreme right of the line. If I pulled even wider, I would be the sole target as I turned around it to get at the tankers embedded behind the defence. If I turned left I would be in the thick of it.

In the event, my attacking line resulted from antics to avoid a hosepiping line of scarlet tracer that was trying to pinpoint the aircraft. I found myself running straight for the bulk of the destroyer and swerving close under the tail of another Blenheim. The ships were bristling with gun flashes. A rattle of hammer-blows told me that some smallarms stuff had found us and Weeky opened up with his Brownings in reply. I dived below the stern of the destroyer, between it and the cleaving bows of the next ship. I had a clear run now for the big tanker. I remember flinching as a prolonged cannon burst ripped and sowed the sea in front. We went through it. I steadied close to the sea for the run-in on the tanker, its massive bulk rising above, the powerful derricks making a frame for the sky beyond. Sparks flickered along its decks as the gunners fought to protect themselves and the sea was spattered around us. I jerked the bomb-release button and heaved the aircraft into a climb for survival.

Another aircraft was lifting past the other side of the funnel. We went over together like two jockeys in a steeplechase. Then the sickening dive for the sea, the belly exposed to the unseen gunfire.

An explosion erupted into an orange ball close beside us and arced like a flaming comet into the sea. I glimpsed the aircraft as it hit, a wall of solid water being thrown up and then falling to deal with the fire, the aircraft and its occupants.

I continued to corkscrew like a man possessed. The sky ahead was empty; it didn't seem possible that we were the only survivor.

Weeky reported an explosion and a skyward rush of flame and black smoke from the tanker, but it was no time for rejoicing. We didn't know whether it was ours or the other poor fellow's bombs that had done the damage.

The following gunfire became sporadic and then stopped, but

I continued eastwards, anxious to put as much distance between us and the ships as was possible and in the minimum time. I called to Benny for a course home and started a long slow turn to the north. I could see the convoy again now, but it was almost completely enshrouded in dark smoke.

Well, we've given them something to think about so now let's get back.

Benny had just started to talk on the intercome when the aircraft gave a kick to starboard. It lurched again and a series of reports told me that the starboard engine was cutting.

'There's smoke coming from the starboard engine!' shouted Weeky, 'and half the bloody cowling hanging off!'

I banged off the ignition switches and groped for the fuel cock on the other side of the cockpit, the aircraft swerving as my foot came off the rudder pedal.

I made a conscious effort to steady my voice, 'Tell me if you see any signs of fire.'

'Christ! The bloody thing's on fire now!' he shouted. 'What do you think that smoke is? Scotch mist?'

I lifted the safety cover of the fire extinguisher and pressed the button. I heard the plop as the bottle detonated.

'There's white stuff streaming out now!' cried Weeky, 'I think it's petrol.'

'It's fire-extinguishant,' I said. 'Tell me if the smoke's abating.'

'Yeah. Yeh, it's petering out now. I think it's gone out.'

I increased the power on the good engine, trimmed out the yaw and roll and settled the aircraft into a shallow climb on the course that Benny had given me.

It was a long and lonely slog home. I felt empty and hopeless. Weeky kept reporting fresh evidence of damage to the aircraft and I kept a watchful eye on the instruments concerned with the port engine. If that coughed, a ditching was inevitable.

'Do you want me to send a "Mayday", Skipper?' asked Weeky.

'No, keep radio silence. If the port engine starts acting up, then we'll have to, but not before.'

'It might be a bit late then,' he muttered, but I didn't answer. There were a number of German fighter bases on Sicily and if they intercepted a distress call, I had little doubt that their Me 109's would be vectored onto us to finish the job.

Apart from the oil pressure which was fluctuating slightly, there was no indication that the port engine was damaged. While it kept going, so would we – quietly.

By the time we got back to the Island, the rest of the squadron had landed, that is, what was left. There were three other aircraft besides ourselves. Of the ten that went out, six had been lost.

The mood at de-briefing was repressive and even the congratulations of the Air Officer Commanding who had arrived on the scene had little real effect. It was all a matter of time, or luck, and it just depended on which ran out first.

CHAPTER NINE

Last bus to Luqa

WE RETIRED disconsolately to the transit mess and pushed our way into the bar which was unusually crowded, for a number of aircraft had arrived en route for the Middle East.

One flight-sergeant pilot with dark hair slicked down and a thin sallow face was holding forth to the group around him. 'It's just not on!' he announced with some heat. 'We were within three trips of finishing our tour in the UK when we get posted to the Middle East, and now this; shanghaied on this flea-bitten rotten little Island!'

'Didn't you tell them that?' asked an air gunner.

'Sure I did,' he replied, 'but it's my opinion that the postings are fixed before we leave London, and in any case, the whole thing was a put-up job!'

'What do you mean?'

'I had a row with the flight commander after the last trip to Ymuiden. He accused me of ducking the convoy, but he'd brought us in at such an angle that I swung wide; I couldn't help myself. I reckon he was the one that fixed me.'

'Oh, come off it, Dicky!' someone protested.

'You'll be all right here,' butted in Weeky with a sly wink. 'If you don't get in on a convoy one day, they'll have bags more for you to have a go at.'

The speaker stared at him for a moment. 'You on 107?'

'Yep.'

Another hesitation, then, 'You got a bit of a dusting this morning I hear.'

'You could call it that,' said Weeky. 'Six out of ten.'

'What? Back, or lost?' asked one of the group.

'Lost,' said Weeky.

The group shuffled uncomfortably and the flight-sergeant looked down at his feet. 'It's not on,' he repeated tremulously. 'I've been bloody lucky to get away with it this far!'

'Well, cheer up and have a drink,' said I. 'Tomorrow is another day.' And drink we did until the bar closed, for no one had much taste for lunch.

Now in a more cheerful mood it was generally agreed that we would go to our quarters for a quick siesta, then freshen up for a night on the town, and by five o'clock we were jogging along in a horse-drawn garry past the Marsah Sporting Club and up the hill to Valletta.

We passed through the worn sandstone arch, part of the original fortifications behind which The Knights of Malta had fought so bravely in another war 300 years previously, into Kingsway crowded with the natives and troops who milled about from bar to bar or stood in groups studying the windows of the giftshops.

We joined them for a while before finding a bar in a side street which rejoiced in the name of The Elephant and Castle. The bare walls and tiled floor offered cool if not luxurious surroundings, and it was already crowded with troops who had obviously made a start somewhat earlier than we. A three-piece band composed of pianist, drummer and accordionist beat out the popular tunes with more noise than expertise and one or two couples were dancing with various degrees of abandon, including two sailors who shuffled around in close embrace oblivious to the ribaldry aimed in their direction.

Roger Waller, a member of the most experienced crew on the squadron, having been on the Island for three weeks, explained that the chaperone system still operated in Malta, and that no decent girl would be allowed out with a man unless a sister, or an aunt, or some other member of the family went along. The women in the bars were no better than they should be.

I studied the scene with fascination before becoming aware that a dark woman sitting alone at a near-by table was staring straight at me. She smiled and I responded somewhat nervously and immediately tried to re-bury myself in the table talk, but I felt, rather than saw, that she was coming over to our table.

She dragged up a chair noisily and sat down beside me. 'Hello, dearie, having a good time?' she said with a smile.

I thanked her politely and said that I was.

'How long have you been here? On the Island I mean.'

I told her the truth. 'Oh,' she said, 'that's nice. Would you like to buy me a drink?'

I didn't really see why I should, but not wishing to be offensive I nodded. She murmured something to a waiter who had appeared silently behind us.

I was never at my best with strangers, particularly women who asked for a drink on such short acquaintance, but I need not have worried for she had a continuous if rather insipid line of small talk. She asked me if I was married and what my age was. When I told her twenty, she made me feel slightly uncomfortable by saying, 'Oh you *are* young!'

I was conscious that the others were giggling and making silly remarks in unnecessarily loud voices beside me. This embarrassed me, but she didn't seem to notice. It was almost a relief when she asked me to dance, but this proved to be even more embarrassing. She put both arms around my neck and contrived to hang herself against me. I was conscious of the pressure of her well-filled blouse and the softness of her thighs which brushed against me in a gentle rhythm as she moved.

My table companions were getting a great deal of amusement from my predicament and were making disgusting signs with their hands whenever they caught my eye.

She was obviously aware of the situation for she said, 'Your friends aren't very nice, are they? I think you're nice though.'

I thanked her for the compliment.

'Do you like me?' she asked.

'Er, yes. Of course,' I said somewhat stupidly.

'Would you like to come home with me tonight?' she asked, wriggling her body against mine so obviously that I thought the whole room must see. 'I'll give you a good time.'

'No thank you, I can't.' I was beginning to sweat. 'I have to meet somebody.'

'Oh. Not another girl!' she said in a manner calculated to be roguish. 'I would be jealous!'

I thought that was a bit presumptuous, but I said, 'No. Of course not!'

The music stopped with a crash of cymbals and she took my hand and led me back to the table. With a single movement, she downed the glass of pink liquid that had appeared in our absence and then leaned across to whisper confidentially, 'Perhaps tomorrow night when your friends aren't here; OK?'

'OK,' said I, and to my relief she stood up, slipped her handbag over her wrist and sauntered over to a curtained doorway beneath a crudely painted sign announcing 'Toilets' and disappeared. I was anxious to get away before she came out again and vastly relieved when someone suggested moving on to another bar.

It was a surprise to find it quite dark out in the street. The sirens were wailing and unseen shapes were scampering for the shelters. We fumbled our way downhill and turned into what I learned later was Straight Street, Strada Stretta in the local language, or 'The Gut' as the troops knew it.

This was the most notorious alley on the Island and judging by the confusion of noise coming from the now darkened bars, things were hotting up. A husky voice from a doorway croaked, 'Come inside Air Force; *exhibish!*' It was a mystery to me how she knew what we were, for in the narrow street the darkness was total. However, we bundled in through the blackout curtain and found ourselves in a bar similar to the first.

A soldier was giving a rendering of Eskimo Nell, the pianist providing a light background while the rest of the band swigged from beer bottles and talked among themselves. It was the most obscene poem I had ever heard, but delivered with gusto to the delight of those at the tables around him.

Our party were arguing as to what to drink next having decided that the local beer was of doubtful origin, but Benny settled it by announcing, 'What was guid enough for Rabby Burns, is guid enough for me. I'll ha' a Scotch!' So Scotch it was all round, my first encounter with the stuff.

The initial 'wee dram' tasted like methylated spirit and I said so. 'Och ya Sassenach!' derided Benny. 'You southerners don't know how ta drink. Ha' another and it'll taste better.'

I did, and it did. By the fourth or fifth, it was sliding down my gullet like a sharp golden nectar and I felt the warmth glowing up from my belly and a growing sense of well-being that made the noisy scene around not only acceptable but delightful.

A fresh-faced sailor looking even younger than ourselves weaved his way to a position in front of our table, waved his pint pot in the air and cried delightedly 'Hiya, Air Force.' Then lost his balance and toppled across the table with a crash of breaking glass. He slipped to the floor laughing uproariously although there was blood streaming from his hand. It was liberally diluted with beer, so it probably looked more serious than it was.

Willing hands hoisted him onto a chair. Someone pointed out that he was bleeding. He held up his hand and studied it uncertainly, then he licked it with some relish, 'Good!' he shouted, waving the arm aloft. 'Good bloody English blood!'

A petty officer came across, his peaked cap set back on a shock of curly hair, 'Wash he up to? What ya doing, Pinkey, you little bashtard?' He bent down and peered into the sailor's face and they both roared with laughter. The PO drew up a chair. 'We've jush got in,' he announced thickly.

'What, that convoy that got in this morning?'

'Yep! And a right bloody mess Jerry made of us too!'

We had heard about it. German submarines had got amongst it near Pantelleria about 200 miles west and rumour had put the casualties at anywhere between forty and eighty per cent. The version given to us by the mariner was pretty shocking: it made our adventures of that morning seem less of a holocaust. We listened with sympathy. The young sailor had fallen asleep on the table.

'You wouldn't catch me doing ten knots with the Navy,' murmured Weeky.

'You wouldn't catch me up in the sodding air,' shouted the petty officer. 'I reckon you blokes 'ave got guts! Guts!' he shouted, waving his fist.

Some more sailors joined us with noisy scraping of chairs and shouted demands to the waiters. Trays of drinks arrived in glorious confusion until the two tables pushed together were covered with bottles, glasses and beer. Stories were traded which seemed hilariously funny and I nearly choked when the normally restrained Benny climbed unsteadily on to a chair and led the singing in

> She's a big fat cow.
> Twice the size o' me.
> Hairs on her belly
> like the branches on a tree. ....

Riotous applause followed, then a burly sailor of an older vintage produced a contraceptive and started filling it with beer. Curiosity turned to shrieks of delight as the contents of more and more bottles were poured in. He had to stand on a chair, so distended had it become, but even so the bulbous bottom was bouncing on the floor. He then took a good grip on the end and began swinging it round his head. There was a confused scramble to keep clear of the missile as it stretched to an incredible length, swinging around the room at ever-increasing speed. A waiter made the mistake of rushing across to stop the antics and was caught full in the face, the device bursting and dousing him with beer.

The curtains at the entrance door were thrust aside and in pranced a gaggle of servicemen linked in line astern weaving erratically in a conga. Our party scrambled to join in and I found myself being swung round as the procession made for the door again. The waiters were shouting excitedly to be paid, but were sent flying over chairbacks by the sheer momentum of it all.

I stumbled down the steps into the street, hanging desperately to the swaying body in front. The men's shouts were echoing up the sides of the buildings. The black chasm was suddenly lit by a series of brilliant flashes and filled with the noise of anti-aircraft guns, but the column staggered on shouting the rhythm: 'Aye, Aye, Conga. Aye, Aye, Conga!'

I looked up just as an orange flash incongruously silhouetted a line of washing that fluttered between two wooden balconies. 'Aye, Aye, conga . . .' The shells exploded in the sky like celebration rockets but with a mean 'wrack, wrack' sound.

The whistle of shrapnel came clear along the alley, and some of the leaders, in an instinctive effort to duck, fell down in a guffawing heap. But the column weaved on. 'Aye, aye, conga . . .' defiant, committed.

I heard some shrapnel rattling from a balcony roof. A massive explosion accompanied by a flash of daylight brilliance announced the impact of a bomb near by. The leaders let out a cheer and we all cheered. 'Aye, Aye, conga . . .'

The man behind me let go and fell down, but I was quickly grabbed by other hands. Would it never stop? I felt I daren't let go. Swaying, staggering, inextricably tied in with a line of strangers, comrades, fellow drunks – would nobody cry stop!

The shouts ahead became more confused as we staggered onto the rubble of a building. I tripped over a piece of wood which cracked my knee, and fell sideways. The man behind held on and began to tumble about me. I kicked and pummelled myself free as we rolled down a pile of broken masonry. Then I was lying on my back, staring up at a black sky. I felt sick

The sky was rent again with flashes and guns exploded close by. I scrambled up with a new sense of urgency. Somewhere I had to find sanity. I staggered across the rubble until I felt a clear pavement beneath me, then I ran across the road to the shelter of a wall the other side.

I heard voices coming from a short distance, traced them to a blackout curtain and pushed through into a lighted bar. The few occupants looked up in surprise. Then I was pushed violently in the back as a massive soldier burst through, fell over a chair and took a spectacular nosedive on to the floor.

Then came oblivion, mercifully.

I awoke to the jabber of Maltese voices. I was lying on the floor with the bartender and his wife standing over me, arguing fiercely. I got the impression that she wanted me the hell out of there. Climbing slowly to my feet, my head heavy with pain, I made my way to the door without a word and was shocked on pulling back the curtain to find the street filled with sunlight.

I squinted at my watch. The time was a little after 6 o'clock but the streets were already alive with people. The shutters were being taken down from shops that had been spared for another day, and in the side streets stalls were being erected and garnished with wares. A surprising number of people were issuing from the open doors of the many churches that populated the area, many of them dressed in black and the older women almost hidden in *faldettas*, the huge framed hoods contoured with whalebone.

While one section of the populace prepared calmly for another day, in other areas I came upon new bombsites where willing helpers were still turning over the smouldering rubble with an urgency indicating that a person or persons were missing. All I had to show for it was a hangover, and I slunk by with a feeling of guilt.

At the terminus in Floriana, I found a bus about to leave for Luqa and there followed an agonising ride on which I was the only passenger, explosions erupting in my head each time it jarred in a rut or collided with a rock in the long, untidy road. I got the driver to drop me off on the hill that led to the airfield, and as I wandered into the Poor House, I found that most of the others were already surfacing in a rather delicate condition, for the squadron was to be on stand-to that morning.

Benny appeared surprisingly fit and Weeky was having a great deal to say for himself, though I had a sneaking feeling that it was largely bravado. I don't think I had ever felt so ill, and I hoped that I would soon die, preferably before lunchtime. On arrival in the crew-room, my mood worsened on realising that I needn't have come to the airfield at all, as our aircraft was still unserviceable and not included on the battle order.

'I'm not surprised,' observed Weeky, 'after the state we left it in.'

I sank into a chair seeking oblivion.

'Och, come on, mun!' cried Benny, kicking the chair. 'Rouse yuursell! You're nae dying!' I suddenly began to dislike him, and scowled.

He didn't seem to notice and went on, 'Why don't we go oot to disperesal and see how they're getting on wi' our machine?'

'Good idea,' said Weeky; 'I need some air.'

They moved off and I struggled up from the chair and followed. It was a longish walk around the perimeter track to the dispersal area, the heat and the glare of the sun adding to my discomfiture, but I trudged along behind the others more because I hadn't the initiative to take a line of my own than for any other reason. The airfield was very active, with transit aircraft leaving for the Middle East and others arriving from Gib. As we approached our squadron dispersal, it became apparent that the ground crews were busy too, for ours hadn't been the only aircraft damaged in the previous day's attack, though it did seem to be in greater disarray than the others.

The flight-sergeant fitter was wiping his hands on a rag as we approached, but the glistening of sweat showed that he had only just taken a breather. He nodded. 'You certainly made a fine mess of this one yesterday,' he said with a grin.

'Well, actually, it wasn't us that did it,' put in Weeky. 'It was that other lot. They didn't seem to like what we were trying to do.'

'Flight!' called one of the airmen from the top of an inspection ladder. 'What do you want me to do about this rockerbox?'

'Take the bloody thing off, of course!' called the flight-sergeant. Then, nodding to us, 'Come and look at this.'

We made our way round to the starboard engine, which was stripped of its cowlings and appeared to have a few other things missing as well. Where numbers 2 and 3 cylinders should have been there was a gap and the ports in the crankcase were exposed.

The flight-sergeant pointed, 'You must have taken a shell inside the cowling ring. Two of the pots had their sides missing, and the pushrods and the rocker box of number 3 had just disappeared.'

'Is that why it caught fire?' asked Benny.

'Sure it was. You'd have your fuel-air mixture being pumped out over the hot engine.'

'Yeah. I switched off the fuel-cock and banged the Graviner as soon as I could,' I said.

'Just as well you did,' he went on. 'It's no use using a fire-extinguisher until you've quenched the source of the fire.'

'What beats me,' I complained, 'is why they had to put the fuel-cocks on the far side of the cockpit. The whole layout must have been designed by a man with six-foot arms. Just when I wanted to get at them in a hurry, I had full left rudder on to keep the thing straight, and as I stretched over to shut off the fuel, my foot slipped on the rudderbar and we nearly lost it.'

The flight-sergeant nodded sympathetically. 'You want to see the engine,' he said. 'You need to be a double-jointed midget to get at anything behind the crankcase.'

'How long will it take ta fix?' asked Benny.

'Well, you won't have it on the flight line today, I promise you that!'

'That's tough!' Weeky chuckled.

'Would it nae be quicker to put in a new engine?' Benny persisted.

The older man picked up a tool box and climbed on to the inspection ladder. 'If we had one,' he said. 'We haven't had a spare for weeks. There was supposed to be a consignment coming out by sea, but it's probably gone to the bottom by now. We have to pinch the spares off the transit aircraft and patch up as best we can. There's a running battle going on between the E.O. here and

Headquarters Middle East. They want to know what's happening to all the spares that should be arriving there. They've got their problems too, I guess.'

I walked round behind the wing and climbed up the cat-walk to where the airman fitter was wrestling with the damaged rockerbox on the number 2 cylinder. I watched as he struggled to loosen a nut, the spanner slipping as he exerted pressure and banging his fingers against the adjacent box. His knuckles were stained with a mixture of black grease and blood.

'Having trouble?' I asked rather fatuously.

He pushed himself into an upright position, 'Not 'arf, Sarge. The whole assembly's bent over yer see. There must have been an explosion between the two pots. The tears in the cowlings are outwards.' He pointed with a spanner to the now misshapen sheet of metal that lay on the ground below the engine.

'Got a 5/8" Whitworth there, Spike?' called an airman from ground level. The fitter sorted through his tool box selected a spanner and dropped it into the waiting hands. 'The number 2 mag's had it as well,' he said, tapping the offending piece of equipment. 'The drive's completely sheared.'

'How long is it going to take you to sort this lot out?' I asked seriously.

'Gawd knows, Sarge. We just keep cracking until it's finished.'

'What, no time off?'

He looked at me directly and shook his head, 'I haven't been off the camp for a fortnight.'

I watched him as he returned to his task, bent over the engine, his hands straining in its entrails. He was gasping with the effort, the sweat running straight down into the open neck of his denims – probably the only garment he was wearing. I felt a sting of guilt that I had always taken aircraft servicing for granted as a sort of supplementary activity to our own. On the squadron in the UK one did strike up some rapport with the groundcrew, though one seldom saw them off duty, but here, where they had to work on whatever aircraft was in trouble and most of them were in transit anyway, no such opportunity arose. I determined that I would do something about it – provided I was around for long enough.

Eventually, the call of hunger found us on the road back to the mess, but as we passed the operations block, the sergeant from the orderly room called us over.

'Did you know that you were being moved?'

I felt a surge of exultation. 'No!'

'Yes, the whole squadron's going out to Marsaxlokk – aircrew that is. The transport'll be at the Poor House at 1400 hours.'

'That's great!' said Weeky despondently, as we went on our way. 'Now we're going to be out at the other end of the Island, miles from anywhere!'

'I don't expect Ron'll mind not getting into town so often,' Benny chuckled, giving me a sly look.

I didn't reply. I didn't think it was very funny.

CHAPTER TEN

Sortie to Sicily

FOR THE FIRST few days in our new quarters, we were left in peace while the CO wrestled with the problems of getting the complement of aircraft up to something like squadron strength. Signals flew between HQ Malta and the Air Ministry asking for permission to detain more transit aircraft, despite the pleas from HQ Middle East in Cairo. Meanwhile the ground crews worked on, improvising as best they could, appropriating spare parts from transit aircraft when no one was looking and even grounding one machine completely by cannibalising it – stripping it of its components in order to make other aircraft serviceable.

I was incensed to learn that it was our aircraft that had been degraded in this way. Including the preferry trials, the journey out, and our squadron time, we had been flying it for about a month and had become attached to it as one does. Although it probably flew exactly the same as any other Blenheim IV, we felt a personal preference for it, particularly as it had got us back under very difficult conditions. It seemed like the putting down of a favourite horse. However, it had been found that the crankcase of the starboard engine was cracked. A new engine was the requirement and there just wasn't one.

By the time we were summoned to the airfield again for an operational briefing, the squadron boasted no less than ten aircraft and eleven crews. We found ourselves down as reserves, and after briefing we went out onto the airfield to watch the take-off. It was a fine sight to see so many aircraft streaming out of the dispersal area, and the sky was full of noise as they circled the airfield and formed up. The target was reputedly two merchantmen and a frigate, so the dice didn't seem so heavily loaded, and the crews went off in good spirits.

Three hours later they returned, two neat vics of three and two stragglers. Two others failed to return.

The following morning found us in the briefing-room before daybreak, and the fact that maps were being distributed instead of charts caused a certain amount of conjecture as to what the target might be, but the hum of conversation died away as the CO stood up and rapped on the table in front of him.

'Gentlemen, the formation is as laid down in the Battle Order – two vics of three. The bomb load will be four 250-pounders with eleven-second delays (must be low-level . . .), and the fuel load, inner tanks only – 280 gallons (can't be very far . . .).

'If you unroll your maps, which I see some of you already have done, the target is circled half-way up the east coast of Sicily. Catania Aerodrome.' There was a murmur of excitement from the crews.

'Take-off will be at 0730. The time is now 0628 precisely. Synchronize your watches, gentlemen.' He paused. 'The start-engine signal will be given by a double green Very light from the tower at 0715, and the leading aircraft should be taxying out by 0722. Form up over the field, not above 500 ft and leave by Sliema Creek going straight to sea-level.

'The first course is three-five-zero degrees to Cape Scamaria, and the same course will take you slap over the town of Vittoria. Three miles farther on, you come to the river valley and turn northeast up the valley itself.' He was now pointing out the details on a large-scale relief map which had been pinned up on the board. 'About here,' he jabbed the spot with his finger, 'you will see an obvious secondary valley to the left and this will lead you up between the hills at Armerna and Lentini. From here it is downhill all the way to the basin, with the town of Catania on the right and the airfield straight ahead. If you're not sure where you are, look up a bit, for Mount Etna, all 10,000 ft of it is straight ahead,' he said to appreciative laughter. 'You will bomb in close formation,' he went on, 'so as to get a good concentration over their aircraft parking areas. Break to the right after the attack and this will bring you across the edge of the town; then proceed along the coastal plain inside Augusta and Siracusa – the Intelligence Officer will you tell you why.' Turning to the man in question he said, 'Perhaps you would like to take over at this point, Jimmy.'

The flight-lieutenant pushed the spectacles farther on to his nose, picked up a pile of glossy photographs with nervous fingers, coughed and began, 'Well, chaps, we have had intelligence reports that the Eyetyes are getting a bit cocky as we haven't been over there for a while, and they are not bothering to disperse their aircraft. As you can see from this picture,' and he held up a fullplate black-and-white photograph, '– or perhaps you can't see it from there, but you can have a close look afterwards – there are a number of Savoia Machettis and some Junkers 88's parked in a nice line lying southwest to northeast along the airfield. Should be a piece of cake.'

'What about the airfield defences, Sir?' someone asked.

'Well. Uh.' He coughed again. 'The airfield is quite well defended and I have marked in the machine-gun and ack-ack positions on this other photograph. However, we are hoping to achieve some surprise effect by getting there around dawn, and they probably won't be expecting you at low-level.'

'Won't the coastal defences have alerted them?' someone else asked, not unreasonably.

'Possibly so,' said the flight-lieutenant. 'But they will only have about fifteen minutes warning at the most.'

'That'll give 'em plenty of time to get some up the spout and be ready for us,' whispered Weeky loudly in my ear, and I was inclined to agree with him.

But the flight-lieutenant was talking again: 'Why we have chosen the particular routeing is because we think you will catch the coastal defences by surprise, and according to our information, they don't have much up in the hills. During the run-out, you will be behind the coastal guns at Augusta and Siracusa, and only have the small stuff to contend with.'

'Any questions?' asked the CO.

'Sir. I would have thought it would have been better to go into the attack individually in all directions and distract the aerodrome defences,' said Dicky Wilson somewhat aggressively.

'No it wouldn't!' retorted the Wing Commander sharply. 'I want that target carpet bombed with slow sticks from each aircraft; no salvoes. If you want to split up on the way out then that's up to you, but if they manage to scramble their fighters, you have a problem.'

The general hubbub developed again as the crews went about their preparations, the navigators plotting in the tracks and measuring distances, the wireless-operator/air gunners drawing the Syko code machines and sheets and noting the colours and letters of the day while the pilots gathered round the intelligence officer to examine the reconnaisance photographs in more detail.

There were some good low-level shots of the airfield as we would see it in our run in, and I studied it closely in order to fix the picture in my mind. Map-reading wouldn't be on at that stage; one would have to identify the target and go for it, and as I was leading the second vic, I wanted to know just what to look for.

On the trucks that took us out to the dispersals, the crews seemed stimulated by the prospect of a low-level on an airfield; nothing could be as daunting as a shipping attack, and to be able to blow up some enemy aircraft and perhaps enjoy the results on the Island for the next few days was attractive.

We had been allocated one of the aircraft that had just been ferried out from the UK and it looked and smelled new as we busied ourselves with the pre-flight checks. The first faint suggestion of dawnlight was colouring the landscape as the engines fired and the peace of the early morning was shattered. The blue tongues of exhaust flames were visible in the grey light darting out of the stack pipes, smoke curled up over the busy scene and there was an exciting tang of high octane fuel in the air.

The earphones in my headset hissed and crackled as Benny's voice came through – 'Testing the intercom, Skipperrr.'

'OK, hearing you five-by-five. How about you, Weeky?' A slight delay, then a remote voice, 'OK, loud and clear.'

The air around us was now becoming murky with rising dust as the pilots started to carry out their engine runs. I checked the cylinder-head and oil temperatures and signalled to the dim figure of the airman who stood in attendance to one side of the aircraft, then pulled the control column hard back and opened up each throttle in turn. The aircraft bounced about and hammered against the chocs, trying to break free as I switched off each magneto in turn to check the drop in engine speed and then increased the power to a throaty roar at full throttle. Boost OK at plus-9; rpm – 2,750; cylinder-head temperatures not above 210°; oil pressures flickering around the 80 mark with temperatures still low; fuel pressures $2\frac{1}{2}$–$3\frac{1}{2}$ lb – it all looked good.

I took out the plus-9 override and throttled the engines back to idling speed. The aircraft seemed to relax and the noise subsided to a soothing tick-over. The airmen scuttled around the aircraft pulling clear the trolley accumulator and the chocks in response to my signal as the aircraft of the first vic started to move out. I followed them and we snaked our way along the taxi track in procession to the runway.

The take-off sequence was brisk, and we were soon rising in the clear morning air and rolling into a turn to port in pursuit of the leader. The atmosphere was icy smooth, and below us the landscape a uniform blue-grey colour as if still asleep. In the harbour area could be seen three broad trunks of smoke that hung motionless over the results of last night's bombing. Well, we were on our way to take a little revenge.

The leading vic was now closing up nicely ahead, the silhouettes of the aircraft outlined clearly against the lighter sky. I was turning inside them to make ground and my wing men were narrowing the gap between us. By the time the leader rolled out onto the northerly heading, the formation was complete and he lowered his nose as we slipped over Sliema Creek and headed for the open sea.

There would be no long slog to the target today with time for doubts and apprehension, for the crossing would take but fifteen minutes; and it suddenly came home to me how near the enemy crouched to the tiny little Island.

The sea began to shimmer as the sun popped its head above the eastern horizon to see what we were doing, and already visible before us was the southern coast of Sicily.

As we raced in close company towards the shoreline, the hills beyond seemed to rise into the morning sky. Details of the beaches were becoming clear now, and a scattering of houses, but there was no sign of activity.

The shoreline flashed like a snake underneath us to be followed by the poppled blurr of olive trees. My concentration was on the leading vic in order to hold our position about a hundred feet to the right and slightly behind. Beyond him I was conscious of a town standing up in our path.

The next moment we were flashing over the rooftops. The blast of noise must have ejected them from their beds.

The houses tailed off, and the leader went into a graceful turn to the right as he came upon the river. Still there was no sign of opposition. The hills were rising high in front now and taking on a brown tinge as the twilight melted in the path of the sun. The river valley was narrowing and the hills on either side seemed to be closing in. Then I saw the opening to the left and we swung into it, climbing gently parallel to the rising ground, but only a few feet above it. Still no sign of life.

Then the whole formation went into a sweeping curve to the right, and looking ahead momentarily, I saw the long smudge of haze under which the inhabitants of Catania would be making their preparations for another day.

The leader straightened out and the formation slid swiftly down the hillside towards the wide valley. I glanced ahead again quickly and saw immediately the familiar block shapes of hangars in the distance.

We were racing over the flat fields now and closing rapidly with the airfield. In another quick glance I saw a number of aircraft closely parked. Then the defences erupted.

As if by a single signal, lines of scarlet tracer started coming towards us from a number of points on the airfield boundary. Then it was among us, streaking in red dotted lines right through the formation of aircraft. There was a rattle on the side of the fuselage as we took our share. An anti-aircraft shell exploded right in front of the leader's nose as if to bar our way. The firing was frantic, as if delivered in panic.

The leader's flight was not so steady now and the formation was jiggling and becoming untidy. But the target was dead ahead. The sparkle of guns could be seen firing at us from the far side of the airfield. Weeky's twin Brownings racketed as we flashed over the boundary fence.

The air seemed crowded with arcs of whipping tracer. We were bearing down on the parked aircraft in a last onward rush. Then I remembered with shock. I'd forgotten to fuse the bombs. For one mad moment, I looked down at the bomb panel and fumbled for the nose-fusing switch. When I looked up, we were turning towards the leaders and out of the corner of my eye I saw my number three veering away.

Benny was to drop the bombs in quick succession by rotating his

'Micky Mouse' lever. The next moment, the aircraft were underneath us. I had a shockingly close glimpse of a black German swastika. The aircraft were flashing past like coaches in a railway train so closely were they parked.

'Bombs gone!' Benny shouted on the intercom.

Then the leader pulled up sharply over a hangar that suddenly blocked our path and went into a steep turn to the right.

He caught me unawares and in pulling up late, I over-reacted and climbed rapidly above him. Two hundred feet up in the blue sky seemed much too high, and the licking prongs of tracer that flashed past my ears confirmed this. I dived for the ground again, losing sight of the leader in the steep turn. I kept turning to ensure that I didn't close with him and then rolled out flat just above the terrain. The first three aircraft, no longer in a neat vic, were in the distance and on a course that was taking them away from us. Ahead the ground was rising, and a puff of very black smoke came from a gun position. This lent urgency to my turn to the left. I was conscious that my number three was still with me, but I didn't think there was an aircraft on my starboard side.

I pulled the plus-nine override and held the aircraft down in pursuit of the leaders; they seemed to be getting away. They were passing behind the outskirts of Catania, and black puffs were dirtying the sky around them. The firing died away as we reached the open coastal plain, and I pulled off the power as we rapidly overhauled the leading vic.

Once stability had been restored, I glanced round to the right looking for the wing man, but there was only blank sky.

I switched on my microphone, 'Weeky, can you see number two?'

'He went in.'

'Christ! Where?'

'On the airfield itself.'

'Well you might have told somebody!' That was a silly thing to say, for there was nothing I could have done about it.

'But we got our own back though,' Weeky went on. 'Fixed up their Air Force good and proper!'

'Was it a good prang?'

'Not arf!'

We were streaming past the outskirts of Siracusa, and there was some desultory fire from some machine-guns mounted on flat roofs, but they had a full deflection shot to contend with and it mostly fell behind us.

During the run down to the south coast, we saw nothing and I had an uncomfortable feeling that before long there could be some angry fighters in hot pursuit, but we made the open sea without incident, and it wasn't long before the outline of Malta began to rise out of the distance.

As we closed with the land, the leader lifted slowly to 500 ft and we with him; then, as the airfield came into view, he lowered his nose and we followed in a dive and flashed across the field very low, 'flying the squadron flag'. On the far side, he waggled his wings and his wing men broke away, number two rolling dangerously close to my nose. Then I gave the signal and pulled up to follow the leader who was now the only one in sight.

After landing, I reached up and slid back the hatch for the sun was gaining strength now and I had my Irvin jacket on. The cool air was refreshing.

We taxied into the dispersal area where the faithful ground-crews were waiting to marshal us into position, and after the final manoeuvre I cut the engines, unfastened my straps and parachute harness and climbed up in my seat with my head out of the hatch.

I looked round just as Weeky's head appeared up through the hatch in front of his turret. He grimaced and pointed back to the tail fin where six or eight jagged holes were clearly evident.

'Did you see what happened to number two?' I asked. Distressingly, I couldn't think of the pilot's name. He was one of the new boys who had arrived from the UK a couple of days earlier. Bad luck to go down on his first trip.

'Well, you know when we caught that first burst of machine-gun fire,' Weeky was saying, 'we got hits on the port wing and along the fuselage. Then he swung across behind us missing our tail by bloody inches with smoke coming from his port engine. The next thing I knew, he was sliding along the ground in a cloud of dust and smoke.'

'Did it look as if he had made a controlled belly flop?'

'Well, yeah. He certainly didn't dive in.'

The fitter called up from where he had been examining the

fuselage near the wing root fillet, 'Sarge, these were a bit near your backside, weren't they?'

Weeky hung over the side to get a better view. 'I know,' he said; 'I lifted my flaming feet up when we got that lot.'

When we got down to examine them, we found a line of surprisingly concentrated holes right along the fuselage under the turret position.

There was a great deal of chatter as we swopped our impressions of the sortie in the dispersal truck that took us back to the operations block. Inside the CO, the Adjutant and the Intelligence Officer were waiting, and in response to their question as to how it had gone, there was a confused gabble in reply, but one man emerged spokesman.

'It was great,' he said. 'The aircraft were parked just as you said, and we got a good run right along them.'

'Did you see any hits?'

There was a confusion of affirmative replies. All the gunners who had the best view as we left the target agreed that the whole area had been plastered.

'What happened to Clements?' asked the CO. Now that he mentioned it, the name came back to me.

'He bought it on the run-in, Sir,' said Weeky. 'His port engine was smoking and he did a belly flop.'

'Did they get out?'

'I didn't see, Sir. We were over the target a second later and I was too busy having a go.'

'Good man!' the Wing Commander was obviously in a cheerful mood. 'Did anyone else see if they got out?' But nobody had.

The Intelligence Officer beckoned us to his table for the individual crew interrogation, and we gave him our version of what happened. We confirmed that he had been right about the disposal of the defences and he was particularly interested in the exact location and type of guns that composed the airfield armoury. It was difficult for me to say exactly where the fire was coming from, as I had been concentrating on holding station on the leading vic, but Benny was able to pinpoint one or two positions on the photograph provided and so did Weeky.

When it came to assessing the damage inflicted, Benny and I

The Blenheim Mark IV was considered to be a medium bomber, and with its excellent handling characteristics and top speed of 270 mph it was ideal for low-level daylight operations. The Bristol Mercury XII engines drove three-bladed propellors. The hydraulically operated gun-turret mounted two Browning .303's. There was a further Browning in the port wing fired by the pilot and two more guns under the nose fired by the navigator, turned forward for low-level work. The bomb load consisted of four 250-pounders, and its range without overload tanks was around 1,000 miles.

Aircraftmen working on Blenheims at an operational airfield.

Malta from the air. The key below shows the principal places on Malta mentioned in the book

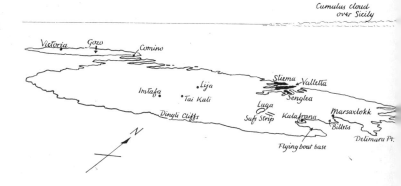

Cumulus cloud over Sicily

Victoria — Gozo — Comino

Imtafa • Lija • Tai Kali

Sliema — Valletta

Senglea

Luga

Dingli Cliffs — Sufi Strip — Kalafrana

Marsaxlokk

Billets

Flying boat base

Delimura Pt.

N

Nearly every day brought bombs in the airfield. Squads filling in the craters were a constant sight

The observer of a Blenheim bomber in his nose position peering ahead for the target

Mast height attack on a convoy in the Heligoland Bight: a direct hit amidships on a 500-ton ship left it well alight

Small-arms fire like this made my airgunner lift his feet

Tanker and trailer on the Africa Road after receiving a direct hit. The crew have taken a dive for the pole at the side of the road

A near miss – but the *Dorset* reached Malta safely

The long main street of Senglea, Victory Street, nothing but a shambles – with every home and shop shattered

The first bomb exploding in an attack by Blenheims of the Mediterranean Command on an Italian motor vessel. A crewman can be seen leaving the starboard side. The ship was sunk

At anchor with its guns apparently unmanned, this escort vessel was a sitting target

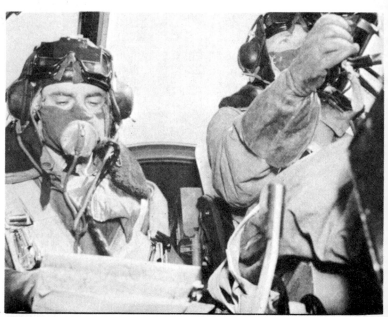

The cockpit of the Blenheim. A temporary seat beside the pilot allowed the navigator to move aft from his nose position

had no idea, for the target was behind us on the run-out; but Weeky was emphatic:

'It was perfect!' he said, jubilantly. 'As we came away in a climbing right-hand turn, the whole lot went up almost together. There were bits of wing and tailplanes flying in the air, and there were bomb-bursts along the whole line until they were completely covered in smoke.'

'About how many aircraft do you think there were?'

'Oh, I don't know; I didn't have time to count 'em but I should have thought about a dozen Savoias and eight or ten 88s.'

'I'd agree with that,' cut in Benny. 'There were a few more aircraft tucked away in a corner, but I didn't get a good look at them.'

'Did you get the impression,' the Intelligence Officer persisted, 'that the aircraft already had an operational load and that their bombs went up as well?'

Weekly slowly shook his head: 'It's hard to tell. There were certainly some mighty explosions, but I've no idea whether they were all our bombs or some of theirs.'

The flight-lieutenant started to make notes and spoke without looking up: 'Did you see any signs of activity around the aircraft. Were there crews there or refuelling vehicles or whatever?'

'I saw some men as we approached,' replied Benny slowly. Then he chuckled, 'But by God they ran awful fast when they saw us coming!'

'Were there any vehicles in the area?' asked our interrogator, looking up.

We shook our heads. We couldn't remember seeing any in our wild dash overhead.

He went on doggedly, 'Was there anything you can recall which might suggest that they were ready to leave on a sortie?'

'How could we know that?' asked Weeky somewhat irritably. 'We just about wrecked the lot; I should think that was all that mattered.'

'That is not all that matters,' said the officer slowly and deliberately. 'We had an intelligence report indicating that the Catania squadrons were planning a maximum effort on a particular installation at a particular time this morning, that's why you were sent there. I just want to check the accuracy of my information if I can.' I found myself wondering just how effective was our espion-age network in the area. It came as a surprise to me to hear that we were getting such detailed information, but he was changing the subject. 'Now what about damage to your aircraft?'

Weeky explained in detail the position of the line of bullet holes that had passed close to his seat.

The Intelligence Officer smiled and said, 'They must have come a bit close to your accoutrements!'

'Don't worry, sir!' laughed Weeky, 'I'm no fool. I always sit on my tin hat when we start the run-in.'

'You reckon your personal equipment is more valuable than your head then?'

'Not arf! If I get my bleeding head knocked off then that's the end of it, but I'd hate to be running around without my marriage assets!' The debriefing session broke up in general laughter.

As we were about to leave the crew-room, Sergeant Murphy and his air gunner came in. They were looking somewhat crestfallen, and we did not learn until later in the day that a cannon shell had exploded in the nose compartment of their aircraft mortally wounding the navigator. By the time they had landed and an ambulance had got to them, he had died from loss of blood.

CHAPTER ELEVEN

The cost of conviction

THE FOLLOWING DAY, the squadron stood down, and most of us relaxed in the autumn sunshine at our new quarters, reading, writing letters home and enjoying a few sociable drinks in the mess at lunchtime.

I slept soundly in the afternoon, and was surprised on waking to find that it was already dark. Having washed and refreshed myself I went in search of the others. I knew where they'd be: in the Nissen hut that served as the NAAFI, the focal centre of such social life as we now enjoyed.

I made my way down the hillside lit by a full moon; a bomber's moon. The craggy nature of the distant headland was exaggerated by the cool light and the grey shadows, and from its base, the silver track of the moon's reflection quivered across the water almost to my feet.

I could hear the noise of conversation coming from the hut even as I approached, and pushing aside the blackout curtains I found that most of the squadron were already there, a number slumped in chairs forming a circle around the iron stove, some perched on a trestle table, and others squatting on the floor with their backs against the wall. As the squadron's numbers had become depleted – there were twenty of us now, six full crews and Murphy and his air gunner who had brought back their navigator dead the day before – we tended to draw closer together.

A crude bar across the corner was manned by a Maltese youth we knew as Mitzi, and among the debris on the counter were several candles mounted in bottles in preparation for the power-cut which would come with the nightly arrival of the bombers.

I prised the top off a bottle of Hop Leaf and leaned with my back to the counter listening to the conversation. The talk was seldom of shop, probably because it was too painful to go back over events best forgotten. They were hardened performers now, these young men, and no longer spoke in awe of what they had seen, but raised instinctive barriers and sought for other subjects.

However, the talk on this occasion was about the defensive tactics of enemy convoys and it was becoming quite heated when the drone of the generator outside began to fade, and with it the two bare bulbs that hung on wires from the ceiling. This was the usual prelude to the air-raid warning: the generator was shut down as it interfered with the sound detectors at the gun emplacements on the hill. Shortly afterwards we heard the distant wail of the siren in Valletta that each night led the doleful chorus. Someone commented that our sortie of the previous day did not seem to have had much effect. The conversation continued as I passed the candles down from the bar to be disposed in strategic positions and Mitzi said quietly behind me, 'I go now,' as he slipped under the counter and made for the door. It was self-service from now on.

Robbie Robinson, the big Australian, had become the centre of the discussion and was finding it necessary to defend himself from a number of assailants.

'I don't care what you say, those boys don't take a deliberate bead on you 'cos there's no point when you're jinking like mad.'

'I wouldn't care to put a bet on it,' said Maxie dubiously.

'Look,' Robbie went on, 'when you've got a tanker and five or six flakships fanned out on either side, they might aim with the big stuff as you come into range; the formation's a solid target of aircraft at three to four miles, but during the run-in, when everyone's taking violent evasive action, they just hosepipe the smaller stuff.'

Several people began to argue at once, but Dick Carter, Dave's navigator, prevailed. 'Put yourself in their position. If you were a ship's gunner and you saw a bloody great Blenheim coming your way with a belly full of bombs, wouldn't you take aim?'

'There's no point in trying to follow a particular aircraft when the pilot's doing his nut,' Robbie continued. 'With the concentration of small arms fire that they can put up, all they need to do is spray it around and you've got to fly through it.'

'What's your suggestion then,' Dave demanded, 'that we don't take evasive action at all?'

'Yes.'

This brought a storm of derision from the crews, and Dave was heard to say, 'That's just asking for the chop.'

'Listen, mate,' chipped in Ted Slater, 'evasive action's good for my morale.' This brought a number of heartfelt 'Hear, hear's'. 'If there is something I have no ambition to be, it's a sitting bloody duck. Skipper can turn our kite inside out as far as I am concerned. He'll get no complaints from me.'

'It depends on the situation,' persisted Robbie.

Arthur Madden who, at twenty-five, was normally given the respect due to an older man, put his case mildly. 'Surely,' he said, 'the object of evasive action is to prevent the enemy taking steady aim. In trying to follow an erratic flight path, the gunner has the greatest difficulty in keeping the machine in his sights, let alone laying off for a deflection shot. When the pilot puts the wing down and kicks on opposite rudder, the aircraft goes into a skid and fools the gunner because it's no longer going in the direction it's pointing. All this is accepted practice and it makes sense.'

'But what I'm trying to say,' Robbie came back somewhat testily, 'is that these jokers are not aiming most of the time. You're just as likely to fly into something when you're slinging the aircraft around as if you went in straight.'

'Good theory,' said Digger Grey, 'but that's all it is.'

Robbie bridled. 'Well I'm entitled to it!'

At this stage, the anti-aircraft guns began to open up from their positions on the hill above us, and we all ducked when a piece of shrapnel cracked on the iron roof and whined off into the distance.

'Talking of probabilities,' said Bob Turner wrily, 'we're more likely to get our hair parted by a bit of British shrapnel than we are to see a sodding Hun shot down!' The corrugated roof went some way to bearing this out, for it was pitted with little holes through which the flashes of the local guns could be seen sparking intermittently.

During a lull in the activity outside, I said my goodnights and left. The party was getting raucous by this time, and I felt tired and somewhat depressed. There had been no letters again for me that morning, and the radio had told of the continued bombing of London.

We were on stand-to the following day, and by 0730 our dilapidated bus was creaking and lurching its way towards Luqa. There was little conversation around me and I sat in morbid silence, barely seeing the stony landscape which was unpleasantly familiar. Eventually the bus stopped at the guardroom gates and a service policeman climbed aboard, a peaked cap set straight on a neatly cropped head. 'What squadron?' he asked peremptorily.

'— Sergeant,' said Madden quietly.

'— Sergeant,' repeated the policeman, fiddling with his red arm-band of authority.

Madden gave him the squadron number, adding, '-and Airman, there are just three squadrons on this airfield; you should have got to know this by now.'

The SP climbed down from the bus without a further word.

'Bloody marvellous, aren't they!' said Weeky as the bus moved off. 'How could we win the war without them?'

Once in the Operations Room, we made for the notice board, and there, sure enough, was the 'Battle Order', the names of the pilots on the day's operations set out in V's in the formations they would be flying.

Weeky dug me in the back. 'Are we on the execution list?'

'Of course!' He grimaced.

'Gentlemen!' A shout from the intelligence officer as the Wing Commander bustled into the room carrying a roll of charts.

'Good morning, gentlemen,' he said quietly. 'I think it would be easier if you gathered round the table.'

He spread out a map of the sea areas east of Malta and jabbed a finger at a pencilled cross. 'We have intelligence of a German convoy reported in this position. It would appear to be of a fairly usual formation, one tanker with an escort of five flakships and two of what appear to be corvettes.' I heard someone whisper 'Christ!' fervently. I had my hand on Benny's shoulder as I leaned over the chart and was surprised to feel his body trembling.

'The bomb load will be the usual four 250-pounders with eleven-second delays and it will be a full squadron effort, that is, two vics of three. Incidentally, Sergeant Murphy, I hope to have a replacement navigator for you tomorrow. I'm borrowing him from a transit crew.'

'Thank you, Sir,' said Tim without enthusiasm.

'It's the mixture very much as before,' the Wing Commander went on, 'and of course, it's the tanker we're after. The tanker we must get.'

'I like the *we*!' Weeky whispered loudly in my ear; a reference to the fact that the CO no longer flew on operations.

'There will be total radio silence, certainly until the target area has been cleared. If, after that, you're in trouble and you think that breaking radio silence will help, well, that's up to you. Certainly in that area you will be out of range of enemy fighters, but of course you've got to think about them on the way back. Our information is that there are three squadrons of 109s at Palermo and if you advertise your position on W/T, it's quite on the cards that they'll come out to meet you.'

'Now for a time check. It's 0810 and twenty seconds – now! You haven't much time so you had better get cracking. With a take-off time of 0900 hours, the convoy will be getting to the limit of your range when you get there; that's allowing for a cruising speed of 210 on the way out, a full bore run-in from about ten miles, and a slow cruise home. Engines will be started on a green from the tower at 0850 and you will taxi out in formation order. That's all. Good luck.'

We stood to attention as he left the room and the Operations Officer took over to brief the navigators on the forecast winds, identification letters and colours of the day, and give them code sheets for their Syko machines.

I helped Benny with his navigation log while Weeky went to collect the rations. These were little cardboard boxes containing such goodies as a bag of crisps, a packet of biscuits, an apple, an orange, and on good days, a hardboiled egg. Geoff King once told me that he was so agitated on an outward trip he ate the crisps bag and all.

Benny was a slow and thorough worker. He didn't like being rushed and invariably we were the last to climb aboard the dispersal truck accompanied by shouts both encouraging and abusive from those already on board.

'What's our position?' asked Weeky as we bounced and rocked over the hard surface on our way to the aircraft dispersals.

'We're number two to Robbie,' I said.

'Are we, by Christ! I hope he's sober this morning.'

'He wasna drunk last night,' Benny protested gently in his singsong Glasgow accent. 'He just had a theeery.'

'Well, he can keep it,' said Weeky as the truck stopped by our machine. 'Come on, we've got about ten minutes.'

There was no time to exchange pleasantries with the ground-crew, but the rigger climbed on to the wing and helped me to load my parachute into the bucket seat asking, 'What's the target today, Sarge?'

'A tanker convoy about 250 miles out.'

'Sooner you than me,' he said fervently, and patting the top of the fuselage. 'Don't get the old girl knocked up, I've got a date tonight.'

Benny was struggling to get himself and his equipment installed in the narrow nose compartment while I checked the electrics and the instruments and set up the bomb-fusing panel. For this type of operation, the pilot dropped the bombs himself purely on visual judgement. There would be neither the height nor the time to use a bombsight.

A crack from the control tower caught my attention as a green Very light arced in the morning air. I opened a side window and shouted for the fitter. He was hidden under the nose but came scrambling out answering my 'Clear to start?' with a thumbs-up sign.

The port engine fired immediately, spewing black smoke around the wing. The starboard propeller turned over sullenly for some time and I began to think the engine was overprimed when it back-fired through the intake with a boom and a spout of flame, coughed twice, and then picked up.

I signalled for the trolley accumulator to be pulled away and then checked over the engine instruments. Weeky came over the intercom in a voice both muffled and metallic, 'Can you hear me, Skipper?'

'Yes, OK. Can you hear me, Benny?'

Benny looked back from his compartment and nodded seriously, then remembered that he had to respond verbally for an intercom check and pulled his oxygen-mask across his face fumbling noisily with the microphone. 'Yes. Heeering you OK.'

'Hey! Robbie's taxying out!' called Weeky, and surely enough, his aircraft was moving out of the dispersal with roaring engines and a cloud of dust. I signalled to the groundcrew urgently to pull the chocks away.

'I haven't had time to do an engine run.'

'But it's only two minutes to take-off time,' said Benny mildly.

'He doesn't have to go bloody mad!' cried Weeky, and I was inclined to agree.

I caught up with Robbie's aircraft as it turned onto the runway and fell in alongside in the number two position, then went through the pre-take-off drills.

Hydraulics – selected ON; Trim – neutral; Mixture – RICH; Pitch – Fully Fine; Fuel – main tanks ON; Flaps – Up; Throttles – friction nut TIGHT.

I looked up from this routine to see Robbie excitedly indicating 'Clear for take-off'. I stuck up my thumb; number three was in position, and almost immediately, Robbie's aircraft began to move. This was all too rushed.

As the aircraft gathered speed, I kept to one side and slightly aft of his tail by juggling with the throttles and the rudder. The ground was flashing by at an increasing rate, but I was concentrating on his centre section. If we got too close, our aircraft would get caught in his turbulent slipstream. If we swung wide, we would go off the edge of the runway.

Fully laden, the machines took most of the run available, and about 200 yards before the end, he lifted off. I followed, sinking momentarily below before pulling up to his level. I looked away briefly to select the undercarriage up, and then concentrated on tucking in behind his starboard wing.

I was generally conscious of the surrounding scene rather than seeing it directly. The rough sandstone landscape slipping away underneath, a pall of black smoke rising slowly from a burned-out building; the sea sparkling almost invitingly beyond the coast, and the number three aircraft rising and falling gently as the pilot concentrated on holding station. On crossing the coast, Robbie eased his nose down, and we followed in a gentle dive towards the sea; three hunters in search of prey, and some of them hoping they wouldn't find it! The other vic would be behind and to the left.

At something less than fifty feet, Robbie levelled off and we raced together over the dazzling wavetops. Once clear of the Island, I pulled away and stood off at about two spans. It would take rather more than an hour to reach the target area, and I felt I wanted to relax. Some pilots felt that to stand off made it harder to keep station as relative movements between the two aircraft were not so easily detected, but at least it gave more room for slight variations. Tucked in at half a span, there was only about eight feet between the trailing edge of the leader's mainplane and the leading edge of the wing man.

In this position I had the chance for a quick look around the scene. It was quite without feature. The lightly ruffled ocean met the deep blue of the sky in a straight line at the far horizon. The fair-weather cumulus clouds had not yet appeared and the sea undulated and sparkled in innocence, limitless and empty.

As time went on, I felt myself relaxing. The excitement of the squadron departure had faded. Once under way it wasn't too bad; that is, until we saw something. As a lad, I had always suffered mental agony in a dentist's waiting-room and on more than one occasion nearly lost the moral fight to stay there and take what was coming. I had now got to this stage on anti-shipping attacks. I have to confess to sneaking hopes that the convoy had been wrongly reported, or that it had moved out of range, and as time went on without a sighting, my hopes rose.

When we had been running for over an hour, I asked Benny for a check on our position. After a pause he said, 'About 230 miles out according to my reckoning. We should be seeing them at any time.'

'You always were a bloody pessimist,' said Weeky.

I began to close in on the leader again, and so did number three. Robbie eased his aircraft down closer to the sea to avoid radar detection and we followed.

The waves were flashing by like sheets of corrugated glass and I could see Robbie's slipstream beating the water. His gunner was swinging the mid turret round in a continuous scan, the end of his woolly scarf fluttering in the draught.

No one broke the silence of the intercom. All eyes were scanning now. I concentrated on holding station about a foot above the leader's wing. He was so close to the sea, it would have been fatal to fall below him.

A microphone crackled into life. I felt myself stiffen. The intercom hissed for several seconds before Benny said slowly, 'What's tha?',

Weeky came in, 'Where, Benny?'

Robbie's gunner swung his turret abeam and scanned ahead.

'Just off to starboard,' said Benny. The intercom continued to hiss.

'Is it smoke. Or a bit of low cloud?' asked Weeky.

There was a long pause, 'I don't know,' answered Benny slowly. With a shock, I realised that Robbie was signalling a turn to starboard. He had seen it.

'It is, you know!' said Weeky raising his voice. 'This is it!'

Robbie's aircraft seemed to crouch even nearer the sea as we speds toward that faint indeterminate smudge on the horizon.

I took a quick look ahead; it certainly was smoke.

Robbie's aircraft began to pull away as he accelerated for the run-in. I opened up the throttles but had difficulty in closing the gap. He must have been using nearly full throttle himself, leaving me very little in hand. Number three had fallen even farther behind, but we were tucked in laterally.

In such perfect visibility, the ships' superstructures began to appear over the horizon even though they were some fifteen miles away, then we would see the bulk of the hulls as we raced towards them. Conversely of course, they would also see us!

Weeky began to count from his turret 'One, two three, four, yes seven of the buggers!' I stole another quick glance ahead. They were still hull down on the horizon, but the big tanker stood out clearly. There were three smaller ships aft, and three in front. They appeared to be stationary, waiting for us.

Had they seen us yet? Could they, with us as close to the sea as we were? Foolish hopes of a surprise arrival were suddenly shattered. A fountain of water shot up in our path directly ahead. They had seen us all right! That was the first of the big bricks; the 12-pounders.

Another spout erupted just to our starboard, the spray glistening in the sun. We were running into their range now, but Robbie kept straight. Three more columns shot up in quick succession, one so close that I thought it must get number three, but he was still flying.

The ships were looming large now. It was time we were taking some sort of avoiding action. Immediately ahead, the sea began to break into little holes. We were running into the anti-aircraft stuff. In a second it was all around us, the sea boiling viciously.

I pulled away from the leader, kicking the rudderbar to put the aircraft in a series of violent skids.

Scarlet lines of tracer arced gracefully towards us, then gathering speed, whipped by in a deadly dotted line.

I realised with a shock that the ships were not line astern. They were deployed in a V-formation with the tanker at the bottom, and we were flying into it.

I began to corkscrew with such force that I could hear the ammunition belts slamming about in the turret. Weeky opened up his guns with the microphone switched on. The deafening roar gave urgency to my actions. I could smell the reek of cordite. It seemed very personal.

I was ill-treating the aircraft, diving it to within an ace of the sea, then pulling it up in a skidding climbing turn only to push it down so violently that my harness tugged at the shoulders.

We were in the crossfire now and it was murderous. The sea was being chopped to pieces by the hail of metal. Above it, the way ahead was criss-crossed by a lattice of cannon fire. Anti-aircraft shells were injecting their dirty puffs in the sky around us with that 'rock, rock' sound you hear as they get closer.

Then I glimpsed Robbie's aircraft, well ahead, low down, and going dead straight. In that moment tracer was flying gracefully all around him, but the aircraft appeared to fly on unperturbed.

I now dived below deck level as we passed the first of the two flak ships so that they couldn't fire at me without hitting each other. I could see from the stuff leaving them that it was aimed at the aircraft following behind, but I was running into a hail of head-on fire from the tanker. It now looked huge. It sat massively in front and barred the way. Countless flashes sparkled along the super-structure as the guns spat out a defence.

I was now at the same height as Robbie. He was still flying dead straight. I nearly lost control of a skidding turn to port and slid behind his tail. He was attracting a cascade of Bofors fire from the tanker, but miraculously it didn't seem to be hitting him.

I threw my aircraft down to sea-level now for the final bombing run. The tanker loomed above me like a great black cliff. Smoke was pouring from its funnel. It certainly wasn't stationary. I winced as a stream of tracer from amidships raked my flight path from left to right. Unbelieving, I saw Robbie's aircraft above me still flying straight and level.

A second later, I jabbed the release button and let my bombs go as a salvo into the ship's side. I pulled up in a skidding climbing turn to try and clear the ship.

I glimpsed Robbie's aircraft as it flew straight into the middle of the bridge deck. The explosion was immediate. A great ball of flame that spewed out debris. I ducked instinctively as we shot through it.

One only needs about 150 ft to clear a ship, but the climb seems to take all the steam out of the aircraft's performance. It hangs there above the masts and the derricks and the lifeboats, and in one intimate glimpse you see a gun-crew swing round frantically.

Then the dive over the far side, pushing down so violently that both engines fade momentarily due to fuel starvation. The punitive fire is coming from behind now; tracer streaming by on either side lends urgency if any more were needed. Then the cry from Weeky, 'We've got it! We've got the bloody thing! But someone else has gone in on this side!'

Gradually the sky clears of missiles. 'Are we out of trouble, Weeky?'

He looks back from his mid-turret position, 'I reckon so.'

'Can you see any others?'

'Not a sod!'

'I don't see how anything could have got through that lot,' Benny said. 'I don't know how we did.'

'You've got to thank the evasive action for that,' Weeky said. 'Thank Christ you didn't do a Robinson.' But I was too sick at the man's fate to reply.

Benny gave me a course back to the Island, and we settled down close to the sea for the lonely run home. Weeky reported that most of the damage was superficial; a number of shrapnel holes in the wings and the fuselage and a larger hole in the base of the fin, but although the skin was missing there for about a foot, he could see the ribs and the sternpost undamaged.

Eventually, two more Blenheims were seen coming up astern and we slowed down to let them formate on us. In fact, we learned later that one other aircraft had made its way home separately. To lose only two out of six against such opposition was better than we could have hoped for. Perhaps it need have been only one; who knows?

As someone said at de-briefing, 'What a price to pay for a conviction!'

CHAPTER TWELVE

The Africa road

THE FOLLOWING DAY, the squadron was on standby, and we dozed in chairs outside the briefing block only half relaxed in the knowledge that a Maryland aircraft of the reconnaissance squadron was scouring the eastern Mediterranean looking for further work for us to do.

I lay back with my eyes closed enjoying the luxury of the sun's warmth on my face, and gradually the incessant jabber of the Maltese workmen engaged in rebuilding a near-by barrack block subsided into a distant murmur, to be followed by oblivion.

This peaceful state did not last for long before Weeky's voice uncomfortably close to my ear called, 'Wakey! Wakey! There's work for you to do.'

I struggled into consciousness, irritable at having been disturbed, then seeing the men filing into the briefing-room I recalled with a sudden rush of anguish that we were on standby and that something had come up.

'We suspect,' announced the Intelligence Officer, 'that there is an enemy convoy south of the Island heading for Tripoli. The recce aircraft this morning has failed to sight it, but going on last night's intelligence, it should be about here.' His finger traced a vague circle on the map north of the African coast.

'We're going to carry out a square search in the area,' broke in the Wing Commander, 'to see if we can find it. The Briefing Officer will give the navigators the tracks and distances. If by the time you get to the southern end of the sweep you have found nothing, cross in over the coast and beat up the road from Homs to Misurata. Save your bombs for any petrol tankers going east, they will be carrying loads to the front. Beat up any other military traffic or installations you see, but leave the Arabs alone; it pays us not to antagonise them. If you come across a camel train, give it a wide berth. According to our information there are no anti-aircraft units in the area and the nearest Luftwaffe squadron is based about ten miles west of Tripoli. Any opposition will probably be from small-arms fire.'

Examining the battle order, we were surprised to find that we were down to lead the squadron on this sortie, and Benny became apprehensive at the thought of his greater responsibility as navigator leader, though for my money he was the best in the squadron.

Within the hour we were airborne, and I climbed in a wide circle around the Island while the other aircraft caught up and tucked into a vic of five, all the serviceable aircraft that could be mustered.

Rolling out onto a southerly heading, I eased the aircraft into a dive across Island and shot over the cliffs at Dingli. In the lead position at fifty feet, I was able to look around me and check on the shape of the formation. Numbers two and three were tucked in at half span, the only relative movement being a gentle rise and fall in the light turbulence, and the shimmering discs of their propellers. I could see the details of the aircraft clearly in the unfiltered sunlight, and the pilots' faces half covered by their microphone masks intent on keeping station. Numbers four and five were out on the wing, their undulations following those of the inner aircraft though somewhat delayed and amplified. The sea jazzed past underneath – we were a spearhead aimed for an identified point in the Ocean – 33° 10′ N, 14° 25′ E.

Benny fumbled with his microphone switch. 'According to me, the forecast wind is about 180° out.'

'How's that?'

'Well, I've just taken a drift with the bombsight and it's about 3° east. The forecast was from 160° at 15 knots which would give us drift the other way.'

'Take the evidence of your eyes, Benny,' I suggested. 'They're a bit more reliable than guesstimates.'

As the sweep area was approached, I led the formation down nearer the sea until we were skimming just over the surface. I couldn't look round now; it was up to them to keep in station.

At the appropriate time, Benny gave me an easterly course, and I eased the aircraft up to fifty feet to give the wing man a bit of height and hand-signalled a turn to the left. Glancing to port, I found myself looking down the wings of number three and the wing man, forming a line that pointed diagonally down to the sea. Looking out to starboard, I saw the machines of the number two and his wing man poised above me and describing a graceful arc against the background of the hard blue sky.

After a run of fifteen minutes east, we turned southwest until due south of the start point of the sweep, then east again only to return diagonally to a point even farther south of the start. To and fro we ranged covering an area of about 250 square miles, but it was vacant. As we neared the southern limit of the area, the North African coast began to show as a low brown line on the horizon. By the time we were on our last run east, some details were visible: rock mounds rather than cliffs and stretches of featureless beach, while in the distance one could see a long dark smudge which was the suggestion of Tripoli.

Without a word I turned south and headed for the coast, the formation following like a pack of hungry animals. As the details of the land rapidly clarified, the air became hotter and with it came turbulence.

We crossed the coast low and fast and came immediately on a convoy of grey vehicles trundling eastwards. There was time for only a short burst of machine-gun fire as we flashed over the road and went into a long turn to the east to pick up the road farther on. It ran dead straight as far as the eye could see, but there was a telephone-line along the lefthand side which obstructed one from getting really low. Benny and I opened up with the front guns as we ran onto a further line of trucks. The occupants bounced over the sides like little black balls, diving for cover. I saw some answering flashes from machine-guns. As we shot over the tops of the lorries I glimpsed a number of dark heaps on the ground. They could have been kitbags or humans, such was the remoteness.

But there was no time for contemplation, for a much larger formation was visible ahead. They had been alerted by the noise of our gunfire and were frantically deploying into defensive positions. It was an important convoy with what looked to be about twenty tracked vehicles towing sizeable guns. Some of the vehicles had stopped and the crews hastened to bring the guns to bear as we rushed in on them. This lot certainly merited a 250-pounder, but our bombs had eleven-second delay fuses for the anti-shipping task. If I dropped one now, the following aircraft would be likely to catch it.

All of our guns were racketing as we raked the convoy, our tracer richocheting off the vehicles as the crews scrambled for cover. By the time we reached the first vehicle, I had made a decision. This was too good a prize to let go. I swung the aircraft into a long turn to the south. As we came round, the other Blenheims could be seen racing above the road and heavy fire was being exchanged. I hoped this might distract the Jerries from what I was doing. I followed the contour of the sand dunes as closely as I could until in a position to turn back for another run. I swung the aircraft in a low steep turn towards the road just as a massive explosion sent a column of black smoke and debris erupting into the air above the middle of the column. One of the others had had a go.

I flattened out just above the road and groped for the bomb switch panel with my left hand, moving the master switch from salvo to single and tripping the nose-fusing switch for number one. I let it go as we approached the confused scene and pulled up into a steep climbing turn to avoid the column of rising smoke from the vehicles already burning.

The other aircraft were out of sight by now, but this was to our advantage for a number of units that they had attacked were just coming out of cover when we took them by surprise.

With events happening at such speed, one's memory tends to retain individual pictures of the more startling images.

We were approaching an oasis of palm trees that straddled the road and just short of it lay a number of crude tents. A single figure stood in the road looking in the direction that the other aircraft had disappeared. Suddenly he heard us, dived into the nearest tent and pulled the flap across.

A short distance farther on, we came upon a camel train stopped in some confusion beside the road. Several of the riders waved their rifles with white flags tied to them as we approached, and bearing in mind the Wingco's briefing we flew past without firing. It was at this point that my battledress blouse which I had stowed on a shelf behind me fell onto my head. I pushed it back irritably, but it was not until later that the true significance of the incident came home to me.

Another huge explosion ahead marked the passage of our companions, and when we approached the spot, the seething black smoke laced with flame that writhed skywards indicated only too clearly that someone had bagged an oil tanker.

We had one or two more minor skirmishes before the outline of Misurata came in sight and I swung south looking for the small airstrip there. Apart from a windsock and some huts there was no sign of aircraft, so I let go the remainder of our bombs along the line of what looked like the strip and turned north for home.

It was some time before we saw the other aircraft ahead and another ten minutes before I managed to get in front of them and assert my leadership. But there were only three. This bothered me. It would be absurd to lose an aircraft on an outing such as that, and I wasn't too happy that I had spent most of my time as leader bringing up the rear. I was tempted to break radio silence to ask the others if they knew where it was, but this would have been too much of an indiscretion.

Apart from a vague worry about the fate of the fifth aircraft, I felt well pleased with the trip, so much so that on crossing the coast at Kalafrana, I signalled the formation to close up and dived across the airfield in a neat box of four.

Back in the dispersal area, I switched off the engines and slid back the hatch as the fitter scrambled onto the wing.

'Had a good trip, Sarge?'

'Yeah, not bad!' I said cheerfully. I was switching off the fuel-cocks when he said, 'Jeese, that was a bit close!'

I craned my head round and saw him pointing to a clean bullet hole in the side of the fuselage just behind the top of my seat; in fact, within a foot of where my head had been.

'Look at this, Weeky!' I called. He scrambled up beside the fitter.

'Here! You know how that happened!' I studied his face.

'It was those bloody wogs!'

'Wogs?' I said.

'Yeah. You know that camel train that we flew alongside?'

'Uhuh.'

'Well, as we went past they lowered their guns and fired. I would have opened up on the buggers but I wasn't quick enough!'

'They couldn't have made a deflection shot like that!' I protested.

'Well it's on the right side, isn't it?' said Weeky.

Then the incident came back to me. I picked up my battledress blouse and examined it quickly. There was a neat bullethole in the waistband and in the back.

I held it out to the others silently with my finger through it.

Weeky began to laugh, 'What a bloody fine line you can shoot when you're wearing that!'

'Wassa matter?' asked Benny, who had scrambled up to join us.

'That!' I said showing him the damage. 'By courtesy of a wily oriental gentleman.'

He looked serious, then turned slowly to the gunner, 'Aw, come on now, Weeky!' he said. 'This is nae laughing matter! Tha's a wee bit too damn close for comfort!'

'Well, I wish it was mine,' retorted Weeky, still laughing. 'I'll swop you mine for it, Ron.'

Our attention was distracted by a crack from the control tower and we turned to see a green Very light describing an arc onto the airfield. Approaching from Valletta was the fifth Blenheim. Its wheels were down and there was something strange about it. As it turned overhead, the sun was reflected from it in a series of odd patterns.

'What's happened to him?' asked Weeky.

'I don't know,' I said, watching his progress; 'the skinning appears to be damaged.'

The dispersal truck arrived with the other crews just as he touched down, and the series of bounces that followed brought whoops and shouts of delight from the onlookers.

It wasn't until he approached the dispersal that the full extent of the problem could be seen. All of the skinning of the underside of the wings and the fuselage was sagging in between the formers and the ribs.

The pilot was Tim Cummings, who had been tail-end Charlie.

'Who got that petrol tanker?' I asked.

'We did,' said Arthur Madden.

'Was Tim behind you?'

'Er yes. I think he was.' We looked at each other until I saw the realisation dawning in his eyes. Tim had flown into his bomb blast. . . .

Despite the unnecessary damage to the fifth aircraft, the Wing Commander seemed well pleased with our report of the sortie, and we climbed into the old bus that took us to our billets in the village of Marsaxlokk in good humour.

Our driver was a young Maltese with a shock of black crinkly hair. He was unusually small, so much so that his feet couldn't reach the pedals from the driving seat and he used to crouch over the wheel and dance on the clutch and accelerator like a dervish.

His driving was wild even by local standards and I got the impression that as he was the driver for a squadron of low-level bomber pilots he felt he too should live dangerously, or perhaps he thought we would never have it any other way. In this he was certainly encouraged when in our wilder moments we exhorted him to get us back to our quarters in the minimum time.

So it was this afternoon.

'Golliwog! There's a quid that says you can't get us back in twelve minutes!' shouted Digger Grey.

'You wanna bet,' the airman grinned over his shoulder. 'I do it easy! You see. You see. I do it in ten minutes!'

The game was on. We careered along the narrow twisting lanes clearing the low stone walls by inches. I found myself praying fervently that we would meet nothing coming the other way. The old bus creaked, rattled and slammed over the rough surfaces and the bodywork twisted visibly. Raucous cheers greeted every gear-crashing slide around the more awkward corners, and in his cab the little Malt bounced about like a monkey, spurred on by the shouts of the men behind him.

The road down to the village was very steep and ended in a T-junction at the sea. One either turned right or left. Even in his quieter moments our Golliwog, as Digger called him, took the hill at an unnecessarily fast canter. On this occasion, spurred by the news that he had only a minute to go, he excelled himself. Children and chickens flew in all directions as the vehicle bounced and hurtled down the hill in its own duststorm. Golliwog pumped on the ancient rubber-bulbed horn and the shouting of the airmen added to the din. Some were urging him on and others crying out for him to stop. But the situation was out of control.

We heard the tyres scraping as he locked the brakes. He wound furiously on the steering-wheel as the junction presented itself.

The bus started to lurch sideways but the wheels lost their traction on the loose surface. It wasn't going to go round the corner. It was sliding diagonally and fast towards the water.

The front wheels hit the parapet and the bus reared up.

'Get the stick back!' someone shouted. 'Let's have a stall!' But the nose fell and the back kicked up. It dived into a mass of barbed wire. The noise was excruciating. The front flopped into the water and immediately started to sink. The Golliwog scrambled excitedly through the open back of his cab to escape the rising level and a general evacuation set in. There were small sliding windows along the sides, but it is amazing what the human body can do in a tight spot. As someone said afterwards, Digger Grey, who was fourteen stone, came through a window a foot square without even touching the sides. We scrambled ashore through the gap in the barbed wire still laughing uproariously while the natives rushed to the spot shouting to each other in alarm. Their reactions changed to astonishment when a couple of the chaps grabbed the little driver and swung him shoulder-high, cheering. The little Maltese looked incredulous, then caught the mood and threw back his head in laughter and waved his fists jubilantly in the air. He was borne away in triumph along the road to our quarters.

Subsequently, in a gross miscarriage of justice, the court of inquiry found that the brakes had failed, and the driver was exonerated.

A fairly wild party followed in the mess and by dinner-time, the end was in sight as far as I was concerned and I staggered up the hill to the low stone barrack block, collapsed on the bed and took my leave of the conscious world.

When I climbed out of bed, still fully dressed, at around 0730, all of the others were still asleep, some in uniform and one in his pyjamas curled up on the stone floor with a pair of boots tucked under his face for a pillow. I made my way to the ablutions, hitched my shaving mirror onto the window catch and prepared to revive myself.

I became conscious of a noise in the distance. It approached rapidly and I realised that it was cannon- or machine-gun fire. By the time I had struggled with the catch and flung the window open, the cacophony was with us.

I saw the bright Italian markings of a Savoia Marchetti flash past, its guns spitting orange. Another streaked along the shoreline below me firing at nothing of importance. A third skimmed the rooftop in an explosion of noise; then they were gone.

I stood with my razor still at the ready. What the hell was all that about? There was nothing worth shooting up here in the village except the barrack blocks. Maybe they were sent over for a primary target but funked it. And the warning hadn't gone. Maybe the alert from last night was still on.

I shrugged and prepared to get on with my toilet when I realised that my mirror was missing. In thrusting open the window I must have knocked it down. It lay on the stone 'floor, the frame surrounded by a pool of finely broken glass. The sight made me curiously apprehensive.

I went back into the sleeping quarters to see if I could borrow another, but surprisingly, no one had stirred. It occurred to me that if one really wanted to win a war, then all that was necessary was to drop a continuous supply of booze on the enemy.

As we were on stand-down I had decided to take up an offer made to me by a friendly Anglo-Maltese in the village bar, a splendid establishment which rejoiced in the name of the Honeymoon Hotel. I ate my breakfast alone before making my way to the harbour in search of him. Edgar was already down by the quayside launching the little craft, and he took some trouble when going through his fishing-tackle to make up the best set for me and to advise me where to go in the bay. I rowed slowly away from the shore in the gentle heat of the autumn sun until the land noises began to fade and blur, and the cries of the children at play softened into a counterpoint to the murmur of the village at work.

On Edgar's advice, I rowed to a point some two miles out, and when I stowed the oars, the rattle of wood on wood seemed loud in such a silence. The tinkling of the water against the transom was too soothing to be considered a noise, and well content, I settled down to bait the hooks and get them overboard. The sea was completely calm, and silver and blue in the sunshine. A slight haze smudged the now distant shoreline, and the hills that rose beyond were topped with fair-weather cumulus clouds, white and fluffy; sent to decorate the scene, for nature seemed to be in a kindly mood.

Although my friend had assured me that Lampuki fish abounded in this part of the bay, none came near my lines. Perhaps they realised that I was an incompetent stranger. In any case I wasn't at all sure that I wanted to be disturbed. I had had a letter from home the previous day telling me that all was well and expressing more concern for me than for themselves despite the fact that London was still being bombed continuously. Home seemed so very far away and I found myself wondering if I would ever see it again.

The supply of relief crews from the UK had dried up during the past week, and our squadron numbers were being whittled down daily. Oddly enough, we were now an all-NCO squadron. Officers didn't seem to survive with us, that is except one, Ivor Broom, a Welshman from the Rhondda Valley with immense courage and a quiet unassuming manner. A likeable fellow, but with a clear stamp of character on his boyish good looks.

Oddly enough, I had been called to the CO's office earlier that week and to my astonishment, was asked if I wanted a commission. The Wing Commander's taciturn nature had given me the impression that he didn't have much time for crews in general and me in particular, so the shock was all the greater.

He explained that any recommendation would have to go to Headquarters Middle East Command in Cairo and that events might take some time to catch up with me. 'You might be back in the UK,' he said, 'or' – rather ominously – 'anywhere.'

He insisted that I keep the matter confidential, and I pondered on it a great deal during the next few days. I couldn't really see why he should have made such a gesture, and in the circumstances there didn't seem much point, for by now I had a growing conviction that only my documents and not me would be sent home from Malta. I even got around to thinking that he had probably done the same to all the other pilots as a subtle boost to the sagging morale.

The sheer peace of the scene around me only added, in a strange way, to my inner sadness. Tomorrow would be another day. We would go to the airfield. The briefing-room would be a bustle with activity. The hard-faced Wing Commander with a frightening sense of urgency would explain to us the task that had to be done, and we would go out together to do his bidding. Then would come the holocaust, and we must go in. It was luck rather than skill which dictated whether you would survive. And how much longer would the luck last? The squadron was down to six crews now from a maximum strength of twenty-nine. There had been talk of a relief squadron coming out from England, but no one took that very seriously.

I was lost so deep in my reverie that the enormous happening in the bay beside me seeped but slowly into my consciousness. I was vaguely aware of a hissing noise that grew in intensity to a low roar. Rising from the water not a hundred yards away was a black, glistening shape. In a moment of ridiculous panic, I cried out, 'Christ! It's a whale!'

I jumped up, lost my balance in the rocking dinghy and fell backwards over the thwart. By the time I had scrambled up for another look the long snout was clear of the water, to be followed by the taller structure of a submarine's conning tower. It slid almost silently towards the Kalafrana shore and a rumour that had been going around the crew-room was now confirmed.

We had heard that aviation fuel was getting desperately short on the Island due to the toll being taken of British convoys coming from Gibraltar, and that submarines were to make the journey from England with fresh supplies. This particular vessel was the *Thunderbolt*, though it was better known before the war, when under the name *Thetis* it had sunk with the loss of ninety-nine souls. Recovered and renamed, it was now doing a stealthy and vitally important task in this theatre of the war.

I watched it until it docked against the refuelling jetty of the flying-boat base and then pulled in my fishing lines and made my way back to the village. Edgar came down as he saw the boat approach and helped me pull it up clear of the water. He laughed at my lack of success, explaining that on some days when it was very bright, they didn't eat at all.

We went into the dark coolness of the parlour of the Honeymoon Hotel and my eyes wandered around the mass of Victorian bric-a-brac as he prised the tops off a couple of bottles of Hop Leaf. His mother, a large, jovial woman, brought us plates of eggs and chips; three eggs for me 'As I had to keep my strength up!' She roared with laughter as she said this, and disappeared into the kitchen still shaking her head at the thought of it.

In the late afternoon, I wandered back along the shoreline to our quarters. The steward was asleep on a chair outside the door of the mess, his head lolling and his mouth hung open like one bereft of bone structure. The mess was deserted, but my attention was attracted by a piece of paper pinned to the notice board which fluttered in the breeze from the open door.

It was headed, 'Adjutant's Office' and stated:

> CREWS WILL REPORT FOR BRIEFING
> AT 0600 HRS IN THE MORNING
> A SPECIAL TASK HAS BEEN ALLOCATED
> BY COMMAND HEADQUARTERS

CHAPTER THIRTEEN

A very close call

THE JOURNEY to the airfield the next day was made in studied silence. We noted as we turned up the hill in the centre of the village that our old bus had been removed from the sea. The one that had called for us that morning was not new but different and so was the driver. He drove slowly and awkwardly, making heavy work of the gear changes. The message – 'A special task has been allocated by command headquarters' – nagged at the back of our minds and the fact that we no longer had our old squadron bus but were being driven slowly to the airfield by a stranger took on a special significance, or so it seemed.

In the briefing-room we found quite a line-up waiting for us. The Station Commander was there, and a naval captain who watched us file in with disconcertingly intense eyes. We realised the significance of his attendance when we heard of the target, the naval base at Cephalonia. Three enemy destroyers and a number of other vessels had been seen in the harbour of Argostolion there, and according to our visitor from the Senior Service, 'Such a concentration will make an absolutely splendid target!'

'The man must be mad!' murmured Benny. Certainly he knew nothing about the technique of air-to-surface shipping attacks. In the open sea, ships in convoy had to keep at a respectable distance from each other and this had the effect of dispersing the protective fire of the escort to some extent, but a group of capital ships moored cheek by jowl in a protective cocoon of shore batteries could bring devastating fire-power on anything that approached.

For six Blenheims to go in at low level in daylight was suicide; but worse was to come. On arrival, we had not had time to study the battle order pinned to the notice board, and the briefing officer now read out the names of the pilots and their positions in the formation. Dick Wilson was appointed to lead.

He was the man who felt so badly about being posted to Malta when he was within three sorties of the end of his operational tour in the UK, and his nerves were completely shot. He openly admitted to being LMF (in official parlance this meant 'lacking morale fibre') and on the last shipping attack he had been seen skirting his way around the convoy to drop his bombs into the sea. Nothing had been said by the other crews on return, and it was not known what story he had given at de-briefing, but surely the CO must have had some inkling of the situation.

As all the crews had a comparable measure of experience it was the custom to give each pilot a turn at leading the squadron, but today's combination was a lulu! My foreboding that had been growing for the past few days now closed in. With five crews behind him, he just couldn't sneak around the target, and when he came face to face with the hornet's nest, there was no guessing what he would do.

The feeling of apprehension was general and when briefing was over, an anxious group formed outside the crew-room door.

'It's not bloody on!' said Ted Slater tremulously.

'What do we do?' Arthur Madden asked. 'Tell the CO that Sergeant Wilson is LMF; that we saw him turn away the other day and said nothing?'

'But it's just plain lunacy!' protested Digger Grey. 'What the bloody hell does the CO think he's doing?'

'Hasn't it occurred to you that he's probably the best leader we could have for a trip like this?' cut in Weeky. The group looked at him incredulously. He went on. 'The chances are that when he sees the opposition, he's not going to go in, is he? And after all, we have to follow our leader, don't we?'

At that moment, Dicky Wilson came through the door with his crew. He was white-faced as he walked past the group to the dispersal truck.

'Come on,' said Weeky with a sigh. 'Let's get this show on the road.'

When we arrived at our aircraft, the fitter was just refastening the cowlings after his daily inspection. 'Caught us on the hop this morning, Sarge,' he called cheerfully. 'Not used to this crack-of-dawn stuff.'

'Neither am I,' I said; 'but we're going after a naval base this morning, and they want us to get there before the poor buggers have a chance to escape!'

'Jesus!' he said sympathetically 'Rather you than me!'

I lowered my chute into the bucket seat and slid down through the roof hatch into that strange hospital-like smell that all military aircraft have clinging to them. For once it was cool, the rising sun not having had time to turn the cockpit into a greenhouse.

I found myself fumbling with the fastening of the safety harness and my mind went back suddenly to that day in wintry Scotland when the adventure was about to start. But that was a long time ago, and then there was hope.

The explosion of Weeky's guns as he fired a test burst into the ground brought me back to the present and I set about doing the cockpit checks. The metal parts were cold to touch, and my breath was steaming up the inside of the windscreen.

Ten minutes to go – time to start engines. I signalled to the fitter who was waiting to one side and got the thumbs-up. I pressed the starter button and the cold engine began to turn over sluggishly. After two or three hesitant revolutions it fired, spat back through the carburettor and stopped.

At a second attempt it chattered into life, blue smoke spilling from the exhaust stacks. The starboard engine gave less trouble, and with both of them turning I slid the roof hatch shut and settled down to wait for the rise in cylinder-head temperatures before doing a power check. This waiting period was always the worst. Looking around, the aircraft on neighbouring dispersals were centres of activity, propellors turning, engines firing and ground crews scampering around disconnecting the ground batteries and pulling them clear. I looked across at the leader's aircraft and to my surprise noted that neither engine had been started.

I switched on the intercom, 'Dicky's leaving it a bit late.'

'Maybe he's going LMF here,' said Weeky.

'Aw! Give the mun a wee chance!' pleaded Benny and as he did so, the port propeller began to turn.

My cylinder-head temperatures were now coming up to the 100° mark and I leaned forward and switched off each of the four magneto switches in turn. The drop in engine revolutions was nominal. By a rotating movement of the hand I indicated to the fitter that I was about to do an engine run and he signalled that it was all clear behind.

I pulled the control column hard back so that the tail would not come off the ground as I increased the engine power, and carefully pushed the port throttle open to the plus-5 boost setting. The aircraft shook and bounced on its wheels and the control column butted against my stomach like something living. I switched off each magneto in turn but a drop of only fifty revs reassured me. At full throttle, the engine was achieving maximum power, the cylinder-head temperatures, oil pressure and temperature were all within limits; what more could you want? I throttled back the port engine and repeated the process with the other, but all was well.

The ground crew kicked away the chocks from the wheels, dragged them clear with the ropes and stood with thumbs up indicating that all was ready for taxying, but the leader had yet to do his engine run. The other four aircraft like ours were ready to go, and a couple had even started to taxi and then stopped, waiting for the leader.

An unnecessarily long time elapsed before his port propeller began to spin faster and his subsequent power check was slow and deliberate as if he were looking for something special. After both engines had been throttled back and the chocks pulled away, he still didn't move.

I glanced anxiously at the cylinder-head gauges.

'Our plugs will oil up if we sit here idling much longer, won't they Skip?' asked Weeky quietly. I grunted.

I saw that Digger Grey was gesticulating urgently at the leader's aircraft indicating that he should get moving, but there was no ready response.

A further five minutes elapsed before his engine power increased, sending a swirl of dust from behind the tail, and the aircraft emerged slowly from the dispersal. We all followed in a ragged and uncertain line along the taxi track towards the runway.

He lined up first and we all watched as he took his time over the pre-take-off checks.

'Jesus!' Weeky hissed over the intercom with exasperation.

A green light flickered urgently from the control tower and the aircraft started to roll forward, slowly at first as if reluctant, or maybe it was our imagination.

His tail came up about half-way along the runway and then the wheels left the ground and he was climbing. We were number three to take-off but number two swung on to the runway and roared off in a burst of pent-up feeling before I could get alongside him. In the light of what followed this was fortunate.

With the runway to myself, I took my time lining up, had a last look round at the setting of the fuel-cocks, flaps, trims and hydraulic lever, then pushed both throttles firmly through to the take-off gate. One was always conscious of having a 1000-lb bomb load in the belly, and the stick had to be pushed hard forward to get the tail to come up. The aircraft trundled over the rough surface slowly gathering speed. Although the outside air temperature was low, there was little wind and we would need all of the take-off run to get off.

As the needle of the airspeed indicator quivered towards the seventy-five mark, I eased back on the control column, and then further in a positive pull. The aircraft sagged sluggishly into the air.

I had just reached down and felt for the undercarriage lever when it happened. An explosion from the port side sent the aircraft into a violent swing. I pushed on full opposite rudder instinctively. The power surged back into the engine and the aircraft swung back, then it cut again with a crack and I screwed round in my seat to try and hold on full rudder and opposite aileron to keep the thing straight.

As the engine popped and banged the aircraft slewed and skidded. We were dangerously close to the ground and the speed was falling. I saw people scampering out of the aircraft's path.

Contact with the rocky ground seemed inevitable and there was 1000 lb of high explosive that would meet it first.

I grabbed for the jettison bulb without looking down and let the bombs go in a salvo. The engine had lost power completely now. My right leg was quivering with the effort of forcing the rudder hard over, but we had insufficient speed, and the aircraft was turn ing slowly but inexorably into the dead engine and towards the village of Luqa. There was no climb performance and at such low speed the rudder effect was not enough to keep the machine straight. As if by some malignant and irresistible force, the aircraft was being turned towards the complex of buildings, and below roof height.

I felt stupified and incredulous. At training school we had been taught that it was fatal to turn into a dead engine. But I couldn't get her to turn the other way. My options had run out. It was either disaster now, or loss of control perhaps clear of the buildings.

I eased off the rudder and the aircraft swung eagerly to port in a flat skidding turn and the nose started to drop. The line of buildings slipped past giddily and I flinched as the bulk of a church loomed in front. We shot low over a stone-walled road missing a donkey cart by inches.

I was conscious of my port wing almost scraping the ground. People scattered in the churchyard. The ground began to fall away towards the coast and I eased the nose down to gain some precious speed even though it meant almost hugging the rough surface. I was buying reprieves a few seconds at a time. If I could get to the sea beyond Sliema, at least we could ditch.

Benny must have read my thoughts, for he called 'Weeky! For Christ's sake get the dinghy ready!'

The speed was creeping up now, and I could just hold the swing, but the ground ahead was levelling off and from it rose a forest of buildings.

I took a hand from the control-column yoke just long enough to crank on some rudder trim. This eased the load from my leg, which was just about to fail. In the next quarter of a mile over rough ground, I managed to gain a few feet of height. There was a wall of buildings ahead and rising ground to the left. I couldn't get to starboard.

I could only ease the stick back in a last effort for survival. If we lost too much speed, then control would also be lost and the buildings would claim us and probably a few more people too.

We shot close over the clutter of the first roofs, then saw that the manmade skyline was rising ahead. With falling speed, the machine began to resist my control forces. The port wing was falling and we were turning to the left again.

Trembling, I saw kaleidoscopic flashes: flat roofs cluttered with assorted junk; a line of washing flashing by; an astonished woman with mouth agape; even a scattering of chickens.

Then we topped the highest rise and I saw the sanctuary of the sea beyond.

I dived down the castellated contours of the remaining roof-tops, across the coast road and flattened out just above the water. This sort of low flying was more familiar. I noted thankfully that the airspeed was now over 90 mph. I could even take off a little rudder and keep straight and ease her into a flattish climb.

We gained about 300 ft by flying straight out to sea then started a gentle turn back towards the Island. There was a cloud of black smoke rising from behind some buildings, which was strange as we had just passed that point.

I broke radio silence and called the tower to tell them that I was returning with engine failure, but got no response. It didn't matter, I was going in anyway. Then I noticed for the first time that the cylinder-head temperatures of the good engine were way up in the red. Even at this height I daren't throttle back yet and I remember muttering 'Keep going you fool!' Benny heard me over the inter-com and looked around the corner from his nose compartment and up at me with anxious eyes above his oxygen-mask.

Slowly we closed the land and positioned onto a base leg for the southeast landing strip. We were still dramatically low, but at least under control. I turned in close to ensure we didn't undershoot and lowered the undercarriage, then came the flaps in quick suc-cession, followed by a steep approach during which I could ease the pressure on the starboard engine.

The landing was safe, if not polished, and as the speed decayed I swung off into the rough and stopped, for it was not possible to taxi with one engine out.

I switched off the starboard engine and told Benny to make his way back to the duty pilot's tent and tell him to put a guard on our bombs which I had jettisoned safe near Safi Strip.

I sank back in my seat, laid back my head and breathed in deeply the fresh air that came through the open hatch. The over-heated engine was tinkling and crackling as it cooled, but other-wise there was glorious silence. Weeky was quiet too in his turret behind me. Perhaps he was praying.

Only too soon, the flight van approached bouncing over the rough surface and I climbed wearily out onto the wing, my legs still shaking. The door came open before the vehicle had stopped and out scrambled the Wing Commander. His face seemed paler than ever.

'What the hell happened?' he shouted.

It seemed a damn fool question and unnecessarily aggressive.

'My port engine cut on take-off, Sir!'

'Well, you didn't have to bomb the bloody Island, did you?'

I was confused, 'I'm sorry?' I said, slipping down off the wing.

His face was unpleasant in his anger, 'What have you been told about not fusing your bombs until you're approaching hostile territory?'

I didn't see what he was getting at, 'I'm sorry, Sir, I don't understand.'

He shook himself with impatience, 'You jettisoned your bombs!'

'Yes, Sir.'

'How?'

'On the jettison bulb, Sir.'

'Then you explain to me how you dropped a live stick across Safi if the nose-fusing switch wasn't on!'

I looked to the southeast where the pall of black smoke was slowly dispersing in the morning sky. Jesus Christ! No wonder he was angry. I looked back at him miserably.

'Well, go on!' he shouted. 'Explain!'

'I went over the bombing panel during my pre-flight checks and I'm sure that the nose-fusing switch was off.'

'We certainly had plenty of time to do the pre-flight checks!' put in Weeky, who had joined us.

The Wing Commander gave him a withering glance and addressed himself to me again, 'What position is the nose-fusing switch in now?'

'I don't know, Sir,' I said stupidly.

'Then go and bloody well look!'

I scrambled up onto the wing and hung head first down into the cockpit, craning my neck until I could see the switch panel on the lefthand side. The switch was on.

When I reappeared, the CO was standing with his hands firmly on his hips: 'It's on! Isn't it?'

'Yes. It's on.'

He turned and walked towards the transport indicating with a peremptory gesture that the driver should do the same. The doors slammed and the van turned away and headed for the headquarters building.

I sat down weakly on the catwalk. I was positive in my own mind that I had checked that panel carefully and that the fusing switch was up. But it was certainly down now.

'Jolly good job they were eleven-second delay,' said Weeky.

I looked at him dully, 'I wonder how many other people we've killed.'

'Well, that's war, isn't it? It's in the lap of the gods. There would have been a lot more written off if you had gone into the middle of Sliema.'

Benny came trotting along the flarepath sweating and puffing. 'Heh, Skipper!' he called as he approached. 'Those bombs weren't safe. They went off!'

'We already know that,' said Weeky scornfully.

'Wha' happened?' asked Benny.

'You tell me,' I said. 'The nose-fusing switch was off when I checked it; now it's on.'

'What bad luck!' he said.

'How long do we have to be stuck out here?' asked Weeky.

'The duty pilot got on the field telephone and asked for transport for us,' Benny replied, then sinking down onto the ground, 'I'm bushed. Must be out of condition.'

'You're entitled to be bushed after what we just went through,' put in Weeky. 'I thought that was our lot!'

We relapsed into silence until we saw the dispersal truck bumping and groaning its way across the field towards us. The groundcrew were in the back and the sergeant fitter climbed out of the cab as it drew alongside. He was grinning.

'Well, that gave the natives something to think about.' I shook my head miserably.

'What happened to the engine?' he asked.

'It cut!'

'Yes, I know that, but any symptoms?'

'It was OK during the run-up, then it cut dead just as we left the ground.'

'What were the head temperatures just before you took off?'

'Normal.'

'Were the engines idling for any length of time?'

'I'll say they bloody were!' cut in Weeky. 'Thanks to that nit Wilson we might have bought it!'

'Aha!' said the sergeant brightly. 'That gives us something to go on.' Then, gesturing to the groundcrew, 'Come on you lucky lads; get those cowlings off and see what we've got.'

'All right if we take the truck?' I asked. 'We'll send it back.'

'Sure, help yourself.'

As we were about to climb aboard, the steady wail of the 'All clear' drifted across from Valletta.

'Was there an alert on as well then?' asked Weeky in surprise.

'They're probably blowing it to get the bastards out of the shelters,' called the sergeant. 'When that lot went off, all the wogs in the maintenance area dived underground and it was no good telling 'em it was one of ours. They didn't want to know!'

Back in the briefing-room, the Intelligence Officer sought me out. 'We're going to need a report from you, old boy,' he said brightly.

'Well, I can only say what I said to the Wingco,' I countered. 'I'm sure the fusing switch was up when I checked prior to starting the engines, and it's down now.'

'Oh, it's not that,' he said. 'It's the Admiralty.'

'The Admiralty!'

'Yes. They've put in a complaint to SASO about your low-flying over their installations at Sliema. But don't worry, old boy, I'm sure you can justify it. Incidentally, your bombs did nothing but make smoke. No one got a scratch.'

I sank into a chair and took the sheet of blank paper that he gave me. He stood looking down for a moment and then said thoughtfully, 'Do you always wear an Irvin jacket?'

'No, Sir; but we had an early start this morning and it was a bit chilly.'

'When you grabbed for the jettison bulb, do you think it possible that the cuff of your jacket caught the fusing switch?'

I looked at the leather sleeve, which admittedly was a bit long and came below the wrist. 'I've heard of it happening before,' he went on.

'I wish you would tell the Wingco.'

'I certainly will.'

By the time I had finished writing my report and been interviewed by the squadron engineering officer, the time was fast approaching when the aircraft were due back from their sortie so we settled down in chairs outside the crew-room to watch for them.

We were in agreement that that was one trip we were happy to miss, but we felt that we would like an excuse next time which was less trying on the nerves. The Blenheim was a great aircraft, but there were no margins when an engine cut at the critical point of the take-off with a bombload on board. A similar thing had happened on a 2-Group Squadron just before we left England, but they hadn't been so fortunate. Whether they had been killed on impact wasn't known, but they were certainly dead eleven seconds latter when the bombs went off.

I was lost in a reverie when the Wing Commander came through the door with the Adjutant. He seemed in a better frame of mind.

'We have just had a W/T message from the squadron,' he volunteered. 'They're twenty miles out and no losses.'

'We would have done better to have gone with them,' said Benny quietly as the Wingco moved off towards the control tower.

'I bet you a fiver they didn't go in,' said Weeky. We both looked at him. 'You see if I'm not right.'

And he was right. When the crews returned, we went back inside to listen to the de-briefing. According to Dicky Wilson, the opposition from the ships and the ground installations was so fierce that no one could have got through and their chances of hitting the target were nil.

There followed an interrogation by the naval captain who had reappeared. He wanted to know a great deal about the shore batteries and details of the ships, but the dialogue came to an abrupt end when Dicky, after close questioning, admitted that the squadron had turned away before crossing the coast of Cephalonia.

'Sergeant,' said the captain, staring fixedly at his victim, 'how can you possibly expect me to believe the details you have given me of the ships and shore batteries when you broke off the attack at such extreme range?' As he turned to leave, I think we all felt sorry for the luckless Wilson.

But that was not to be the end of the story.

CHAPTER FOURTEEN

Into the hornet's nest

THE WING COMMANDER silenced the buzz of conversation that followed with his own announcement. Briefing tomorrow was to be an hour earlier. The target was to be the same. We would take-off before first light and proceed individually to a point fifty miles short of the Island, and then form up for a dawn attack. His face was pasty and his eyes intense.

There was much bitter comment in the mess that evening. No one blamed Dicky for turning away, for apparently the anti-aircraft fire that had been thrown up even before they got within range was murderous.

'I told the Wingco afterwards that I didn't want to lead the squadron again,' said Dicky querulously.

'What did he say?' someone asked.

'"You certainly won't be."'

'The whole thing is obviously at the Navy's request,' said Arthur Madden, 'and the CO's got to commit us whether he likes it or not.'

'Why can't the blue jobs get in there and do their own dirty work?' Ted Slater wanted to know.

'I tell you this much,' went on Dicky; 'if I'm on the battle order tomorrow, I'm going to refuse to go.'

'You can't do that,' said Arthur Madden quietly. 'That would amount to mutiny.'

'I don't care!' replied Dicky. 'It was bad enough today, but to go there two days running is just asking for it. There's not even the advantage of surprise.'

There was little doubt that he voiced the sentiments of all of us, but there was nothing we could do. As Weeky said, with any luck our aircraft would still be unserviceable and we would be off the hook.

But we weren't. On arriving for briefing, the engineering officer told us with some pride that the groundcrew had worked all night replacing a cylinder-head that had blown off and that the engine had been ground run and found to be satisfactory.

'Shouldn't you have to do an air-test after a major job like that?' asked Benny when the Squadron Leader had gone.

'You should really,' I said, 'but with the Wingco's present mood, I don't think it's on.'

'The bloody engine nearly killed us yesterday,' complained Weeky. 'Surely to God we should try a take-off first without a bombload!'

The arrival of the Wing Commander broke up the discussion and we were soon being treated to a very detailed briefing. The harbour of Argostolion lay in a hook of land at the south end of the bay of Ormos surrounded on three sides by mountains. As the briefing officer said, as there was little possibility of surprise we might as well make our approach in such a direction as would lead to the easiest escape route.

The attack on the previous day had been made directly from the sea. It was now proposed that we circle around to the north of the peninsula and then come south over the hills to dive into the harbour and then climb out along the southerly valley where the enemy would be inhibited from firing at us for fear of hitting the villages there. It sounded quite comforting the way the man put it.

The choice of Ivor Broom to be the leader was significant. The Wing Commander wanted to ensure that the attack would be pressed home this time. Dicky Wilson was to be the wing man at number three, and we awaited his reaction, but there was none. He climbed onto the dispersal truck with the rest of us, silent and grim.

Ivor had been on the squadron longer than anyone else and had actually got to the end of his tour and been offered a posting home, but he had refused to go. His commission had come through shortly after we arrived on the Island, and as the only officer on the squadron, he had, as a lowly pilot officer been made the CO's deputy and as such he was kept in reserve for very special tasks.

It was quite a novel experience doing our pre-departure checks in the dark for we had not flown at night since our training days.

I had even forgotten where some of the cockpit and instrument lighting switches were.

The sky was as black as jet velvet but encrusted with the silverest of stars and the air was sharp. Not a light showed across the Island for it was silent and asleep, the nightly raid having been over for an hour or more. The torches of the groundcrews flitted like fireflies among the olive trees in which the dispersals lay. A rude flash from one of the aircraft as it backfired during start-up announced the beginning of another day of war and the silence of the dark hour before the dawn was shattered.

I peered out of the side window and found the fitter's hand with upturned thumb illuminated by a torch in the distance like some disembodied symbol. I groped for the starting switches and brought our own aircraft into life. In a dimly-lit cockpit, noise and vibration appear more intense than during daylight; one feels like a prisoner in a hostile world.

The instrument panel danced in a blur of pale blue light and outside the cowling rings were glowing and the exhaust stacks emitting stabs of orange flame. The next aircraft was showing a red and a green light on opposite wingtips. I thought how attractive they looked in the darkness, then remembered that my own navigation lights were not on, and groped for the switch.

I had just finished my power check when the outside world became diffused with a brilliant white light. The leader had switched on his landing-light to help him find his way along the path that led through the olive trees to the main taxi track. We took up positions behind and followed him like large nocturnal insects crawling through the undergrowth.

Take-offs were to be carried out individually at twenty-second intervals, and as I was leading the second vic of three, I watched the first group get off, their exhaust flames flickering and fading into the distance as the navigation lights lifted slowly above the line of sight. Then they too disappeared into the distant darkness.

As I turned onto the runway, at the back of my mind was a nagging worry that I hadn't asked to do an air-test before going off with a bombload. Had I insisted, then we could not have got off with the rest of the squadron for this operation, and my motives might well have been misconstrued. In any case, I am sure that the Wingco would have overruled me. In these situations, the normal regulations had to be pushed aside.

I lined up between the two rows of flickering gooseneck flares that converged in the distance, applied the parking brake, pulled the stick right back and began to open up the throttles to the half power position. I was conscious of more tension than normal, probably due as much to the strange night environment as to the prospect of another drama at lift-off. After all, the engine had performed perfectly during run-up, but then it had yesterday as well.

All the instrument readings appeared normal, the brakes hissed as I released them and the machine started to trundle forward. I pushed the throttles fully open, pulled down the plus-9 boost override and concentrated on steering straight down the centre.

The goosenecks flashed by the side windows at an increasing rate until they became a blur. The dimly lit airspeed needle moved steadily round the dial towards the unstick figure. The number of goosenecks left was diminishing. The narrow gap at the end had widened and was coming towards us. Beyond that was Safi Strip.

I eased the control column back and we became smoothly airborne. Now get the head down on instruments. Concentrate on that panel twenty inches from the nose; that vital source of changing information as to how the aircraft is performing in relation to the dark and shapeless world outside. The altimeter began to show a positive climb. Grope for the undercarriage lever. The green lights go out and the red lights come on, and then go out in sequence. Three hundred feet, retract the take-off flap, check the sink with the control column and gently re-trim the attitude. Passing 500 ft, push off the boost override, reduce power to the climb value, and relax!

Initially we had to proceed at 1000 ft on an easterly heading and already there was the merest suggestion of a dawn in the sky ahead the base of the blackness relieved by a faint tint of indigo. During the next twenty minutes I watched, enthralled by the birth of a new day.

The sky, where it kept a private appointment with the sea, changed slowly and gracefully from indigo to bluey-grey, then the blue faded and left it sullen for a while until the approaching sun infused it with a flush of ochre above the lightening sea. An arch-way of pale pink now developed, which with its warmth began to melt the lower reaches of the dark sky.

My reverie was rudely burst by the sudden hiss of the intercom.

'We're passing the first vic over on our left, Skipper,' said Weeky. There was a hint of reproach in his voice.

There were the grey shapes of the three aircraft neatly tucked into formation, their navigation lights extinguished.

'Any sign of our chaps?' I asked.

'Yeah. Number two is about to close in on your starboard side, and number three is something like a mile behind. They've both got their nav lights on.' I reached down and switched off my own navigation lights.

'Ah. Both their lights have gone off now,' said the gunner.

The night was over. The day was about to begin and maybe it wouldn't last long for some of us; nor be followed by another.

I throttled back slightly and took up a position behind and to the right of the leading formation. As the light improved they sank down towards the sea until its grey mass was streaking past just underneath us.

Against the lightening sky, the outline of the Greek mountains began to emerge, and the leading vic went into a smooth curve to the left onto a correction course.

The grey silhouette of the island of Cephalonia developed sharper details with the emerging light. Crags and ravines appeared on the hillsides and varied tints of dark green and lighter greys began to show. As we closed the northern corner of the island, the vague outline of hillside villages could be seen, and away to the right I saw a lone fishing-boat hugging the coast.

The formation described a wide circle about two miles from the northernmost point and then turned into the bay of Mirtou.

We were rushing straight towards the base of the mountains now and they were growing rapidly in stature; then the leader swung to the left as he spotted the valley that carried the road up through the mountain pass and down into the target area.

His engines sent back twin puffs of smoke as he pulled the plus-9 override and began to pull away. The formation opened out and became untidy as each man crouched low over the sea in a headlong dash to the same gap in the hill line.

We flashed across a sandy beach and into a green valley. Then I saw the leader up ahead drop his starboard wing and disappear round a corner. His wing men followed and we did the same, for he had found the road that climbs up through the pass.

The mountains rose steeply on either side as we weaved our way along the course of the road like children playing follow-my-leader. So far we had seen no opposition or sign of habitation. Sweeping round another bend, we saw the saddle of the pass above us and beyond was the open sky. We climbed rapidly to this bridge of land and shot over the top like projectiles in swift succession.

The ground dropped away with dramatic suddenness. Below was the bay of Ormos and looking to the left I saw the complex of buildings, ships and smoke that was the naval base at Argostolion.

Immediately, cannon shells began streaking up the hillside towards us. The leader banked steeply to port and went into a dive towards the harbour, but to my surprise one of his wing men turned to the right and set off across the bay towards the hill on the other side. I swung hard left to keep close to the hillside. We had 1000 ft to dive off and the engines were howling.

The harbour was erupting like a set piece at a firework display. Black puffs pitted the sky around us. Rapid tracer was coming straight up the hillside regardless of the cottages in its path. Both Benny's and Weeky's guns were racketing. I corkscrewed around the hillocks and houses on the descent. There were three large destroyers anchored in a group. Their decks were ablaze with vicious cannon and ack-ack fire. The batteries on the quays were firing with a frantic intensity. We were diving through a lattice work of whipping tracer streaks.

Digger Grey was below me and going straight for the centre of the harbour. Suddenly, a flame erupted from his port engine and streamed back like a comet's tail. He continued in a clean dive over the last destroyer and was extinguished in a mountainous explosion of water just short of the quay.

Despite the steepness of the dive I was still some 300 ft above the harbour mouth. If I dived to deck height, I could never pull out. I pushed the nose down sharply to point it at the looming mass of ships, jerked the bomb release, and wound the aircraft into a violent climbing turn to port.

The ground rose rapidly away from the harbour and as we

scrambled up in a frantic search for the sanctuary on the other side, the enemy's fire followed us, the scarlet tracer flashing past maliciously and arcing into the ground in front of us. Our speed was falling drastically in the steep climb. It was like being chased in a bad dream when one's legs won't move fast enough.

Even as we topped the hill with very little flying speed left, several shells burst in our piece of sky with the customary 'rack, rack', as the final insult. I thrust the nose down and dived with the contour of the hill towards the sea.

A couple of shore batteries fired at us in what by comparison seemed a desultory fashion before we turned westwards above a sea that blossomed and sparkled as it was touched by the sun's first rays.

A slight haze lay on the horizon; it was going to be a fine day. I listened dully as Weeky swung round slowly in his turret surveying the damage and giving us a detailed account. The aircraft was flying satisfactorily and we were on our way back. That was all that registered.

There was some argument as to whether the aircraft we saw go in was the leader or his number two; I was pretty sure it was Digger Grey and felt saddened. We had all witnessed Dicky Wilson's peel off away from the attack.

'He's going to have to answer some awkward questions this time,' suggested Weeky. I just grunted. I didn't care one way or the other.

We flew on alone, skimming over the sea, my mind partially elsewhere, my flying mostly automatic. By the time the pale brown outline of Malta had risen out of the sea ahead, we had come upon no other aircraft. In such visibility I felt sure that we would have spotted any that might have been around. The prospect of being the only survivor left me with a feeling of desolation.

I didn't bother to do a circuit but came straight in over Kalafrana and headed for the runway.

The wheels went down with their customary clonk and we sank lower and lower over the untidy landscape. We were landing in the opposite direction to yesterday's take-off, and Weeky whooped as he saw the craters that our bombs had left just outside the boundary of the airfield proper.

I concentrated on the landing, flared off just above the runway, closed the throttles and eased the stick back as she settled. It was going to be a good one. The wheels touched with an unjustified jerk I thought, then we bounced slightly and at the second touch I felt them snatch and the aircraft started a swing to port. I slammed on full right rudder and applied some brake. There was a screech of tortured rubber and the swing was going out of control. We were bouncing crabwise into a ground loop. I slammed open the port throttle but too fast, the engine coughed then backfired before surging into life. By this time we were off the strip and careering over the rough ground. I had the stick hard back and using as much brake as I could without bringing the tail up.

The aircraft had turned through 180° by the time we stopped in a cloud of dust.

'The port tyre's screwed off!' shouted Weeky.

'Any sign of fire?'

'No. But it's smoking.'

'Get out there with a fire extinguisher!' I said, slamming off the ignition switches and reaching for the fuel cocks.

The aircraft had settled left wing low as we scrambled out to survey the damage.

'Wha' happened?' asked Benny blinking at me. 'Used too much brake on the landing?'

I shook my head. 'That tyre was already blown. I felt it snatch on touchdown.'

I climbed back on the wing and sat on the top of the fuselage. There was a rank smell of hot rubber and deep wheelmarks had scored a curved path from the runway to our position.

The tinkle of a distant bell attracted my attention to the fire wagon which was trundling towards us a bit belatedly I thought, when Weeky called out, 'Look! There are two aircraft on finals!'

They were Blenheims. I felt my spirits rise at the sight.

At de-briefing it was confirmed that Digger Grey had gone in and another had been lost on the way out, but the surprise was that Dicky Wilson was missing. Ted Slater had seen what happened. Dicky had certainly chickened out and set off across the harbour for home, but as he turned, a direct hit had taken off his port wing. The machine had twisted onto its back and dived into the water inverted.

None of us could be sure that we had hit any part of the target and the Wing Commander listened morosely to our accounts of the attack.

He said without spirit, 'Well, tomorrow we should be able to put four aircraft on the line with any luck, and we have five crews left.'

'What! No day off, sir?' said Ted Slater lightly.

The Wingco's face brightened in a rare smile. 'Yes, you can stand down tomorrow. I think you've earned it.'

CHAPTER FIFTEEN

The beleaguered island

THE DRIVE BACK to our quarters was made in almost total silence and seemed interminable. The bus creaked and lurched along the road that undulated between the low stone walls as if trying to find a way out, and the general untidiness of the landscape was depressing. The shallow hillsides were terraced into miniature fields though they were not fields as we remembered them; no soft green carpet covered the nakedness of the soil, which was the colour of ochre and pitted with stones and rocks. An occasional olive tree served to break the monotony and here and there a cactus stood guard by a crumbling wall.

It seemed as if we had been incarcerated on the Island for a life time, though in fact it was little more than a month, and like prisoners we were being conveyed to our quarters, there to await the further orders of our masters. The depression settled on us the more deeply when we walked into our barrack block, for tonight there would be nine more empty beds.

The four stone buildings that were stepped down the hillside had been built each to accommodate twenty beds with two small rooms at one end presumably for senior men. The one at the lowest level had been empty for some time, and about a week ago, those in the third had moved in with the occupants of the top two; but as Weeky said, it was time we had another reshuffle.

There was a convention on the squadron that when a man was lost, his kit would be 'seen to' by a man from another crew whom he had previously nominated, the idea being that the 'executor' would get to it before the Adjutant and his orderlies and remove such things as might prove an embarrassment if sent home. It was also understood that the chosen friend could keep anything which particularly appealed to him, though the more expensive items and those which might have a sentimental value would be left alone.

Inevitably, when a number of crews were lost at the same time, some of the appointed executors would be missing too and then it would have to be agreed as to who would deal with the kit that was unallocated.

For me it was a grisly experience going through a man's kitbag and locker, gaining at times unwanted glimpses of the fellow's private life, but Weeky seemed to enjoy it, not for any sick reason, but merely because he loved to collect things. He used to get a great deal of pleasure in pitting his wits against the rigidity of the Service stores system. He was an authority on exactly what he was entitled to, and never failed to draw it. If he could outwit the system and get a double issue, then his delight would be boundless, and when, as in this instance, he was 'seeing to' another man's kit he would be reluctant to dispose of anything that might conceivably, in the distant future, be used for something.

I was deputed to look after Dicky Wilson's gear and as I stood by his bedspace, a feeling of the deepest sadness came over me. He had tried to beat the system, to escape by surviving until the happy day that a relief squadron arrived and he could go home. But the system was unbeatable. Any escape, if escape there was to be, would be at the whim of an unseen deity. Any attempt to fashion one's own destiny would be dealt with in disaster.

His bed was not made up, but the clothes were thrown back where he had left them on rising in the wee small hours to go through the accepted rites of washing and shaving himself in preparation for another day. But his day had not lasted very long. His aircraft had last been seen entering the water vertically. Right now, the twisted clutch of metal would be rocking gently in the current that moved across the sea bed, and undoubtedly, Dicky was there in the green depths together with his crew.

With actions that were purely mechanical, I made up his bed according to Service instructions. The three 'biscuits' that constituted the mattress stacked at one end of the iron bedstead. The blankets, folded three ways, placed in a pile on top, the last one being wrapped around the others in a final neatness. Then the pillow at the summit.

His kitbag and locker were crammed and I dreaded the task but it had to be done. The contents of the locker were relatively straightforward; shaving kit, hair brush, toothpaste and toothbrush.

I put them in a heap on the floor. They could go back into the kitbag for homeward transmission.

I dipped into the kitbag without enthusiasm; an old copy of *Dombey and Son*, a pair of leather gauntlets – aircrew for the use of, a bundle of letters in an elastic band all in the same handwriting, and underneath a layer of sundry flying gear a rectangular object wrapped in cloth. It was the framed picture of a young girl in an unusual pose. Her head was in profile which outlined the pert little nose, but she was looking sideways out of the picture and at the beholder. The suggestion of the smile had an impish quality. Her long wavy hair fell about her shoulders and on her dress was a brooch in the form of a pair of RAF wings.

I stood looking down at the lovely face that seemed to smile back at me. If she wasn't known to Dicky's parents, then how, and when, would she learn of his fate? I began to feel a compulsion to write to her, explaining as gently as I could what had happened to him, perhaps adding words of consolation. At least it would put an end to doubt; but if I opened one of the letters, the address on it might not be hers. I couldn't be sure. Perhaps his parents did know.

I had no stomach to go on delving into the kitbag and replaced all the articles and the toilet equipment before pulling tight the draw-string, knotting it, and laying the bag gently across the bed springs.

There was a great deal of activity going on around me as the occupants of the next block were moving in with their belongings. It was a psychological drawing together. Fifteen men would only leave five empty beds, and the three uninhabited blocks could be ignored.

In the midst of all the comings and goings, someone discovered it was lunchtime and a general exodus to the mess resulted. Although we had eaten nothing since that very early breakfast, I didn't feel hungry, and neither did most of the others it seemed, for we congregated in the bar.

Since my drunken excursion into the 'Gut', the smell of whisky made me shudder, so the steward fixed me a John Collins which was refreshing as well as giving me a lift. Having been raised in a family where the discipline was Victorian, I hadn't drunk before joining the Service, apart from the occasional few half pints of beer, so I didn't need much of the hard stuff before I began to glow with physical and mental well-being.

This applied to most of us I guess, and certainly within the hour there were no further signs of melancholy. The information delivered with some urgency by the steward that lunch would 'go off' in ten minutes fell on disinterested ears, and when the sergeant cook arrived to remonstrate, he was cornered and forced to take wine with us. He was clearly nervous at the outburst of hospitality, for relations between the occupants of the mess and the cookhouse staff had been far from good. During the past two weeks the food had got progressively worse, and there was never enough of it.

Tackled at lunch a few days previously he said that as the convoys weren't getting through, our rations had been cut back; but it was the private opinion of many of us that some of the goodies that should have arrived on our table had found their way into the black market.

'What a nice gold watch you have!' intoned Ted Slater, pulling back the sergeant's cuff. 'Did you buy it recently?'

'No, as a matter of fact,' he said, fingering the watch nervously, 'I've had it some time.'

'Must have cost a packet!' said Ted deferentially, '– at least 200 tins of Maconochies.'

'Now don't be funny!' said the hapless sergeant. 'I told you, I've had it for some time.'

'I must say I haven't seen you wearing it before,' put in Arthur Madden quietly.

The man's face reddened. 'Well, you see,' he said confidentially, 'I know a chap who's got a jeweller's shop up in the Kingsway and he gives me a discount.'

'That's nice,' said Ted. 'Can we all come?'

'Sure. I'll give you an introduction if you want it.' Draining his pint pot, he made towards the door. His way was barred.

'Have another drink,' said Vic Green in a tone that had a ring of authority. 'Steward. Another pint for Sergeant Basset.'

'That must have been one hell of a course you did at cookery school,' put in Weeky.

'Well yeah. Six months actually.'

'Is that all you got? Six months? Should have been six years!'

He picked up his drink and glared at the assembled company, then changing his mind he banged the pot back on the bar. 'I'm not standing for this bloody nonsense! I've got work to do! But he was pinned in the corner.

'Work? What work?' asked Ted Slater. 'None of us want to eat your lousy food!'

'Look!' said someone, 'the sergeant's sweating.'

'Yeah, he looks hot.'

'Why don't you take a dip?'

'Just the afternoon for a swim.'

The unfortunate fellow tried to push his way past, but the others closed in and he was dragged through the door. There was a large flat rock from which we had cleared the barbed wire in order to use it as a diving platform, and it was on this that two of the party swung the cook to and fro over the water while we shouted in unison. We were joined by a crowd of Maltese who had been working on a near-by building, and when Sergeant Basset was released to fly out and down to the deep water, they cheered lustily.

We watched as he floundered to the bank. 'I'll have the lot of you!' he shouted. 'You'll all be on a charge!'

'Wizard!' said Maxie. 'Then maybe they'll put us in the glass-house for the duration.'

We walked back laughing into the mess only to find that the terrified steward was frantically trying to put up the bar shutters.

'Oh no you don't! You're going to do some work this afternoon. We're going up onto the roof and you are going to keep us supplied with whatever we want,' explained Arthur Madden.

Although it was late October, the sun still had a generous warmth, and we sat around on the parapet stripped to the waist, drinking and yarning in a personal glow that became more golden as the afternoon wore on.

Around 4 o'clock, we heard a distant siren. This was surprising, as it was unusual for Jerry to pay us a call so late in the afternoon. The matinee was normally over by 2 o'clock, and the evening performance didn't commence until it was dark.

The workmen on the next building were scampering down the ladders chattering like monkeys, the tails of their coloured shirts flapping behind them. They had to run past the mess to get to the air-raid shelters, glancing up fearfully at the shouts from the rooftop:

'I'll take four-to-one on red shirt!'

'Evens on the blue-and-white!'

'Six-to-four the field!'

'What's it worth to nobble the favourite!' cried the normally subdued Arthur Madden producing a Very pistol that someone had brought up to keep the cook at bay.

To my amazement, he fired it after the retreating workmen. The two red balls of fire sailed through the air with a hissing sound giving impetus to their already hasty flight. The projectiles hit the ground behind them and began to bounce in pursuit. They screamed in panic, leaping and capering up the path to the shelter where they collided in the doorway and fought with each other to get through. I joined in the general laughter, but in the back of my mind grew an uncomfortable feeling that things were going too far.

It was some time before distant gunfire announced the arrival of our Nazi friends, but when the anti-aircraft gun on the hill just above us exploded its first round, we all jumped. A group of fast-moving black dots could be seen making their way from left to right, then in quick succession they went into their dives, like insects dropping straight from the sky. Near the bottom of their trajectories, smaller black specks dropped away like excrement and seconds later, foul mushrooms of smoke erupted slightly after the sound of the bomb explosions reached us.

Our local gun opened up again and someone shouted and pointed to the left. An aircraft was running fast along the line of the hill towards us. It trailed a thin string of black smoke that was too persistent to be the exhaust. The gull-wings and fixed under-carriage marked it out as a Junkers 87.

As we watched, its line of flight closed with the ground. The anti-aircraft crew were trying frantically to swing their gun around to bear on it. So low and swift was its flight that one had the illusion that it was flying through the rocky outcrops. Then the illusion was shattered. The wheels struck the ground and the oleo legs were ripped off and flung away as debris.

The machine scored into the hillside and slid on its belly for many yards it seemed until the contents of the fuel tank erupted in a sickening 'Rump!' sound, transforming it into a flaming missile. It came to rest about a hundred yards away, burning savagely.

We stood still in a moment of paralysis, then a number of us made towards the stairs. Scrambling up the hill towards the flaming hulk it was clear that no one could have survived the crash, but we ran on stupidly.

The light wind was carrying the heat and the smoke in the other direction and it was possible to get quite close.

The pilot could be seen clearly, sitting upright and still, oblivious to the frantic flames as they engulfed him. I watched with horrible fascination as his flying clothing began to separate into holes, and his body leaned forward under the attack, submissive, shrinking and disintegrating slowly and deliberately.

Some of the jabbering workmen had joined the crowd, and I was appalled to see them laughing and spitting into the flames. Suddenly, there was a series of cracks and flaming catherine wheels detached themselves from the wreckage and flew in all directions. The ammunition was going up.

The Maltese turned and fled shouting down the hillside like frenetic clowns. I followed slowly, too numb to be conscious of the danger. I had never seen a man die at close range, incinerated so effectively and so quickly. My mood had now gone full circle, and as I made my way to the barrack block, I felt a dark depression settling down on me and with it, lethargy. Some of the others who had not run up the hill were already there, sprawled on their beds, all exuberance gone.

I learned that the Adjutant had just departed with a truck loaded with the belongings of our missing comrades, but that he had said a liberty bus would call for us at ten in the morning to take us into Valletta, returning from the Castille at six o'clock. Well, it was a gesture anyway, and I drifted into an alcoholic haze which merged into sleep.

Some time later, disturbed by a general movement around me, I surfaced slowly into consciousness, learning that a group were going into the village for something to eat. The idea appealed and I hurriedly washed and dressed in time to join them. It was a moonless night but clear, and the black velvet of the sky seemed unusually crowded with stars as we made our way along the coast road towards the village.

At one point, a slipway crossed the road and disappeared into the water, but at the top of the slope was a large and mysterious shed. Some two weeks previously, a crew had been walking back from the village rather later than usual when they came upon a great deal of muted activity by the slip. They were surrounded immediately by armed soldiers who materialised out of the darkness. Their identity cards were scrutinised by torchlight, they were searched and then ordered to stand facing the wall with their hands above their heads. However, Maxie, by squinting under his arm, managed to keep the shed in view and was astonished when a large black seaplane bearing German markings was trundled out and down the slip. Immediately it hit the water, the engine was started and it taxied off into the darkness.

The soldiers with their rifles at the ready, then ordered the crew to walk towards the shed where they were taken to an officer for further interrogation. He warned them to forget anything they might have seen and above all to mention it to nobody, not even to servicemen. They felt, not unreasonably, that they had been left in a dilemma; if this was a British intelligence activity, then fair enough. But what if it was something else? Shouldn't someone be told about it, or at least a check made?

They approached the intelligence officer at the airfield the next day and told him what they had seen. He showed no surprise, but taking them into his office and closing the door, he told them that the machine was, indeed, a captured German seaplane, a Blohm and Voss; and that it was used for intelligence purposes, landing off the coast of Sicily at night to drop off, and pick up, agents.

As we approached the shed our curiosity got the better of us, and as there was nobody about, we walked up the slip and shone a torch through a crack in the doors. The shed was empty. This was intriguing and led to some conjecture as to where it could have gone.

A few days afterwards, Maxie asked our Intelligence Officer and he confirmed that one night during the week, the aircraft had taken off for Sicily but had failed to return. The weather had been ideal at the time so it had to be assumed that the brave men had been caught. There was little doubt what their fate would be.

As we walked on to the village, I found myself wondering just how much undercover activity was going on around us. The

Intelligence Officer had told the crew who made the discovery that they should tell no one, but they had passed on the information to the rest of us. Presumably we were good security risks, but there could be people around us who were not what they seemed. Quite a few Maltese were pro-Italian, and sabotage on the Island was not unknown. I, for one, resolved to be a bit more cautious in future.

The only social amenity in the village, and a favourite one, was the Honeymoon Hotel. I am not sure whether there were any living-in facilities for guests, but certainly, the parlour downstairs had been set aside as a café-cum-bar. The Victorian bric-a-brac that crowded the room made it appear even smaller, and a huge flyblown mirror which reflected the dull glow of the single paraffin lamp added little to the apparent size, for it was crowded with images of the countless pictures and a large case of regimental badges on the opposite wall.

The owner was an Englishman of less than average height, weatherbeaten after many years at sea with the Navy. Having served his time, he went to work in the Malta Dockyard and married a Maltese girl before finally retiring and settling in this remote corner of this remote island, two thousand miles from home. The war, in a way, had its advantages for him as it brought an influx of servicemen who boosted the trade of the place; but more than that, he appreciated the company, and whenever we trooped in he would join us at the table, eager to talk and to listen. Edgar, the son of the house, who had let me go fishing in his boat, looked more Maltese than English, but was over six feet tall, an unusual height for a local. He harboured a passionate admiration for the Air Force. On one occasion, during a stand-down around midday, inevitably, Jerry came over and battle was joined very high in a burnished blue sky. I could just see the specks that streaked along at the head of the contrails, but he identified each one as a Hurricane, Messerschmitt, or whatever. Secretly I doubted if his vision could be as acute as this, but suddenly he pointed, shouting, 'Look! That Hurricane's been hit!' I saw a speck that dragged a tail ominously darker than the others. As I watched, it became clear that it was indeed, falling, but it wasn't until it reached the lower levels that I could identify it as a Hurricane. We watched in silence as it made its rapid way down the sky and disappeared behind the rocky outline of

Delimara point. Several seconds elapsed before the black smoke came billowing up above the headland, and the dull boom that echoed across the bay announced its end.

As on other occasions we were entertained by the proprietor's amiable wife who bustled to and fro and with the help of another elderly Maltese lady who I think was her sister, produced a seemingly endless supply of eggs and bacon. The bacon was poor stuff, presumably out of a tin, but the eggs were fresh, having come from the chickens that they kept on the roof. I knew, because I had seen them: Edgar had taken me up there one day to watch a dogfight and I was surprised to find not only chickens clucking around but a couple of rabbits running loose and a mangy-looking dog.

By the time we were on our way back to the mess, our humour had been restored. We had been fed, and drunk enough to regain our equilibrium but not to unbalance it. Besides, tomorrow was a day off and we were going on the town.

The morrow dawned brightly enough and within half an hour of leaving our quarters we were mixing with the crowds that thronged Valletta's main street. At its western end was a small stone archway, part of the original 17th-century fortifications, and beside it the mountainous ruins of the opera house lying desolate in the sun. Much of Kingsway was still intact and bustling with activity, the giftshops being filled with a miscellany of servicemen trying to decide what to send home to their families for Christmas. There were offerings of Maltese lace, locally made jewellery, cheap watches and lighters, and models of Knights of St John. Certainly the shops had a greater variety of goods to offer than those at home and although there were rumours that food was getting short, there was no evidence of any rationing system so far.

We made our way into a narrow side street that led down to the Grand Harbour in a series of cobbled steps. The buildings rose sheer on either side, an unusual blend of Moorish and Italian architecture that told in eloquent silence of the turbulent history of the Island.

Since the time when St Paul was shipwrecked on the northern coast in a bay which still bears his name, Malta has been invaded by a succession of Mediterranean nations, and has been ruled in turn by the Phoenicians, Cathaginians and the Romans. In the

11th century the Normans invaded, and for the next 400 years the little Island was passed around between the crowned heads of Europe until Charles V of Spain granted it on a feudal tenure to the homeless Order of St John of Jerusalem, after the loss of Rhodes.

Most of the sandstone buildings in the trading and residential quarters of Valletta are of simple, almost Arabic proportions, but embellished with the addition of ornate balconies on each floor, many of these being covered in with brightly painted wooden panels topped with shuttered windows.

The street in which we found ourselves had a number of tiny shops at street level; through the open doors wares could be glimpsed in the gloom. Some of the traders sat outside, relaxed in the autumn sun and idly watching the bustle around them as they waited for custom. The noise of half-shouted conversations and of shoes that clattered on the worn cobblestones was edged with the piping songs of linnets and canaries that danced in tiny cages adorning the doorways or upper windows of most of the shops and houses. It was a busy and cheerful scene hardly reminiscent of an island in the grip of siege, but no doubt history had conditioned the Maltese.

We continued down to the end and emerged on to the Custom House Quay which overlooks the water. A Grand Harbour it certainly is, for the water is deep enough to take the largest capital ships and the rising ground on three sides gives snug protection from the weather. At this stage of the war, it was crowded with both merchant and naval vessels, the tenders criss-crossing the gaps between them with their wakes. Several of the ships showed signs of recent damage, mostly to their superstructures, but one large freighter had a floating crane alongside and a crew working to repair a gaping hole just above the waterline. From others came the blue flashes of welding torches and the rattle of rivet guns echoed across the water.

Dockside cranes dipped into the holds continuously, setting their loads down on the quayside and returning immediately for more. Undoubtedly a convoy had come in within the past twenty-four hours and just as surely most of the ships would be filing out through the harbour entrance within the next couple of days to run the savage gauntlet to Gibraltar. We weren't sure whether we felt envy or pity.

It was pleasant standing there in the sun and looking on at the busy scene, but the previous day's debauchery had left us with dry throats and we moved off in search of a bar. We found one built into an archway, but no sooner had we settled down at one of the marble-topped tables than a siren began to blare close by and most of the other occupants left in some haste. The barman did not appear to notice and brought our drinks to us without comment.

'We're nae in a vera guid position at a time like this,' observed Benny. 'The harbour's always a popular target.'

'This place looks pretty solid,' said Weeky between gulps.

'Well, I'm damned if I'm going to spend my day off in an air-raid shelter,' I put in. 'Cheers!'

We soon heard the guns mumbling in the distance, and then the ships in the harbour started up with a deafening racket. One seldom hears noises from the ground in an aeroplane, and we were taken aback at the intensity of the sounds. The firing was incessant, constituting a continuous mighty rumbling like thunderclaps at the centre of a tropical storm. The defence barrage had an almost frantic quality.

We heard the rising whine of a diving aircraft, but if it dropped its bombs the noise was swallowed up in the general cacophony. A piece of shrapnel zipped and clattered across the doorway and we all ducked instinctively.

'Fancy tackling this lot!' said Weeky in awe.

'Worse than Cephalonia?' I asked.

'I don't know.'

The firing stopped as abruptly as it had started like the end of a summer shower, and we took our drinks to the doorway to survey the scene. There was no obvious sign of damage although an extensive cloud of smoke hung over the whole area where five minutes before had been an unmarked sky. Then we saw flames shoot up from the cluster of houses that rose steeply from the water's edge at the far side. The cranes had stopped working and a great deal of activity could be seen on some of the ships but there were no symptoms of a disaster.

The 'All clear' raised its wail into the air and I wandered across the road to the water's edge. In the distance was the stone fort of Saint Angelo, the same structure that had withstood the siege of the Turks four centuries ago; what a fabulous story that was, and in this setting, readily visualized.

The Ottoman Empire was at its peak, and when the most-feared Suleiman, Sultan of Turkey, invaded the tiny island with 31,000 troops in 180 ships it seemed impossible that he could be stopped.

La Vallette, the Grand Master of The Order of St John of Jerusalem had but 640 knights and some 8000 troops, but with the help of the Maltese he provisioned the forts, poisoned the wells in the country round about the city that was to become known as Valletta, and prepared for siege.

When it came, the battle was bloody indeed. It took thirty days for the fort of St Elmo to fall and there were no survivors: all of the 1300 defenders had died along with 8000 Turks. But La Vallette in Saint Angelo fought on. As the castle was pounded by cannon fire, so were the walls repaired by Maltese men, women and children, but they also had the pleasure of pouring boiling water on the heads of the attackers as they tried to scale the ramparts. But day by day, the casualties mounted and the prospect of survival became more remote. The fighting grew even more savage and at one stage, the Knights were cutting off the heads of their prisoners and firing them at the enemy from cannon.

Suleiman was killed accidentally by one of his own guns, and the Turkish force which had up to that time proved invincible began to waver. The final blow came with the landing of 9000 men from the Viceroy of Sicily at Mellieha Bay. The Turks withdrew in disorder and the Island was saved.

That was in 1565, but now, nearly 400 years later, Malta was again in a state of siege. The tiny island was completely surrounded by enemy territory. At the western end of the Mediterranean was an intrinsically hostile Spain; to the north, Sicily and the Italian mainland, to the east, German-occupied Greece; and to the south, nearly all of the African coastline was in enemy hands. Losses among the convoys bringing stores and ammunition were mounting to frightful proportions and the Eighth Army were being driven back steadily towards Cairo. If we lost Egypt then the Suez Canal would be denied to us and with it an important escape route for returning convoys. Would history repeat itself, or could, this time, the tables be turned?

I was brought back sharply from my reveries by Weeky and Benny, who had joined me suggesting that we go up into the town for some lunch. As we climbed the steep narrow streets I was conscious of a feeling of uneasiness moving in on me, and Weeky rebuked me during the meal for being such poor company, so when Benny suggested going to see a comedy film in the afternoon, I agreed readily.

One could never quite get away from the situation even in the cinema, for mines were exploded regularly every thirty minutes in Sliema Creek by the Navy as an anti-submarine precaution; and as we had chosen a picture house which was quite close to the water, not only did loud bangs catch us by surprise each time, but with them came a cascade of plaster from the ceiling. I think we got as much amusement from this as we did from the film.

After about an hour, the screen went blank, and the stopping of the soundtrack brought whistles and catcalls from the audience composed mostly of troops. The hiatus went on for several minutes, then a crudely written notice appeared on the screen –

'ALL MILITARY PERSONNEL ARE TO RETURN
TO THEIR UNITS IMMEDIATELY.'

'Wha' the hell's all that aboot?' asked Benny.

'I don't see how it can apply to us,' said Weeky; 'we're not even on duty.'

Then the house lights went up and a number of servicemen began to move uncertainly towards the exits along with some of the more nervous civilians. Others were still clearly in doubt about the true authority of the message.

Then there was a scuffling at the back of the stalls and a number of military police moved in. They walked down the aisles shouting 'All military personnel report to your units!'

'We're aircrew on stand down!' called out Weeky.

'Makes no difference. You must report back.'

We shuffled to the end of the row, and I asked the nearest corporal what was going on.

'It's an emergency,' he snapped.

'Wha' sort of an emergency?' asked Benny.

'If you must know,' replied the corporal, and his voice was trembling, 'there's an invasion force heading for the Island!'

CHAPTER SIXTEEN

View from the ground

IN THE BRILLIANT sunlight outside the cinema there were scenes of confusion. We had a problem in that we weren't sure where we should head for. The obvious place was the airfield but all of our flying kit was at Marsaxlokk. We decided to hitch a lift there.

We took up station on the road to Lupa and in a very short time an RAF 15-cwt truck came swerving round the corner. I stepped into the road and held up my hand and it pulled into the side.

'We're trying to get to Marsaxlokk!' I shouted.

'You're in luck, Sarge!' called back the driver. 'I'm going to Kalafrana; jump in!'

He knew no more about the situation than we, and he seemed to take a singularly cheerful view of the whole thing. As we left the outskirts of the town behind us, I got a feeling that we were moving into isolation and found myself hoping that it wouldn't be too difficult for us to get back into the centre of the Island again.

'We might meet a truck with our chaps in, coming the other way,' Weeky said, apparently reading my thoughts. 'We'd better look out for it and try to stop it if we can.' But the road was empty, and the driver dropped us off at the top of the hill that led down to the village.

In Marsaxlokk itself, the air of general calm indicated that news had not filtered out that far. Some of the older men were sitting on chairs outside their front doors dozing in the sun. A group of screaming children were chasing a frantic dog that had a rat in its mouth, and some of the fishermen were preparing their gaily painted boats for the next excursion out into the bay.

'Think we ought to warn 'em?' asked Weeky as we hurried past.

'Negative!' I said. 'That really would cause a panic and we don't know the true form ourselves yet.'

We saw as we came within sight of our quarters that it was a scene of much activity and that the crews were milling about and stacking sandbags on top of the low stone wall that ran along the side of the waterfront road.

'Did you see anything of the others in town?' called Arthur Madden as we approached.

'No. We were lucky to get a lift right away,' I replied. 'What's the score?'

'Well, apparently they've sent out another recce aircraft as there appears to be some doubt as to where the ships are. Going on the first report, it looked as if they would arrive off Gozo at dusk. We're supposed to stand by here.'

'What's all the sandbag bit then?' asked Weeky.

'Well, it's bloody obvious, isn't it? The coast's got to be defended. They're sending us a load of rifles and ammunition as soon as they can.'

'Bloody hell!' murmured Benny.

Without further comment we joined the work force in taking down the sandbags from outside the mess windows and carrying them one at a time across to the wall. Even with our jackets off, it was hot and thirsty work, so it was with surprise and pleasure that I spied Sergeant Basset appearing round the corner of the building bearing a tray of beer-bottles. In silence he offered us each one in turn, and we took them with various degrees of embarrassment.

'Sheer bloody flannel,' murmured Ted Slater, putting the bottle to his lips and tilting his head back. He took a long swig then wiped his mouth with the back of his hand and waited until the sergeant cook had moved out of earshot. 'He's just trying to get round us. Another six of these and he'll succeed as far as I'm concerned.'

'Look!' called Weeky, pointing out into the bay with his bottle. 'What did I tell you!' There were two fishing-boats in line astern heading for the open sea. I felt a twinge of conscience, but as I watched, an air-sea rescue launch from the flying-boat base at Kalafrana appeared around the point and creamed off towards them. It had no difficulty in heading them off and the three boats bobbed about in unison. After a time the two boats turned around and made their way back towards the village and the RAF launch described a swift clean curve through the water and slid out of sight behind the headland.

'You see!' said Weeky, 'you might just as well have told 'em. Saved 'em a bit of petrol.' I shrugged. I could well imagine the panic that would be triggered off when they arrived back with the news.

Shortly afterwards, a truck arrived from Luqa with a load of rifles and ammunition and these were issued against a signature on the inevitable triplicated form.

Although I had been in the Service for eighteen months, I had never handled a rifle. Arms drill had not featured in our crowded curriculum and although we had learned to clear stoppages and dismantle a Browning machine-gun, the Enfield 303 was a stranger to me. Weeky exploited my discomfort when I admitted it, but he gave me a useful briefing nevertheless.

As the glow of the sunset faded from the sky, I took up my position with the others squatting in a line behind the sandbagged wall, and laying the barrel between two of the bags, I braced the butt against my shoulder and squinted along the sights.

This really was a hopeless situation. I had never fired a rifle in my life, and when I did, it would probably knock me over backwards, but the targets were for real. When they came swarming up the beach they would be Germans and Italians, trained fighting men, part of a massive invasion force.

There were fifteen of us plus three of the cookhouse staff, and as darkness settled in, the talking became more subdued and the hiss of the restless sea on the shoreline asserted itself. To our right, the silhouette of the anti-aircraft gun on the hill was clearly visible against the deep purple of the sky, its barrel pointing stolidly seawards, and the sounds of the crew calling to each other came over clearly on the still air. We thought them unnecessarily noisy, but eventually they too settled down to watch and to wait.

With the coming of total darkness, the temperature dropped markedly and I began to shiver. After a while it was agreed that we would, in groups of two or three, make our way back to the barrack block to pick up our Irvin jackets and the odd blanket in order to make the long night bearable. Some of the men draped the blankets over their heads like shawls giving them the appearance of nomadic Indians crouching in the darkness. I felt that we were not an impressive company, and situated as we were on a sparsely inhabited stretch of coastline, very vulnerable. To our certain knowledge, the only other people around were the complement of the flying-boat base about a mile away and beyond the next headland, the gun-crew on the hill, and the occupants of the fishing village half a mile in the other direction.

In the all-enveloping black silence, I felt a great sense of loneliness. How swiftly could fate change direction. For the past few weeks the conviction had been growing that my crew and I must take our turn in the process of elimination: I even knew how it would come, as I had seen it meted out to so many others. Now, quite suddenly, it was clear that it was going to be different. Against such ridiculous odds, there was not even the faintest hope of survival. One would just have to keep firing until the end came. Perhaps one would be working so hard that there would be no time to contemplate fear.

As I turned the situation over in my mind, the earlier feelings of self pity dissolved in the heat of a rising anger. I felt that again, I had been pushed into an untenable situation. But the real force of my feelings were being re-directed at the bastards who had started all this and were coming to get us now. For the first time in my life, I felt hatred. If I was to be overrun, then I determined that I would concentrate on getting everything that came into my sights until my faculties were stripped from me. Having squared up to the inevitability of my fate, this decision came easily and was even satisfying.

But the long waiting was endless. Despite the stars, the blackness beyond the coast had a cloying velvet quality. Occasionally, the odd flash of phosphorescence on the gently moving water attracted one's eyes, but the darkness which immediately followed reclaimed and concealed the secret. The anxious search went on but was frustrated from finding something tangible; only hints and tantalising suggestions at irregular intervals served to consolidate the belief that something was there.

I squinted at the luminous dial of my watch, and was dismayed to find that it was barely midnight, I began to feel the twinge of hunger, but there was no question of moving now. No one spoke or even stirred. At one stage I must have dozed off momentarily with my cheek against the rifle stock for when my mind swum back to consciousness, it was with a pang that I realised that this was no dream but the bitter truth. Finally my mind began to float in vague suspension, enveloped in the limitless dome of the dark night and lulled by the unintelligible whispering of the sea.

A telephone bell tinkled distantly in the mess hall. Immediately the nervous tensions re-crystallised.

A voice was heard talking, briefly. What news was this?

Someone was walking down the track towards us. A conversation broke out at the end of the wall. People began to stand up.

'What's the score?' 'What's up?'

A voice came in reply 'Stand down.'

'Stand down!' several cried in unison.

I pushed my way towards the bearer of the message. He was explaining, 'They just said emergency terminated – stand down.'

'Who's they?'

'Operations.'

'How d'you know it was operations?'

'It's got to be, Sarge; that's a tie-line.'

Relief was diluted by a feeling of incredulity that such a situation could evaporate so quickly and completely on the strength of a telephone conversation.

We made our way to the mess and stood around in the hall, a group of worried and tired men. Arthur Madden summed up our feelings, 'You can't have a bloody great invasion force sailing for the Island one minute, and then suddenly the emergency's over!'

'I for one won't sleep tonight anyway,' said Maxie.

'There's only one way to put our minds at rest,' I said and took up the telephone. A voice answered abruptly. I recognised it as the Adjutant's, and I explained our concern.

A normally pleasant fellow, he became irate. 'The position is perfectly clear,' squeaked the small voice. 'The emergency is over. You will all stand down. I am not prepared to offer any further information.' A click terminated the encounter.

We wandered off disconsolately to the barrack block, each trying to reconcile his mind to the fact that he could now sleep safely in his bed.

Weeky lay down fully dressed, and lighting a cigarette he inhaled deeply, paused, then ejecting the smoke noisily he watched as it writhed towards the ceiling. 'It just doesn't make sense. A full-scale alert. Panic. Man your defences until the end and all that crap and then it just fizzles out.' He turned to me, 'Did he say anything about reappraising the position in the morning or anything like that?'

'No,' I answered; 'just, "The emergency is over."'

I was undressing. Reaction had set in and I slipped wearily between the rough blankets. The discussion meandered on in a desultory fashion until, for me, the talk receded into the distance and dissolved into the silence that dreams are made of. If the enemy was coming tonight, then I, for one, had lost interest. . . .

It was lunchtime before we surfaced and gathered in the mess the next day, but there was still no further explanation of the previous night's hiatus. Someone had walked down to the village during the morning and discovered that they were still in a state of panic. Most of the doors had been barricaded and the waterfront street was deserted. Apparently, the local policeman had moved inland to the main station at Casapola the previous evening and hadn't been seen since, and it occurred to no one to tell this tiny outpost of the Island that it was all over.

We were on standby the following day but the Adjutant and the Intelligence Officer weren't talking either; there was a distinct atmosphere about the place. We hung about in the crew-room for a while and then some of the chaps started carrying their chairs outside to sit in the sun. I was about to do the same when I noticed Tim Cummings sitting glumly in the corner. He had been very quiet and depressed-looking for the past couple of days, and then I suddenly remembered that on the morning of the invasion scare he had not had a day off but was detailed to fly a reconnaissance.

'Hey Tim,' I said; 'I've just thought. You did a recce the other day; did you see anything of this supposed invasion fleet?'

He moved his hands in a gesture of impatience and raised his eyes to the ceiling. 'Don't talk to me about it,' he said miserably. I sat down on a chair beside him.

'Well, did you see anything?' I asked anxiously.

'Unfortunately,' he replied, fixing me with a woebegone expression, 'I did.'

It took some prompting to get the complete story.

Apparently nothing had been seen in the area that he had been told to sweep, and he was on his way back at about 8000 ft above partly broken cloud when he saw a large fleet of ships heading for

the Island and about fifty miles out. Being that close, he assumed
that it was one of our convoys, and knowing that the Navy was
pretty trigger-happy, he didn't go in for a closer look.

When he mentioned this at de-briefing, the balloon went up.
There was no Allied convoy expected for a week, so obviously it
must be the enemy. Another reconnaissance aircraft was sent off
but failed to make contact. At dusk, the two Wellington squadrons
were deployed to drop flares in the area and bomb anything within
sight. They found nothing.

By this time, any such force of ships would have been within
spitting distance of the coast and a motor torpedo-boat was sent in
search, but reported no shipping of any kind.

At a high-level conference, Tim was further interrogated and it
was finally decided that what he had seen was a mass of cloud
shadows on the sea. The cloud in the area at the time was fracto-
stratus, and it was not inconceivable that it had thrown long narrow
shadows.

Thinking back on what we had suffered that night my first
reaction was one of anger, but he was so clearly crestfallen and had
so obviously taken a pasting from the top brass that I held my
tongue. After some persuasion, he came to sit outside and volunteered his story to the rest of the chaps. After the initial shock, they
started to laugh and eventually he found he had to join in, though
somewhat ruefully.

'Talking of dropping clangers,' said Maxie, 'during my initial
training, there was a chap on the course who was always putting his
foot in it. He went off on a cross-country flight in a Tiger Moth
one day and got lost. However, he very sensibly force-landed in a
field before he ran out of petrol and then phoned up the airfield to
say where he was.

'They told him to go back to his aircraft and stay there until he
was rescued. Meanwhile, the chief flying instructor and the lad's
instructor set off in another Tiger to find him. They spotted his
aircraft eventually, sitting upright and undamaged but in the
smallest field they had ever seen.

'There was a bit of a conference over the intercom apparently,
but the two pundits decided that if a pupil could get down in a
hundred yards, then so could they. They made a precautionary
landing approach over the lowest hedge, but there were trees at the

other end, and at the last moment they funked it and went round again. The second time, they dropped it in over the hedge but realising that they weren't going to be able to stop in the distance, they opened up and took off again, missing the trees by inches.

'By this time they must have been pretty rattled and developed a fixation that they had to get it in at any cost. They dumped it expertly enough inside the hedge, found they couldn't stop in time, ground-looped the thing, hit a treestump and the machine went over on its back.

'The pupil had been watching all this in growing alarm and he rushed over to try and get them out. Apart from a few bruises and the fact that they were shaken, there was no other damage, though the aircraft was a write-off.

'When the CFI had recovered his composure he said, "What I don't understand, Bloggins, is how you managed to land a Tiger in a field this size without damage."

'"Oh, I didn't," said the bright one. "I landed in the next field and bounced over the hedge!"'

When the general laughter had died down, someone told the story of a Sikh who used to fly in a bright blue turban instead of a helmet, and stick the Gosport tubes up underneath. One day he was having trouble getting the Tiger down after a solo flight. Finally, he hit the ground, bounced about thirty feet then put a wing down and slid straight into the ground, the aircraft flying into its component parts. He stepped out shrugging off the debris and when he was asked what happened he said, 'Well, Sirrrr, you tell me that if I am too high on landing I should sideslip off my surplus height.'

We were thoroughly enjoying our reminiscing when the siren on the airfield began to ascend the scale. We rose, and more in sorrow than in anger carried our chairs back into the crew-room. Jerry must have caught the early warning system by surprise, for almost immediately we heard the guns at Rabat open up and we crowded in the doorway to see what was happening, for there wasn't time to make the air-raid shelter even if we wanted to.

On the far side of the airfield were six Wellington bombers neatly lined up and ready for their air-tests prior to going off on a night's trip to the North African front. The temptation was too much for the German pilots who put their aircraft in a dive towards the helpless Wimpeys.

The Junkers were about half a mile away as they came in, but we saw clearly the bombs leaving their bellies. There was an undignified scramble for any cover we could find, under tables, behind chairs, or even cupboards. A rapid cascade of explosions vibrated the stone floor under our feet and what was left of the glass in the windows was projected into the room to the accompaniment of a tinkling arpeggio.

When the firing of the ground defences had stopped, we came out of hiding to assess the damage. The two Wellingtons at the far end of the line were wrecked and on fire but the rest appeared to be undamaged. We moved outside and looked around the sky, but the Jerries had gone, which was typical of their hit-and-run technique during daylight. The burning fuel from the crippled planes was sending wreaths of oily black smoke rushing skywards. It was appalling to see precious aircraft being destroyed in this way.

'If they don't do something pretty damn quick, the rest of them are going to take fire with the wind in this direction!' said Arthur Madden. 'Does anyone know how to start up a Wimpey?'

'No, but I can start a tractor,' said I, spotting the vehicle which was still attached to the line, and I set off across the airfield at a canter.

I could hear Arthur pounding along after me, then the second aircraft in the line exploded. I felt a savage blow in the chest. The world turned over once completely and then the sun went out.

The ringing in my ears grew louder and was joined by local noises. I found I was lying face down with my back to the aircraft. Arthur was pulling my arm and urging me to get up.

I was surprised to find that my battle dress blouse was neither torn nor bloody, but covered with dust. I scrambled up and staggered back to the sanctuary of the crew-room. According to the men who had been watching, when the bombs on the second aircraft exploded, I was seen to do a complete back flip onto my face. I sat on a chair and rather shakily undid my shirt, but there were no marks and nothing felt damaged. That blow in the chest must have been pure blast.

The CO then arrived and asked what had happened. He didn't seem too pleased but inquired brusquely after my condition and then left. The Adjutant came back to tell us that we were stood-down until the next day.

When we came out of the crew-room again, the third aircraft was on fire, but someone had got to the tractor and was towing the machine away. We heard subsequently that two were undamaged, two destroyed totally, and the other two damaged by shrapnel.

Arriving back at the mess, I was called immediately to the telephone to be told that I was down to fly a reconnaissance trip in the morning.

'That's what you get for upsetting the CO,' Weeky observed. 'You drop us all in it.'

CHAPTER SEVENTEEN

Recce to Pantellaria

THERE WAS, in fact, a small squadron of Marylands at Luqa for reconnaissance work, but they had been losing aircraft almost daily, and when they had difficulty putting one on the flight line, it was not so unusual for our squadron to be asked to supply a Blenheim.

It was not a popular job, for the aircraft were not really suited to it, and on the island of Pantellaria, about 200 miles distant, was a Luftwaffe airfield. It was suspected that fighters from this base were accounting for the losses of the lonely spy planes. My crew and I hadn't been called upon to do one prior to this and I must say it did cross my mind that it was unfortunate that I had brought myself to his attention just when he was looking for a 'volunteer'.

I felt quite uncomfortable the next morning when we taxied out on our own. It was our first sortie into enemy territory without the squadron. I turned the aircraft into wind, got a winking green light from the control tower and pushed the throttles fully open. We had no bombload and she bounced over the uneven surface and became airborne before I really intended.

There was little wind and the air was smooth and clear, ideal for accurate formation-flying. However, we skimmed over the cliffs at Dingli and dived for the sea, for the first part of the trip was to be at low level to avoid radar detection.

I turned on to a westerly heading and the little island was soon disappearing astern. Ahead was a blue and featureless expanse. We flew thus for about an hour and then as we approached our first patrol line which would take us near the enemy island of Sfax, I climbed steadily up to 2000 ft to get a better view.

The Tunisian coast runs due north at this point and in such visibility it could be seen running clear up to Cap Bon. I swung to starboard and paralleled it about two miles out. From here we would see any vessels that might be coast-crawling, but undoubtedly our approach had been observed on radar. It remained to be seen whether they would bother to scramble the fighters for a single aircraft that obviously was not going to intrude.

As we flew north, the dome of Pantellaria Island appeared above the horizon; now that wasn't so good. At the top of the sweep, Benny gave me a course of one-six-zero, and I turned to starboard onto a southeasterly heading. The island was behind me now. I fumbled for my microphone switch: 'Keep an eye on Pantellaria, Weeky.'

'Too right!' he said. 'I'm watching it like a hawk.'

However, we saw nothing throughout that leg and as we closed the African coast we turned back onto a northerly heading and droned on steadily until Pantellaria again came into view.

'I can't help thinking that this is tempting providence,' Benny observed, studying the green-brown of the hills that stood out like a relief map. 'They must know by noo that we're in the area.'

'It's bloody silly if you ask me, sweeping this part,' put in Weeky. 'It's not surprising they keep losing aircraft.'

'If you look at the map,' I said, 'you'll see that it's the direct sea route from Italy and around the west coast of Sicily to Tripoli. If we're going to find anything, this is where it'll be.'

When we were within about two miles of the island we turned southeast again, and so we ranged to and fro above an empty sea for the next two hours.

By now we had decided that the enemy fighters weren't interested today – then Benny made me jump by switching on his microphone and shouting, 'Wha's that up ahead?'

'Whereabouts?'

'Slap bung ahead, aboot two or mebbe three miles and slightly belaw.'

It was several seconds before I picked out the distant dots and identified them as aircraft. I studied them closely and was relieved to find that they weren't growing rapidly larger. They were on the same course as we were and had their backs to us.

There was some discussion as to what they might be.

'They look too big for fighters,' I suggested.

'Don't let's wait to find out,' said Weeky. 'Discretion's the better of valour.'

'It's my opinion they're doing a recce the same as us,' Benny said, and as we closed slowly with them it seemed that he was right, for they were Caproni seaplanes, flying slowly in loose formation.

They obviously hadn't seen us. Up to this time, we had been cruising at economical power but now I opened up the throttles to the take-off gate.

'Hold your fire until we're right up their backsides, Benny, then as we go past, you can have a go, Weeky.'

We were overhauling them fast. Moving in for the kill, and they didn't even know we were there. I could see the sun glinting in their propellor discs now and the bracing wires from the heavy floats to the wings. With stealth we could bag them both.

Then at 200 yards, Benny opened fire. His line of tracer arced in a futile line beneath them. Almost instantly they rolled in different directions. Weeky was cursing Benny profusely. I pulled the Blenheim round in a steep turn to try and hold onto the tail of the nearest one, but with our excessive speed we overshot.

Weeky's guns racketed as we passed behind our quarry, but now the tables were turned. The other one was out of sight behind me. 'Weeky, where's the other one?'

'He's pissed off. Try to get on the tail of this bugger.'

He had dived to sea-level and black smoke was trailing from his engines as he pulled the boost override. I followed him down, and although the airspeed indicator was passing the 260-mph mark, we were gaining almost imperceptibly.

He went into a turn to starboard and I tried to cut inside him but he rolled out on a northwesterly heading, in the direction of Pantellaria.

We raced in line astern just above the wave tops but I couldn't be sure whether we were gaining on him. The aircraft was shaking at the unaccustomed speed and at take-off power it was golloping fuel, no doubt. We still had another hour to go on the patrol line. If we returned early because we had been using fuel playing at fighter boys, the Wing Commander would have our guts for garters.

I pulled back the throttles and turned away, 'It's no good, chaps,' I said. 'We're not going to catch him before he gets to Pantellaria, and anyway we can't afford the fuel.'

Weeky started berating Benny for firing too soon and giving the game away, and Benny came back at him sharply In the end I had to intervene.

We completed our sweep without further incident and turned for home. I was getting hungry and looking forward to my lunch. Weeky came up on the intercom. 'Got a message from Base, Skipper. There's a red warning on. They're telling us to stand off.'

I cursed under my breath but then said, 'OK, we'll cruise at minimum speed until we have the Island in sight, and then stand off to the south.'

I got the speed right back to 90 mph, trimmed the aircraft level and dawdled along, or so it seemed at about a hundred feet.

We saw the anti-aircraft fire even before the Island appeared as a vague yellow blur on the horizon. I began a slow circle to port.

'This is a bloody bind!' objected Weeky. 'I'm hungry.'

'How much fuel do we have?' asked the navigator.

I studied the gauges carefully for a moment. 'Enough for about forty minutes.'

'Jesus, is tha' all?'

'Well,' I said, 'we wasted quite a few gallons chasing those Capronis.'

'If somebody hadn't got excited and opened fire at about five miles, we might have got 'em too,' cut in Weeky.

'You pipe down and listen out,' I admonished him. 'We need to know just as soon as the alert's over.'

Twenty minutes later we were still circling and sporadic gunfire could be seen above the Island.

'Shall I call up Luqa and ask if we can go in yet?' asked Weeky.

'You keep radio silence,' I said somewhat testily. 'Jerry must still be around – you can see the ack-ack, for God's sake. The last thing we want to do is attract attention.'

'What, even when we're falling in the drink through lack of fuel?' I chose to ignore him.

We circled monotonously for a further ten minutes. The firing had stopped during that time but we still had no clearance over the radio. I felt sure they must call us any moment, but the fuel-gauge readings were perilously low. Perhaps they had forgotten us.

'Give them a call, Weeky.'

A minute later he came back on the intercom, 'They say stand by.'

'Ask them if the alert is still on.' I could hear the Morse from his key breaking through sporadically on the intercom.

'They say negative.'

'What's the matter with them for God's sake! Tell them we've got ten minutes' fuel and we're coming in!'

'Roger.' Then a long pause, after which he came back and said slowly and deliberately, 'They still say negative, Skipper. Due to bombing, the landing-strip is out of action.'

I felt the hairs tingle at the back of my neck.

'I'm going in!' I said, and turned on course for the Island.

'Wha' aboot Tai Kali?' asked Benny. I didn't reply. I was already on course for the fighter airfield in the middle of Malta.

As we approached the coast near Comino, three fighters appeared coming from the right. For one nasty moment I thought they were Messerschmidts but then correctly identified them as Hurricanes. They swung towards us, obviously anxious to interrogate. Two flashed over the top of the canopy and one went underneath. Weeky couldn't have seen them coming for he let out a shout of alarm.

I flew on steadily along the centre of the Island, but even as I approached the fighter airfield I knew why the controller had held us off. Several aircraft were burning on the ground and the short runway was pockmarked with craters.

I flew on towards Luqa. We had a problem!

From 1000 ft I could see that vehicles were already out on the airfield disgorging workmen. Looking down from above it was impossible to see a straight run of any length between the holes in the ground. The vehicles and workmen were rapidly adding to the hazards. A red Aldis light was winking at me from the control tower. I ignored it.

Circling to the left, I saw an area on the edge of the field which wasn't quite so heavily pitted. There wasn't a straight run of sufficient length, but if I managed to touch down opposite the operations block and then swerved to the left, I should be able to stop before I got to the edge of the Siggui quarry. I'd better!

I selected the undercarriage down. 'What are you going to do, Skip?' asked Weeky, and he sounded very worried.

'Just tighten your straps and hold on,' I said. 'We've just run out of options.'

I came in low from the Safi end and saw a truck full of men bouncing across my path, obviously very anxious to get out of the way. A double red Very light was fired from the control tower.

I selected full flap and got the speed as low as I dared without stalling. From this low level, the airfield looked in an even more chaotic state.

We shot over the wall just by the motor transport park. I slammed the throttles shut and heaved the stick back. We hit the ground with an awful thump. This was no time for finesse.

Immediately ahead was a pile of rubble that marked the edge of a crater. I slammed on full left rudder, but the tail wasn't on the ground and the aircraft began to bounce and caper sideways.

The flattened curve wasn't going to take us clear. I snatched at the brake lever, but on the loose rough ground, the wheels weren't holding.

At the last moment I slammed the starboard throttle open. The engine cut, then recovered and surged with a roar. We were skidding violently sideways, bouncing in our own duststorm. I never saw the crater as we passed the edge.

There was now a hazard to the left. I slammed the starboard throttle shut, squirmed round in my seat to give it a boot-full of rudder the other way and hugged back the stick to keep the tail down. The brakes were snatching but not enough. A burst of port engine now; but we'd got to stop the flaming thing soon.

She straightened up. I grabbed the port throttle shut and banged off the ignition switches. The engines died. There was just the graunching and grinding noises as the tyres tried to get a grip on the loosely broken surface.

There was just a short run uphill and then the sky. The quarry was beyond. The aircraft was lurching and rolling, then a report from the starboard side told me that the tyre had finally burst. The aircraft swung uncontrollably round to the right, pivoting about the oleo leg, then it hit a large boulder. The tail came up. We were going on our nose. I just hung onto the control column helplessly. We hung there, interminably it seemed, before the tail fell back, slowly at first, then gathering speed to strike the ground with a crash.

We just sat there as the dustcloud settled and cleared.

A lorry driver who had stopped to watch our progress now turned his vehicle away and steered a slow and erratic course across the airfield towards the centre of activity.

No other vehicle came in our direction though we sat there for some time. There were more important things to attend to. Our problem was minimal.

A superficial examination of the aircraft showed that the flaps on both sides had been damaged by stones thrown up by the sliding wheels, and the tyre on the starboard side was completely chewed up and wrapped around the wheel hub. There was still a pungent smell of hot rubber.

'The Wingco's nae ganna like this,' observed Benny quietly.

I shrugged. 'We could have bailed out and let it drop in the sea, Benny. Both fuel gauges were showing empty when we turned on to the final approach.'

'We're about as popular as a pork chop at a Jewish wedding,' put in Weeky, looking across at the headquarters buildings. 'Nobody wants to know us.'

A further fifteen minutes elapsed before a tractor came bouncing across the airfield towards us with the groundcrew clinging to the sides.

'Sorry we didn't get here sooner,' said the sergeant-fitter who had been driving, 'but two replacement aircraft came on the strength this morning and we were busy getting them to operational readiness when we heard you had a problem.'

'Two new aircraft?' asked Weeky.

'Yeah. They arrived just before Jerry this morning.'

'They're not likely to be the forerunners of the famous relief squadron we've been hearing about for the past two weeks?' I suggested.

'Nope. Just two odd bods who thought they were going through to the Middle East.'

'Aha! Victims of the old Shanghai!' grinned Weeky.

'That's right,' the sergeant went on. 'I told 'em, but they wouldn't believe me. One crew kept insisting that they wanted to leave all their gear on board as they were on their way to Cairo in the morning. They were still arguing when the warning went. I haven't seen 'em since.'

'No risk of our getting a lift back to headquarters, I suppose?' asked Weeky.

'No chance,' said the sergeant. 'Every vehicle we've got has been pressed into airfield repair work. I was looking for a 15-cwt to bring out some gear, but MT wouldn't play. What's the score?' he called to the riggers who were crouching by the starboard wheel.

'It'll need a retraction test at least, Sarge,' one of them called over his shoulder. 'I think the leg's strained at the main spar attachment points and there's a lot of flap damage.'

'Jesus!' muttered the sergeant. 'That's all we need!'

'We're going to leave our gear in the aircraft,' I said. 'We'll come back for it as soon as we can get transport.'

He nodded as we moved away.

We walked on over the rough ground in silence for a while, then Weeky said, 'Well, that'll keep us off the battle order for a day or two.'

'I wouldna' count on it,' Benny replied. 'They've got a full complement of groundcrew and only five aircraft to work on.'

'Seven,' I said.

'Aw, big stuff!' added Weeky. 'We can put up a box of six again now.'

The new arrivals were in the crew-room talking animatedly among themselves when we got there. One of the air gunners had known Weeky during training apparently and called out when we walked in, 'What the bloody hell goes on here?'

'Everything!' replied Weeky cheerfully. 'How are you, matey, haven't seen you since Upwood.'

'A bit cheesed off,' answered the gunner. 'We were supposed to be going to the Middle East.'

'Ah, they all think that!' Weeky was enjoying himself. 'Anyway you wouldn't like it there with all those flies and things.'

'I'm not so bloody sure I'm going to like it here either, if this morning's anything to go by,' he said.

'You know it's not really on!' cut in a red-haired sergeant pilot with the suggestion of a moustache on his upper lip. 'We were definitely posted to HQ Middle East. I saw the signal. They just can't do this sort of thing!'

'Wanna bet?' The conversation was cut short by the arrival

of the Wing Commander with the Adjutant in close attendance. His face looked even paler than usual.

He stopped in front of me. 'What the hell happened to you?' he demanded.

'We were running out of fuel, Sir. If I hadn't got down then we would have had to ditch.'

'According to our calculations,' he went on, 'you should have had at least another twenty minutes' fuel left. Were you holding at the minimum power setting?'

'Yes, Sir, I was, but the fuel gauges showed empty.'

He glared into my face, 'Then they must have been misreading. Mr Johnson,' he said over his shoulder to the Adjutant, 'have those tanks dipped.'

'But we must ha' used quite a few gallons when we chased two Capronis,' put in Benny. I could have kicked him.

The Wing Commander glared at him. 'You were chased by two Capronis?'

'No, Sir,' explained Benny carefully. 'We – chased – them!'

The malevolent eyes were turned on me again. 'What the hell were you doing chasing other aircraft around when you were supposed to be on a reconnaissance! Had they attacked you?'

'No, Sir, but it occurred to me that they might also be on a recce and could have seen something.'

'You were supposed to keep your eyes open and keep quiet,' he went on. 'You could well have attracted attention to yourself and we would have lost another aircraft. Did you see anything else?'

'No, Sir.'

'Right. You'd better report to the briefing officer now.' He marched out of the door with the Adjutant in hot pursuit.

'That's nice!' observed one of the new crew members quietly. 'Is he the CO?'

I nodded and moved towards the briefing-room.

'Hang on,' Weeky called to his gunner friend. 'We shan't be five minutes, then we'll take you to the transit mess.'

The Intelligence Officer showed us some silhouettes of Italian seaplanes and we were able to confirm that they were Capronis. 'They usually go out on reconnaissance in pairs, one to protect the other.'

'Well, the one we chased was rather left out on a limb,' I remarked. 'The other one just pushed off.'

'Ah well,' he explained smiling, 'they're Italians!'

As Weeky had forecast, the briefing was over quickly and we took the newcomers along to the transit mess. We learned that three aircraft had set off from Portreath, but one had disappeared on the first leg to Gibraltar. Their news of the bombing raids on England was depressing. It didn't seem so bad when one was in the middle of it, but not to know how one's family was faring back in the Old Country was a constant source of nagging worry.

The morale of the newcomers didn't lift very much either after Weeky had regaled them with stories of life on a Malta squadron, but after two or three drinks had been downed in quick succession, the conversation turned to lighter things, and by the time we moved into the dining hall, it was positively cheerful.

No sooner had we sat down than the lunchtime siren wailed into life. Immediately two NCOs rose, carried their chairs to the doors at each end of the room and sat down, effectively blocking the exits.

'What on earth are they doing?' asked the red-haired pilot. I explained that they were on door duty. Their task was to stop the waiting staff escaping once the warning had gone. Two of the Maltese stewards started to harangue one of the NCOs excitedly, but he merely settled down to study his copy of the *Malta Times*. The waiters retired to the kitchen shouting at each other.

It was late afternoon before we were finally allocated a truck, retrieved our flying gear from the aircraft and climbed aboard the bus for the drive to Marsaxlokk.

It was now raining and I looked out dully at the passing landscape. The six new crew members were very quiet, and two of them had fallen asleep. I had forgotten that they must have taken off from Gibraltar before dawn to have arrived at Malta by midmorning. Those that were awake looked very depressed and I felt sorry for them. Apart from the air-gunner who knew Weeky, they were all straight from the operational training unit. They had not yet seen any action, and this was certainly not the best place to start.

No time had been lost in getting them operational either, for during an interview with the CO after lunch, they learned that their names were included on the battle order for the following day. As Weeky had prophesied, 'a full box of six'.

I too felt flat now that the effect of the lunchtime drinking had worn off, and I decided to write a few letters and have an early night. For obvious reasons, I never mentioned the operations in my letters home, but concentrated on the interesting things on the Island and the doings during our lighter moments. They must have got the impression that I was having a gay old time; or did they?

By 9 o'clock, I felt unusually tired and went back to the empty barrack block, climbed into bed and went to sleep without delay. I heard nothing of the others when they came in in their usual noisy fashion no doubt, but in the small hours of the morning I woke up sweating profusely.

It had been rather chilly the previous night and I had used the full complement of blankets when making the bed, but now I pushed them down and was grateful for the coolness of the night air on my body. I could hear the rain spilling from the guttering. It was odd that it had turned so warm.

I couldn't stand the heat. The noise in my head was beginning to pulse in time with my heartbeats and was making me feel dizzy. With an impatient kicking I freed myself of the bedclothes completely and found that my pyjamas were soaked and becoming chilled. I felt a desperate need for fresh air and started to get out of bed, but it seemed to gyrate under me and I lost my balance and fell back.

There was a growing nausea. I had to get outside before I was sick. I got myself up on one elbow, made a conscious effort to sit up but overbalanced and slid off the edge of the bed onto my knees. I knelt there panting in the darkness. I started to vomit then managed to gain control. Impelled by the thought that I must get outside, I forced up into a crouching positon and fumbled my way to the end of the bed. I picked up my dressing-gown, then abandoned it and launched myself off towards the door between the row of beds.

I found myself weaving dizzily from side to side and collided painfully with the end of one of the beds. The occupant just grunted and mumbled in his sleep.

I made the door at the far end, pulled it open, swung round it colliding with the jamb, and almost fell down the two steps into the ablutions.

The stone floor was delightfully cold, and on the far side I could see the vague outline of the doorway that gave onto the path. I had to get to it. I felt, rather than saw, the shadowy details of the washbasins and shower cubicles which seemed to be swinging round me. I was becoming disorientated. The floor was tilting crazily first one way, then the next. With arms outstretched for protection, I was staggering like a drunk and I couldn't make any ground towards the doorway.

The motion got wild; I remember falling. There was a flash of shattered lights and then oblivion.

I must have lain there for several hours as Maxie found me lying on the floor when he came out to the toilet just before dawn. The next thing I knew was being borne by strong arms and lifted gently on to the bed by the door. There were four or five men around me and the lights were on, but their voices were confused and distant.

Then I began to tremble uncontrollably. I was deadly cold and I felt myself being covered with blankets. I remember Benny's face looking concerned and hearing someone saying that they had phoned for an ambulance.

I must have dozed for some time, for when I woke it was daylight. Several of the chaps were standing by the bed fully dressed. Arthur Madden bent over me, 'How are you feeling now, old boy?' he asked quietly.

'Better.'

'We phoned for a flaming ambulance two hours ago,' he went on, 'but there's still no sign of it and the transport leaves for the airfield in ten minutes.'

I didn't want to be left behind. 'Will you get my clothes,' I asked weakly, 'and I'll come with you.'

'Jesus! You're not going to be crazy enough to think of reporting for duty, are you?' demanded Weeky.

'Of course not; but I can go sick from up there.'

I felt terribly weak and dressed with difficulty and certainly needed help to walk slowly down the path to where the bus was waiting. During the journey, I began to shiver uncontrollably again and was only vaguely aware of what was going on around me.

I remember at one time being surprised to find that a navigator from one of the new crews was sitting beside me looking worried. It seemed odd that a newcomer should seem so concerned.

When the bus got to the airfield gates, I vaguely remembered a lengthy discussion outside the bus between several crew members and the airmen of the guard as to where I should be taken, but it had no interest for me. I felt that I was just existing in vacuo. It was finally decided that I should sit on a wooden bench outside the guardroom and wait for the transport which would leave for Imtarfa, the military hospital, in half an hour.

The new navigator was one of the group who helped me down the steps of the bus and conducted me to the seat. He buttoned my jacket solicitously. He was the last to leave me, and on boarding the bus he turned, put up his thumb and winked encouragingly. He seemed very kind.

I never saw him again. He was one of those who died later in the day.

CHAPTER EIGHTEEN

Under the red cross

I MADE the journey to the hospital sitting up in the back of the ambulance with half a dozen other assorted souls. On arrival, there was a long wait before I was seen by the medical officer and I barely knew what was going on around me and cared even less.

I was examined eventually by an army major who referred to me as 'sarnt', announced that I had a fever, shouted for the orderly and said sharply, 'Isolation'. I was given a coloured card, taken outside and given directions to the isolation ward which was in a distant wing of the hospital.

'Will you be all right?' asked the orderly doubtfully. I nodded dumbly. He went back inside and I set off unsteadily for my goal. I was only half conscious of the sights and sounds around me. I knew that I was weaving along the pavement, but I was making progress in the right direction. To my surprise, I came upon the entrance as described, but half-way up the stairs my legs began to tremble. I pulled myself up slowly with the help of the banisters. The door to the ward was open and a nurse coming out of a side room caught sight of me. She led me to a chair, helped me into it and took away the card that I was still clutching.

She was Maltese, small and neat. Within a moment she returned with the sister who was angular and English. She peered first at the card and then at me through her wire-rimmed glasses.

'All right, Sergeant Gillman,' her voice was very shrill, 'Nurse will show you to your bed.' And then as an afterthought, 'Where is your small kit?'

'I haven't, er, got it. I - I forgot.'

'You know the rules, Sergeant. Whenever you report sick, you should bring your small kit with you.' I nodded bleakly.

'Very well, Nurse,' she said. 'Put the patient to bed.'

I was on the last lap. With trembling hands I found my way into the coarse flannelette pyjamas that had been given me and sank back onto the bed. The nurse lifted my legs from where they hung over the edge, gently pulled up the covers and I sank into merciful oblivion.

From then on, my disorientation was complete. Sounds and sensations were mostly in the blurred distance, only occasionally to come fitfully into focus and then to fade into the muted confusion. At times I was vaguely aware of something pulling at my body, of a man's voice, steaming heat, a sudden clear glimpse of an uncurtained window, the confusion of voices around me and long periods of dark, thrumming, throbbing numbness.

I heard the familiar urgent sounds of an air raid in the distance, then not so distant, but it could have been a dream. I was tumbling in the warm flood, mostly immersed and in darkness; but occasionally, as if an ear had broken the surface, I suffered an injection of local sounds before sinking swiftly beyond their range.

I don't know how long this state continued, neither did I recognise the transition back to sanity, but one morning I found myself looking at the scene around me. The picture was no longer confused. Several nurses were busying themselves cheerfully with preparations for another day. There were two lines of beds in which men were propped in varying attitudes. No one seemed aware of my existence. My body seemed weak and cool, but my mind was pleased with what I saw. I was happy to lie and watch.

A small dark nurse came hurrying along the ward. I recognised her. She looked at my bed with absent eyes as she passed, then stopped. She came over slowly as if not sure that I was awake, then she smiled, put her head on one side and said, 'Hello. Feel better?'

I nodded slowly.

'Anything you want?'

I tried to answer, but my voice wouldn't come at first, then it broke and was too thick to be understood.

She fussed with the bedclothes. 'You lie still,' she said quietly, 'and I'll get you a drink.' I felt good.

A short time later I heard footsteps returning, but now she was following the sister. The Englishwoman was wearing a crisp white headdress and the eyes behind the glasses were quite penetrating. 'How do you feel now, Sergeant?' she demanded in a voice that was both brisk and strident. I smiled and nodded my head.

She took my wrist between her thumb and forefinger. 'You

have had quite a time,' she said more quietly, studying her fob watch. Then after a pause, 'Keep covered up, we don't want you catching a chill. The doctor will be here shortly.' She turned to the nurse: 'Give the patient plenty of liquid but nothing else yet. Record his temperature once an hour.'

'Yes, Sister,' replied the young Maltese girl meekly.

As the senior woman left, she poured a glass of cordial from a jug. 'You like a drink?'

'Please.'

I tried to sit up but there was no force available. She slipped her arm under my head and raised it towards the glass. She smelled lightly of disinfectant. Her arm was slim and golden brown, the sleeve of her uniform rolled neatly above the elbow. I drank slowly and gratefully and when I had finished she laid my head back gently and disengaged her arm. I looked at the ceiling as she rearranged the covers. My mouth was foul. I wanted to ask her if I could wash, shave and clean my teeth, but I lacked the initiative.

The doctor arrived as she was taking my temperature for the second time. He was younger than the major I had seen on arrival and was less peremptory. Taking the thermometer from my mouth he shook it several times and held it up to the light. 'That's a bit better. You're coming off the boil,' he smiled. 'How do you feel in yourself?'

'Fine.'

He turned to the Sister and the staff-nurse who were standing in attendance and gave them some diet instructions before moving off. I watched them slowly making their rounds until sleep reclaimed me.

I awoke to the rattle of cutlery; it was lunchtime and the staff-nurse called from the bottom of my bed, 'Would you like some soup?'

I cleared my throat: 'No thank you, Nurse. I'd like to clean my teeth.'

She smiled. 'Sure. Just let's get the lunches out and we'll be with you.'

The toilet gave a lift to my morale and was worth the effort, for by the time I was sitting propped up against the pillows the thought of food was becoming attractive.

My thoughts must have communicated themselves, for the little nurse, who had told me that her name was Magda as she had helped me wash and combed my hair, asked, 'Would you like something to eat now?'

'I'd love a bowl of soup.'

'Sure,' and she gave a brilliant smile.

When it arrived, I ate it with relish. I don't think that chicken soup had ever tasted so delicious. There was incessant gunfire rumbling in the distance. I lay back and listened; it was still going on, then.

During the afternoon, the little bright-eyed one and another nurse busied themselves straightening up my bed, chattering and giggling over a private joke. Then Magda turned to me: 'Your air gunner and navigator came to see you yesterday,' she said.

I put my hand to my face. During the washing process I had been conscious of an unusual growth of whisker.

'Yesterday? How long – how long have I been here then?'

She smiled slowly but her eyes were serious. 'Three days.' I shook my head and sighed.

I dozed intermittently for the rest of the afternoon and between whiles, lying with my eyes closed, I was pleasantly conscious of the activity around me. I bestirred myself to take an interest when the high tea came round, but although most of the others were given a savoury, for me there was a bowl of broth.

Gradually the colour drained from the rectangle of blue sky that I could see through the lofty window opposite my bed, and there was much noisy activity as the nurses struggled to get blackout frames in position urged on by ribald comments from some of the men. There was a great deal of laughter which was snuffed out when the Sister appeared in the doorway and stood watching the scene.

The bare lightbulbs that hung under metal dish reflectors were poor substitutes for the Mediterranean sun that had flooded the ward with a certain gaiety during the day, and the fall-off in general activity had a depressing effect.

The fellow in the bed on my left seemed to spend all his time sleeping, and the soldier on the other side, a gunner from the Devon Regiment, was not very communicative. We both made a desultory attempt at conversation and then lapsed into silence.

The arrival of the last hot drink of the day provided a welcome diversion, but I was disappointed to see that the little dark-eyed nurse was no longer on duty; she had been replaced by a taller girl whose good looks were quite negated by a sullen manner. Most of the staff had the dark colouring of the Maltese, but their voices were inclined to be guttural when they jabbered in the local language. As the lights were dimmed for the night, I settled down comfortably, for I was quite ready to sleep again.

I didn't hear the siren. The first I knew of the raid was my bed rattling unaccountably. My mind must have just surfaced when the next explosion gave the building a teeth-rattling jar. The flash was visible through the gaps in the blackout frames. A scuffling noise attracted my attention to the other side of the ward, in time to see a patient slide under the bed in the dim light. I heard his tin hat scrape across the floor.

Judging by the commotion at the far end, others were doing the same. I propped myself up on an elbow listening with a pounding heart; waiting for the next one. I heard the dull unhurried drone of the bomber. Surprisingly the anti-aircraft fire was light and sporadic. The noise of the aircraft was fading.

The night-nurse came running into the ward. She seemed agitated and on discovering several of the men under their beds, she ordered them back in a shrill voice.

I shrank down under the clothes. The bombing had not worried me particularly before, but now I felt trapped. I lay listening for a long while, and eventually, with dread, I heard the guns open up again in the distance. The firing was more intense this time. The guns sounded like a pack of angry dogs barking at the prey that defied them in its slow movement overhead. The noise of the bomber's engines was deliberate and moving steadily nearer.

Then there was a rustling sound and an almighty bang in the valley, it seemed, but not as near as the first one. Then a whistling, the note falling to end in an explosion that was louder and nearer than the first. Then two more, the noise and shock doubling in size. The man was laying a stick of bombs across the valley and they were coming in the direction of the hospital.

There was a general scramble to get under the beds. The fifth attacked the ears with sound shock. The lightbulbs were swinging. The next one was for us. I tried to scramble out of bed but my feet were caught up in the clothes. I fell off the side and on to the floor with my feet still on the bed. Another explosion seemed to rattle the teeth in my head and a huge piece of ceiling plaster crashed into the gangway and erupted into a large cloud of dust that dimmed the light. I kicked my feet free and rolled under the bed as the next one cracked right alongside the building. It was followed by an ominous rumbling that continued for several seconds. I cowered under the bed expecting the walls to come tumbling down, but there was silence apart from the inevitable drone of the aircraft.

The firing stopped and the heterodyne beat of the bomber's engines faded slowly and deliberately into the distance.

I was trying to climb back on to my bed when the Sister hurried into the ward, her voice loud, shrill, but quite calm.

'Now come along you men, get back into your beds.' She was picking her way through the pile of rubble. 'Is anyone hurt?' There were mumbled answers from the far end. I could now hear the shouts of men outside the windows; heaven knows what had happened there.

Two more nurses came hurrying in, followed by the little dark one fastening her uniform at the neck. They reacted quickly to the Sister's orders, two of them going out again in search of brooms and buckets. One stripped the counterpane covered in rubble from an unoccupied bed.

'Don't shake that, you stupid girl! Do you want to choke the patients with dust? Go and get a bucket of water!'

Several of the walking patients gathered around the Sister with offers of help, and under her control they and the girls began to restore some sort of order out of the chaos.

I caught the eye of the man in the next bed. 'It's getting worse,' he said.

'You mean this has happened before?' I asked in surprise.

He nodded, 'Every night.'

I looked sceptical. I couldn't believe that I could have slept through such events even in a fever.

'But why should they bomb this bit of the Island?'

'It's the airfield, you see,' he volunteered.

Of course, Tai Kali was just down the hill from the hospital.

'They lay sticks of bombs across the airfield,' he went on, 'and some of them overshoot.'

'But isn't the hospital marked?'

'It was. There used to be a red cross on the roof floodlit at night, but then they thought that it would give them a landmark, so they switched it out.'

I shook my head slowly. 'You can't bloody win, can you?' I said. He shrugged.

When the mess had been cleaned up and some of the beds remade, the nurses came round with hot sweet tea frothing with bromide. As Magda handed me the mug she asked with a giggle, 'Did you get under the bed?'

'Too right,' I said. 'Did you?'

'I was under the table in my room,' she said. 'Then the light fell on it and the bulb exploded and I jumped up and banged my head!' They started to laugh a little hysterically and the Sister as she swept by called, not unkindly, 'Now, girls, get on with your work.'

By the time the lights had been dimmed again, it was 3 o'clock and I could only doze fitfully until the daily routine started again punctually at 6 a.m. The same nurses reappeared but they looked a little jaded and the toilet and breakfast routines were carried out almost in silence. During a lull in the general activity, I asked the Sister if I could get out of bed to go to the bathroom. She agreed, but walked beside me as I made my unsteady way to the door.

'Was the hospital hit last night, Sister?' I inquired.

'Yes it was,' she said.

'Anybody hurt?'

'No, fortunately. The administrative block was damaged. It's going to cause an awful lot of inconvenience, but no one was on duty there, thank the Lord.'

On my way back to bed, I paused by a window. Imtafa is on the crown of a hill, and the Island, coloured by sunlight, looked incredibly peaceful.

Around mid-morning, an orderly came in and asked something of the staff-nurse. To my surprise she indicated my bed and coming over he handed me an envelope. It was a letter from Benny.

Apparently they had called to visit me the day after I was admitted but were told that I couldn't be seen as I was in Isolation. Benny went on to say that of course they were taken off the battle order after I reported sick and they had watched the box of six take-off for an attack on a convoy reportedly about 200 miles out. Both of the new crews were lost.

I felt my throat contracting and a feeling of uncontrollable sadness enveloped me. They couldn't have known what to expect. Apart from the ferry trip out, it was their first operational sortie since leaving training school, and their last. I remembered the navigator who had shown such genuine concern when he helped me off the bus and over to the bench outside the guardroom. His face had been gentle and it had been comforting. I closed my eyes to stop the tears betraying me, and in my debilitated condition I struggled with myself to stop breaking down. I tried swallowing hard but only succeeded in emitting a series of loud gulps. My body was trembling again and I couldn't stop it.

I was startled by Magda's voice close beside me.

'Bad news?' she asked quietly.

I nodded, keeping my eyes shut tight, 'Sort of.'

'Someone at home?' she persisted.

'No, just friends,' I said, forcing myself to look at her; it seemed a reasonable explanation.

'We're just making a cup of tea. Would you like one?'

I nodded.

With the tea, she gave me a pill to take, and then suggested that I lie down and relax for a while. This I certainly did, for it was mid-afternoon before I woke. I watched in a mood of sleepy detachment as the golden light at the window weakened and faded into a misty grey. Then same the burst of activity as the blackouts were rattled into position and I felt shut in again.

Jerry didn't visit Tai Kali that night and I remember waking in the small hours and being reassured by the sight of the staff-nurse bent over a letter by the subdued light at her table in the middle of the ward, before sinking into an untroubled sleep.

The following day dawned full of golden promise as they all did in Malta, but there seemed to be a general feeling of optimism in the ward. I ate my breakfast with relish, and when the little dark nurse came to take the tray she said, 'That's a good boy. Now you'll grow up to be big and strong.' Her eyes were laughing, but there was a directness in her glance that excited me.

During the ritual of the doctor's rounds I was told to get out of bed whenever I felt like it and to exercise my legs as much as possible. 'Sandfly fever usually lasts only for a few days,' he said, 'but it's very weakening. What we have to do now is to build you up.' Later on that morning, I was conducted to the service room at the end of the ward and told to climb on the scales: the pointer stopped just short of nine stone.

However, my strength seemed to be returning with each hour that passed, and the moral and physical weakness that had brought me to the very edge of a breakdown was now a receding memory. With it came an increasing optimism which only dimmed momentarily when I thought about the time when I must return to the squadron. I moved about the ward during the ensuing days taking an interest in the other occupants and helping the nurses. I began to feel part of the community, and on several brief but tingling occasions, I found myself alone with Magda.

One afternoon, I was sitting out on the balcony but happened to catch her eye as she passed a window. Shortly afterwards she came through the door and looking round hastily to see if the Sister was about, she sat down on the bench beside me.

'It's a lovely view from here,' I said. She nodded and relaxed visibly. On the right was the noble walled city of Mdina, standing with dignity on the hill it had occupied for over a thousand years, but to the east the land fell away to the plain of Marsa and in the far distance was the smoky outline of the city of Valletta.

'Where do you live?' I asked her.

She pointed across the plain. 'In Lija, not so far from Luqa.'

'Do you get home at all?'

'About once a week,' she said, then turning her lovely dark eyes on me with their ever-present hint of warmth, she asked quietly, 'What's it like in England?'

'Not a bit like Malta.' She smiled and inclined her head.

'It's incredibly green,' I went on. 'Where you've got yellow sandstone everywhere, we have rolling fields of lush green in the summer, and they're much larger and surrounded by hedges instead of being marked out with little stone walls. The trees are tall and very green too, though in the autumn they go a lovely gold colour. It's all much -- neater, if you know what I mean.'

'It sounds lovely,' she said wistfully, then with a surprising directness she added, 'Will you take me?'

Her eyes were suddenly intense yet with a background of

anxiety. There was no doubting that she was serious. I felt the shock of surprise. There she was facing me with all her youthful innocence; she couldn't have been more than seventeen or eighteen at the most, petite, wonderfully attractive and so very feminine.

'I'd love to,' I said, 'after the war.'

She reached out her hand and I took it in mine. It was small and soft and I found this first innocent contact exquisitely thrilling.

We had only sat for a few seconds when we were startled by a shrill voice behind us. 'Nurse Busitil! What *are* you doing! Get back in the ward at once!' Magda scampered away. The Sister's normally pale face was glowing with indignation. 'And, Sergeant, you should know better. It's clear that you're on the road to recovery. It's time you were sent back to your unit!' She minced back into the ward.

I sat down slowly, my feelings a mixture of elation and apprehension.

During the next two days, Magda seemed to be avoiding me and when we did talk briefly, there was a constraint between us. Although I sought it, no occasion arose when we were alone together.

Just after lunch one day, I was sitting on the balcony in company with a number of the others who were up and about, when the undulating wail of the sirens echoed across the valley. Eventually we saw some black dots falling towards Luqa. They were too far away to make out what sort of aircraft they were, but seconds later, the flashes and eruptions of dust and smoke indicated that their eggs had been laid.

Then we saw them coming towards us across the plain and climbing fast. I could identify them now as Junkers 88s.

'Look! The fighters are on to them!' someone shouted, pointing. Behind and above could be seen the small figures of vengeance, diving. They were Hurricanes. Two of the German machines peeled off to the north and a pair of fighters curved in angry pursuit, but the third 88 continued climbing straight ahead.

He was almost above us when the Hurricane, which was closing fast, opened fire. There was a long deep trill of the guns and the Jerry went into a steep turn to the left. The fighter swung wide, and then tightening its turn he came round on the bomber's tail again. They were low enough for us to see the details.

The machine-guns rattled again and a puff of smoke shot from the starboard engine of the Junkers. Shouts and cheers went up from the growing crowd on the balcony. I was suddenly conscious of a small voice beside me. It was Magda.

'Look!' I cried excitedly. 'He's got him!' As I spoke, a further long burst from the fighter extracted a tail of flame from the damaged engine. My arm was around her now and she was trembling.

More shouts went up from the watching crowd as three black dots fell from the crippled machine. Then the white canopies of their parachutes blossomed. 'Where's the fourth?' I said breathlessly in a half whisper, then to my amazement, the German machine turned into the next attack, and its front guns opened up. The fourth man was still on board and fighting with an engine on fire.

But he had tightened the turn too much. The dark grey Junkers flicked on to its back, the nose dropped gracefully, then it went into a vertical spin which became more vicious with each turn, the black smoke twisting into a corkscrew shape behind it.

Magda buried her head in my shoulder. I slipped my hand under her dark hair, felt the softness of her cheek and gently lifted her face. Her eyes were swimmy with tears. 'Will you come with me?' I whispered.

'Oh! Yes!' and she buried her face again and sobbed.

Then the next good thing happened. The fourth body was hurled from the spinning aircraft. It fell for several seconds, then the parachute cracked into shape behind it. An involuntary cheer went up from the onlookers. Such a man deserved to live.

Magda slipped away in the confusion. We watched the parachute until it disappeared behind the roofs of Rabat. A body was brought into the mortuary that night and the story went around that a Maltese had crept up behind him with a shotgun and blown his brains out.

Later that afternoon, the Sister told me that I was to report to the main medical block at 0900 the following morning. I knew what that meant; I was to be discharged.

To my consternation, Magda did not appear when the supper came round. I asked the staff-nurse where she was and learned that she was not well and had been sent back to the nurse's quarters. I threw caution to the wind. 'I have to see her,' I said urgently.

'Please tell her that I am being discharged tomorrow.' The staff-nurse gave me a withering look and didn't reply.

The rules were so strict that it was going to be difficult to get in touch with her, and I was concerned as to how sick she was or whether she was just suffering a reaction from the afternoon's drama. When the lights had been dimmed for the night, I lay in the silence scheming over ways of getting in touch. After tomorrow, I couldn't be sure what my programme would be. I could say that again!

Then the door at the end of the ward opened. Magda appeared, hesitated, then tiptoed to my bedside.

'Are you all right?' I whispered. She nodded. 'I'm being discharged tomorrow.'

'I know,' she said. 'Staff told me.'

'When can we meet?'

'I'm not off until next Tuesday, then I shall go home – but you can't come there,' she added hastily.

'Can you meet me in Valletta?' I asked, though I wasn't at all sure that I could get there myself. However, there were ways and means if necessary. She nodded.

'There's a dance every afternoon at the Senior NCOs' Club in the Castille; can you meet me there at 2 o'clock?'

She nodded again.

'I'll wait for you at the top of the steps,' I said.

She bent over me. I felt the softness of her hair on my face. Her cool, moist lips touched mine briefly. I tried to put my arm around her but she eluded me, made her way swiftly and quietly to the door and disappeared.

CHAPTER NINETEEN

The last straw

THE DISCHARGE formalities on the following day took several hours and it was nearly midday before I got back to the airfield and reported to the Adjutant.

He glanced at the form that I handed him. 'Feeling fit now?'

'Yes, Sir,' I said without conviction, for my first half day of normal activity had left me feeling weak.

'Well, it's back to the grindstone I'm afraid,' he went on. 'I have to put you on the battle order in the morning as there's a special job coming up.'

I felt that unpleasant tingle in the pit of my stomach.

'I'll arrange some transport for you back to Marsa and perhaps you'll take this copy of the order and make sure that everybody sees it. The pick-up in the morning will be at 0800 hours.'

Once back at Marsaxlokk, it seemed as if I had never been away, though the eight days spent in hospital had seemed an eternity at the time. Weeky filled in the gap in the squadron story for me. Apparently, on the day I went into hospital, the Wing Commander led an attack on a convoy. I was surprised at this, but learned that it wasn't the first time he had ignored the doctors' ruling and got into the air. One of the new crews was lost during the run in, and the other came out with an engine on fire. He managed to douse it, but seemed to be having difficulty in coping on the other engine. Maxie and Tim Cummings held back to escort him, but having gained a few hundred feet initially, he began to lose it again and slowly closed with the sea. They flew in company for some time, anxiously watching the crippled aircraft just skimming the wave tops; then a quick shower of spray indicated that a propellor had hit the water, and almost immediately the aircraft made contact with the next wave crest, soared in the air like a porpoise then dived into the sea a hundred yards farther on. When the mass of water had subsided, the aircraft could be seen floating and figures were scrambling out of the top hatches.

The escorting aircraft circled round but in less than a minute, the metal aircraft had gone. Two figures could be seen crouching in the dinghy which they had managed to inflate.

It was estimated that they were about 140 miles south of the Island, and Maxie climbed in a spiral above the spot, trailed his aerial and got the radio-operator air gunner to send a distress call to Malta. Luqa replied and the operator held his key down so that they could take a bearing on the transmission and pinpoint the area.

Meanwhile, Tim Cummings was still circling low down and his air-gunner divested himself of his life jacket, tied it round a box of emergency rations, inflated it and threw it out of the hatch as Tim flew low past the dinghy. It fell near enough to the dinghy for the two men to retrieve it. At least it would keep them going until they could be rescued.

With their fuel reserves seriously depleted, the circling crews had reluctantly to dip their wings in a final salute and set course for the Island.

At de-briefing it was learned that the radio operator on the airfield had got a good fix on the dinghy's position, and the Wing Commander promised that an MTB would be sent out after dark to retrieve them. However, when Maxie checked up on the following morning, the briefing officer appeared somewhat evasive, but admitted finally that the unfortunate crew had not, in fact, been rescued. This brought a wave of indignation from the other men. In low-level operations, it was most unusual for a crew to survive in this way, as it was not possible for parachutes to be used and the ditching of a damaged aircraft was seldom successful. For two out of the three-man crew to be seen alive in the dinghy and then to be left to their fate was too much. For some time there had been a growing conviction that the squadron was considered expendable. It was a bitter thought to accept although in the circumstances perhaps it was understandable; but now, when there was a chance to save at least two of them, the opportunity had been neglected. This was the last straw.

The men were in revolt. Out of the commotion, Maxie was appointed the spokesman and he promptly telephoned the CO and told him in anger that the crews would refuse to fly on any more operations until something was done for the unfortunate men.

The harassed Wing Commander lost his temper too, exclaiming that this was tantamount to mutiny and that in wartime such people were shot. Maxie put the phone down on him. Within half an hour, the Adjutant rang the mess to say that a transport was on its way there and that the crews were to report to the airfield with full flying kit. Uproar followed, but by the time the bus arrived, the sober counsel of Arthur Madden had prevailed and it was agreed that they would go to the airfield and try to impress their views on the CO.

Tempers had cooled when the confrontation took place, and the Wing Commander explained that the Navy had said that no small high-speed vessel was available at that time. However, he suggested that the squadron should take-off and go in search of the dinghy. If found, supplies were to be dropped, but the searching aircraft should keep radio silence. He couldn't risk the squadron being picked up by enemy fighters. Among the equipment to be dropped was a small radio-transmitter for the use of the two men in the dinghy.

The five aircraft took-off and flew in formation to the area and then split up to carry out individual searches. They flew to the limit of their fuel endurance before returning singly to base, but no trace of the dinghy was found.

Two days later, the crews were briefed for another shipping attack. Their mood was sullen but Weeky's was one of indignation when he found that he was to fly with another pilot whose radio-operator air gunner had also gone sick. His protest was peremptorily overridden by the CO and according to Tim Murphy, who was the unfortunate pilot, he moaned all the way to the target area. However, no ships were found, so that honour was saved.

'And the moment you come back,' said Weeky accusingly, 'we're told that there's a special job lined up. You can't bloody win!'

How special the job was, we learned the next morning. It was apparent that something big was on the moment we walked into the briefing-room, for the Senior Air Staff Officer was there with his retinue. There were more top brass than bodies to do the job.

After my lay-off, brief though it had been, I felt apprehensive and ill-equipped. As the details of the raid emerged I began to feel weak and slightly sick. Apparently, a reconnaissance aircraft had sighted a large number of ships in Tripoli Harbour. 'You might think,' said the briefing officer casting a sideways glance at the Group Captain, 'that we shouldn't have let them slip through in the first place. However, now that we have got them bottled up, we can do something about it.'

Got them bottled up! Tripoli Harbour was known to be a hornet's nest. To send five Blenheims in there was suicide. The crews went through their preparations in a state of shock. This was the worst one yet!

Climbing onto the truck that was to take us out to the dispersals, my legs felt weak. When it started with a jerk, Benny stepped back on somebody's toes and an argument ensued which I just hadn't the drive to quell. I felt myself getting impatient when Benny made heavy weather of getting his parachute pack and navigation bag stowed in the nose compartment of the aircraft, and I ignored a tirade from Weeky about the state in which the fitters had left his turret after servicing.

During my pre-flight checks I found that the port fuel gauge was unserviceable and reading zero. I signalled to the fitter and he scrambled up on to the wing and hung his head down through the open roof hatch. 'What's up, Sarge?' he asked.

'This fuel gauge is U/S,' I said, pointing at the offending instrument.

'Well it was all right when I did the DI this morning,' he replied. 'Give it a tap.'

I knocked it a couple of times with my knuckles but it failed to respond. 'I can't take it like this,' I said uncertainly. 'How the hell will I know what my fuel situation is on the way back?' I began to feel a glimmer of hope.

'Well the tanks are full, Sarge, I know that,' the fitter went on. 'If you know what you've started with and you know the consumption, then you know what's left.'

I had already thought of that. Furthermore, if both engines were run at the same speed, then the indications on the starboard fuel gauge would give me a good idea what was still left in the port tank. However, if the starboard engine was knocked out, I would have to put up the power and thus the consumption on the port engine, and I would have no idea how fast the fuel was going down.

One half of me dearly wanted to scrub on the strength of this argument, but the other half knew that I was trying to get out of going on the trip. In the background of my mind hung the words that the Group Captain had uttered at briefing – 'This operation, gentlemen, is crucial. If we can bottle up the ships or damage the harbour installations, then this will be of inestimable help to the Army which is losing ground at this time.'

'I'll go and dip the tanks, Sarge, and make sure they're full right up,' broke in the fitter in a helpful voice. He didn't want to be clobbered with the responsibility for the aircraft pulling out of the flight line.

A green Very light snaked into the sky from the control tower giving urgency to my deliberations. I must go. I struggled clumsily with the straps of my parachute and safety harness. Weeky's machine-guns racketed as he fired a test burst into the ground beside the aircraft. The fitter darted out from under the wing shouting wildly. Weeky should have checked that there was no one around before firing.

The fitter came white-faced round to the front of the aircraft and responded vehemently to my thumbs-up signal for clearance to start the port engine. The fuel gauge had been forgotten.

I pressed the starter button and the propeller began to turn over sluggishly, but although the fuel was switched on, it showed no tendency to fire. After several seconds, I gave it a rest and the fitter darted in to turn up the rheostat on the starter trolley that was plugged into the aircraft.

We went through the thumbs-up routine again and I had another try. There was no life in the engine and I re-checked the positions of the fuel cocks and the ignition switches.

The fitter indicated that I should try the starboard engine. There didn't seem much point if the port wouldn't start, but in my bemused mental condition I was allowing decisions to be made for me. It fired readily enough with spurts of blue smoke from the exhaust stacks, and the fitter indicated that he was going under the nacelle to try priming the port engine again.

An aircraft pulled alongside and stopped. It was Maxie who was leading the raid. His microphone mask was swinging free and his face seemed angry as he stared at me out of the side window of the cockpit. I stared back. He raised an arm and pointed in an exaggerated fashion at his watch, mouthing words at me. I waved a deprecatory hand and looked away.

With a roar of engines he moved on, projecting a duststorm around the aircraft that were following and rocking my aircraft with his slipstream.

'What's up with him?' said Weeky. 'Niggled 'cos he thinks we're not going with him?' But I was repeating the starting routine on the port engine. It seemed lifeless. Then I tried flicking the ignition switches off and on and it kicked, backfired sending a spurt of flame from the intake, and struggled into uncertain life. The groundcrew scampered around, pulled the starter trolley clear and dragged the chocks from under the wheels. The last of the squadron aircraft were already leaving the dispersal area. I was supposed to be number two to Maxie, but I would have to sort that out once we were airborne.

He was already on the runway and sending twin columns of dust aft as he opened up the engines. The aircraft trundled forward, the tail lifting with gathering speed and gradually the machine and the noise narrowed into the distance. It seemed to be almost at the far end of the runway before the heavily-laden bomber lifted slowly and daylight appeared between the wheels and the ground.

The other three followed at short intervals, and I lined up when the last of them was half-way along the strip. There had been a gap of only ten days since I last flew, but I felt strangely awkward.

I checked around the cockpit for the setting of the elevator and rudder trims, the flaps, mixture control and directional gyro, the hydraulic selector, and yet again, the fuel cocks. I opened up to half power on the brakes, the instrument panel dancing with the vibration, but all the readings were good except that wretched fuel gauge which stood out like a sore thumb, with its pointer on the zero stop. The brakes released with a hiss of escaping air and the machine rolled forward. Well, here we go. Committed.

There was something of a crosswind and I overcorrected clumsily with the rudderbar causing the aircraft to snake. The needle was creeping reluctantly around the face of the airspeed indicator. Acceleration seemed abnormally slow and the details of the little stone wall at the far end were becoming rapidly clearer. I felt unusually tense. For some reason, by the time the speed reached the lift-off value of 90 mph my heart was pounding. I snatched on the control column and we made an awkward lurch into the air. The aircraft jiggled in the turbulence and I steadied it with the ailerons before reaching down for the undercarriage lever. The other aircraft were turning in a long sweep over Valletta, closing on the leader.

I tried to turn inside to overhaul them but failed to check the nose-drop and we lost some precious height. It was unnerving what an effect such a short lay-off had had, but with a total flying time of less than 200 hours in the log book, in a more rational mood I would have realised that this was not really surprising. The leader was still turning across the Island towards the south coast and the plan form of his wings was clear against the sky above the rocky terrain.

As we closed with him, it was necessary to dive underneath to come up on his starboard side. Number four was already there and he turned away to let me in. Maxie was sweeping down towards the sea as I manoeuvred into position. The situation was becoming familiar. My pulse-rate had slowed down now but the sweat on my face and neck felt cold and sticky.

We flew low and swift over the sea for a time, the five aircraft in the vic making slow sensuous movements in relation to each other on the slightly turbulent air. Eventually, Maxie eased up to around 100 ft and we took this as a sign to relax and as a man opened out the formation to about two spans.

This was the familiar lull before the storm, and I found part of my mind wandering. Today was Sunday. What a way to spend the Sabbath! During our drive to the airfield that morning, the air had been filled with the clanging of innumerable church bells as the locals made their way slowly to the places of worship, the younger women wearing mantillas of black lace while the elders carried rather than wore the *faldettas*, the large-framed hoods of black cotton material under which the wizened faces were barely visible. They didn't look up as the military bus rattled by, its horn blaring; they had seen it all before.

Today was Sunday, and on Tuesday I had a meeting with Magda. For me it was an urgent meeting, but it seemed so far away. Perhaps impossibly far away. I felt I must get through this day. There was something to look forward to now.

The intercom hissed into action. It was Benny's voice.

'I've just taken a drift, Skipperrr. There's aboot seven ta starboard. According to ma reckoning, we're going ta mak a landfall aboot five miles ta the west of the target.'

'OK, Benny,' I acknowledged. There was little I could do about it. Weeky was strangely silent this morning I thought.

My mind was wandering off into a reverie again when I realised that we were descending gently towards the sea and the other aircraft were beginning to close up.

'How far to the target area now do you reckon, Benny?' I asked, holding the intercom switch over with my thumb.

'Aboot fifty miles I should say. Seventeen minutes.'

Maxie was closing up a bit early, but perhaps it was just as well. The air was becoming jaggedly turbulent now and one was having to work hard to hold an accurate station. The visibility had gone down to about two miles in the last half hour and the sky had a yellowy tinge. We were probably running into the Gregale, a hot southerly wind that blew straight off the desert.

The turbulence was becoming most marked now, more violent than I had known it so close to the sea, and the other aircraft were rocking and bucketing about in untidy disarray.

'I reckon this is the Gregale,' said Benny, voicing my thoughts. 'The wind was westerly when we left; I hope the leader's taken it into account.'

I didn't answer; my hands were too busily engaged wrestling with the controls to go for the intercom switch.

The run-in seemed inordinately long, certainly more than the seventeen minutes that Benny had suggested. I was sweating a lot and beginning to tire. Then I realised that the leader was coming towards me. He rolled into a steep turn to starboard without gaining height. I struggled to keep inside. I daren't slip below him into the proper position for we were too close to the sea. Nor could I take my eyes off the leader; I didn't know why we were turning. We were slipping in behind him. His slipstream was twisting us towards him. I forced the ailerons hard over and flinched as our port wingtip missed his tailplane by the narrowest of margins.

He rolled out of the turn abruptly. We slid clear and I regained proper control of the aircraft. Beyond him I could see the low outline of the African coast. There were no distinctive silhouettes of large buildings or wharves.

'According ta me, he's turned the wrong way,' said Benny deliberately. I didn't reply. Certainly it was a bad landfall, for Tripoli was nowhere in sight and he was going to have some difficulty finding it in this visibility. At one stage, the leader swerved towards the coast and then turned away again.

'Where the bloody hell is the mun going?' demanded Benny.

'Away from Tripoli I hope!' said Weeky, speaking for the first time.

We had been running west for about five minutes when the leader started coming round in a starboard turn again. This time he did gain a little height, and although I was having to handle the aircraft roughly in the conditions, at least I was able to hold approximately the correct station slightly below him and at about one span out. I daren't look away and over my shoulder to see how the number four man was doing. He was really getting the dirty end of the stick.

'Is the silly bugger turning back or going to look for Tripoli in the other direction?' asked Weeky in some alarm.

'They'll certainly know we're coming now, that's for sure,' said Benny grimly.

The turn continued until he rolled out parallel to the coast again but now going in an easterly direction. This was really going to be something.

I seemed to have been fighting with the aircraft for a long time, and the faint hope was dawning in my mind that perhaps we wouldn't find the target in these conditions and could justifiably turn for home.

But almost immediately, the hope was stillborn. A startling series of flashes dead ahead sparkled in the yellow haze. Black puffs materialised in our path and rushed towards us accompanied by a staccato 'rack, rack, rack'. The sky in front seemed to be miraculously filled with flashes. Then I saw the silhouettes of cranes and a concrete wall. We were running straight into the mole at the western end of the harbour. It was too late for evasive action. In any case, we were already being thrown about violently by the natural turbulence. The entire wall seemed crowded with firing guns. To the right I was conscious of the loom of a large ship, and of buildings beyond decorated with scarlet flashes.

In headlong confusion we shot over and between the line of

cranes. We were now in the harbour itself and the leader went into a turn towards the town. How the hell could we get on to anything from this angle? The firing was coming at us from all directions. An Arab dhow was caught in its slow passage and the sea foamed around it. I hung on to the leader as we headed in towards the shore batteries. It was too late to avoid the conflict. Maxie rolled violently to the left to turn away. Caught out by the suddenness of his manoeuvre I overshot, then wrenched it around in a tight turn to port.

We seemed to hang there with our belly exposed to the on-slaught. I couldn't get the thing round fast enough. We were running on to the far wall of the harbour. There were two ships moored line astern. I tried to roll out and take a line on them but it was too late. We shot past and over the wall. I saw Maxie racing away into the gloom still turning to port and anxiously I followed.

Mercifully, the visibility was worse here and we were soon enveloped in the deep yellow haze. I had lost sight of Maxie's aircraft and was still in a turn to the left when another Blenheim shot across my nose like a projectile. I glanced down at the gyro; we were turning through west. Let's get to hell out of here. I cranked the ailerons hard over the opposite way and brought her round onto a northerly heading.

'What a bloody cock-up!' shouted Weeky.

'Give me a course to steer, Benny,' I said somewhat shakily.

'Eh. Um. Stand by,' he muttered. His wits were still in Tripoli Harbour.

The visibility improved as we ran north, and eventually we saw two aircraft flying roughly in the same direction. We overhauled them slowly and saw that they were the leader and Bob Turner's aircraft.

'Any sign of the others, Weeky?' asked the navigator.

'Nope! Not a thing; but what do you expect?'

Back in the dispersal, I switched off and climbed wearily out through the roof hatch. I sat there for a moment studying the southern sky for a sign of the others, but there was nothing. That was Dave Patchet and Tim Cummings and their crews missing, and for what!

The top brass were waiting for us as we entered the crew-room, and the Group Captain listened hardfaced to the tale of no success.

Maxie twisted the facts a bit. He didn't mention hitting the coast west of the harbour and turning the wrong way initially, but said that due to the poor visibility we couldn't see a line on what ships there were until it was too late.

Under interrogation, none of us seemed to agree as to how many vessels had been there, but it certainly wasn't full of ships as the reconnaissance had suggested.

'What I don't understand,' said the Group Captain, looking steadily at the unfortunate Maxie, 'is why, having got out, you didn't go back in on a better line and have another go.'

'Well, Sir,' stammered the sergeant, 'the defences were fully alerted by that time and the opposition was murderous.'

'I see,' said the SASO quietly, and picking up his gold-braided hat he walked out of the room.

Maxie turned to the Wing Commander. 'It couldn't be helped, Sir,' he said in a voice of appeal. 'The vis and the turbulence were shocking!'

'Yes,' said the CO. 'The Gregale is forecast to reach here by the evening. There's no point in trying again tomorrow under those conditions so you can stand down until Tuesday morning.'

The reprieve seemed nothing more than a sighing space. His mind was already made up. We would be going back the day after tomorrow.

CHAPTER TWENTY

Target – Tripoli

TRAVELLING BACK to our quarters at the southern tip of the Island in the dilapidated old bus, there was an air of brittle gaiety, and it was generally agreed that we should have a wild night on the town; except for me. I felt I just couldn't make it. I felt physically weak and my legs were shaky. I resisted their blandishments and opted for an early night.

'Eat, drink and be merry! For tomorrow we die!' cried Bob.

'Make it Tuesday,' I said dully.

The following day, the wind blew strongly from the south, and the sea surged and frothed against the rocks at Delimara Point at the far side of the bay. Some of the chaps had returned noisily in the small hours of the morning but others were still missing. I spent most of the day in writing letters and reading, though at lunchtime I did join the others in the bar, but found it difficult to get carried away in the general mood. I couldn't get Magda out of my mind or think of our forthcoming meeting without a flurry of excitement. But before that there was the little matter of the sortie in the morning to be dealt with.

I slept badly that night, and lay, for many hours it seemed, staring up into the darkness. I felt a premonition closing in on me when I thought of the job we had to do in the morning. The squadron now consisted of three crews, the lowest ebb it had reached so far. For three Blenheims to be sent back into that holocaust was a merciless act. Undoubtedly it had been decided at command level that what was left of the squadron was hardly worth saving, and tomorrow, knowing the strength of the opposition, must be its swan song.

It was unthinkable that we could come out of it unscathed, and impractical that any further sorties could be attempted with less than three aircraft. The big question was, which of us, in the morning, would be coming face-to-face with our Maker? I felt dully that finally my luck had run out; and it had been luck. However skilful the pilot, in conditions such as we were encountering one needed a charmed life to get through. We had done well to get into the last three, now I felt resigned to the fact that our luck, at last, was going to leave us. A feeling of deep melancholy took possession of me and my mind, probably in unconscious defence, wandered idly around until I drifted into sleep.

All too soon it was daylight, and some of the others were moving around the hut; there was none of the usual banter. They went about their rituals of preparing themselves for another day without enthusiasm and in silence. Not a word was spoken throughout the journey in the rickety old bus up to the airfield, and on arrival we filed silently into the crew-room.

One immediately got the feeling that something was going on behind the scenes. The Adjutant dived into the CO's office and they both reappeared putting on their hats. The Wing Commander seemed pleased about something. He nodded to us almost cheerfully and bid us good morning. We replied in unison as they disappeared along a corridor together.

Perhaps it was all off! A hope began to glimmer in our minds, then was quickly extinguished by the arrival of the briefing officer. He dumped a collection of rolled maps on the table, sucked air slowly through his teeth and said in a toneless voice, 'Well, gentlemen, you know what we have to do today. The target is Tripoli again. The Gregale has blown itself out and it should be easier for you to find what you are looking for.' He gave Maxie a tired smile and then turned his attention to me. 'You will be leading this sortie, Sergeant Maxwell will be your number two and Sergeant Turner will be in the number three position. I suggest that you make your attack directly from the sea to gain maximum surprise effect.' He then went into details.

Benny was clearly very nervous as he fumbled with his protractor and parallel rules, and I helped him in a voice that I tried to make sound reassuring. Bob Turner watched standing with his hands deep in his pockets, a characteristic attitude. Although twenty years old like most of us, he looked even younger with his fresh-complexioned face set in an almost permanent grin, and a lock of dark hair that fell over one eye, completing the boyish effect.

He was grinning now. 'Let's get it right first time today, eh?'

he said to Benny. 'Let's sneak up on 'em and frighten them out of their wits.'

'I knaw one who's ganna be frightened out of his wits,' murmured Benny as he checked the course out for the third time.

A group was coming along the corridor. The first to enter was the Air Officer Commanding, an Air Vice Marshal. We had seen him only once before when he had given us a lecture on morale outside the crew-room during an air-raid. Jerry elected to bomb the airfield on that occasion and we finished up face down in the dust, the A.O.C. included.

The Adjutant put on his official voice: 'Gentlemen! Your attention, please!'

The Air Vice Marshal began to speak in a quiet, almost casual delivery.

'I am sure you will be pleased to know,' he said, 'that your relief squadron arrived in Gibraltar last evening.' The news brought forth a murmur of surprise. 'When you return from this trip,' he went on, 'you will be relieved of any further operational duties on the Island.' 'Hooray!' whispered Weeky in my ear sarcastically. 'You have done a great job here,' the A.O.C. continued, 'working very hard under particularly difficult circumstances, and I greatly appreciate it. I have instructed your commanding officer to make arrangements for your early departure for the UK. Now please don't let me distract you from your preparations. Good luck with the trip.' He left in a flurry of attending officers.

His 'thank-you' speech seemed a bit premature, but ominously final. He was thanking us for what we had done as if we had come to the end. It seemed to me tactless to the point of indifference.

As Bob Turner said with a grin as we bumped our way out to the dispersal in the back of a 3-ton truck, 'He had to get in his stirring address this morning in case there's no one to thank by lunchtime.'

'Do you mind!' complained Weeky. Bob's sense of humour was a bit too much for him. Me, I wasn't feeling anything at all.

I went through the pre-departure checks and the engine starting procedure with a slow deliberation. I had that cold, clear feeling now that had beset me once or twice before when, faced with the conviction that the end was coming, I determined to make my presence felt. It was a viciousness born of anger.

I took off and went into a climbing turn through the calm blue sky, throttling back to let the others catch up. The untidy patch-work of houses and streets took on a dull gold look in the morning sunlight. The Island appeared to be dozing peacefully.

The towers and roofs of Rabat and Mdina stood out clearly on their shoulder of high ground, and then beyond I saw the ugly bulk of the military hospital at Imtarfa. With a twinge I sought out the wing where I had been incarcerated. On the end was the administrative block, still a heap of rubble, and there quite clearly, was the terrace where Magda had stood beside me. She wouldn't be there in all probability. She had no doubt spent the night at home before her day off today. In five hours we were due to meet, but right now I was on my way to North Africa. Let's get it over with! I eased the nose down and skimmed over the top of the cliffs at Dingli and flew past the rocky island of Philfla that was used for practice bombing. The dark shapes of Maxie's and Bob's aircraft were swimming close beside me. The air was smooth and the engines droned on contentedly. Everything was under control.

During the journey south, Benny worked slowly and deliber-ately, taking a drift every quarter of an hour or so, and passing me tiny corrections to the course. He was determined that we should run straight in to the target. After some time, he looked round the corner from his nose position and up at me as he said, 'We're aboot fifty miles oot now, Skipper.' His eyes were full of concern.

I nodded and eased the aircraft down towards the sea. The others followed obediently. The sea was very calm but there was just enough popple on it to help in judging the height. I edged as low as I dared until I thought we were about ten feet up and the sea was flashing by underneath like a pattern of glass rods.

Weeky's microphone hissed into life, 'We're a bit low, Skip,' he warned; 'I can see our slipstreams beating on the water.'

'We're just about right then,' I replied. 'We don't want to give them too much warning, now do we?'

'Too bloody right!'

The visibility must have been about thirty miles, for eight minutes later a dark smudge of smoke directly ahead marked the town of Tripoli for us. After the first sighting, the run-in seemed interminable as it always did. By the time the gantries of some of the cranes were visible, and the superstructures of several ships could be seen above the harbour wall, I felt convinced that we too must be seen and I could not understand why they held their fire.

The answer came soon enough. A column of water erupting dead ahead. Anonymous and silent, it subsided in a shower of glistening water droplets as we shot past. The time had come to confuse the enemy. I waggled my wings to indicate that the formation should be opened out for evasive action.

If the run-in had started fairly gently, the defences certainly warmed to their task in quick time. In the sunlight, the gun flashes were not so evident as they had been in the yellow gloom on the previous occasion, but ugly puffs of black smoke told us that something was being sent on its way. They had got the range quickly, and the sea was being blown up in front of us and then all around us.

I began to work at the controls like a man possessed, hauling the nose up in the air while laying on right rudder and aileron so that the aircraft skidded and juddered over the top then slid swiftly down to the sea again. A mass of water seemed to blow up in my face. The aircraft swung as it hit the port wing, but other spouts erupting in our path lent further urgency.

I could see the bulk of a large ship lying beam-on, but I couldn't tell whether it was against the harbour wall or in the middle. Two others were lying stern-on against the western mole. I decided to go for the big one in the middle.

There were no cranes on the outer wall which was now speeding towards us, but guns were being fired all along it. Light anti-aircraft and multiple pom-pom guns were pumping a mass of shells in our direction. The sea was breaking into holes, and dotted lines of bullets raked rapidly to and fro across our path.

Benny opened up with his front guns and I grabbed the gun button on the control column. The one Browning 303 in the wing of the Blenheim fired slightly high, so I gave it bursts as we dived towards the harbour wall.

I found myself flying past the overlapping harbour entrance and straight for a gun position on the wall. Repetitive flashes showed that it was certainly in action and both Benny and I gave it long rattling bursts. I saw the guncrew frantically trying to swing it round as we shot over the top.

The ship was anchored in mid-harbour. It stood out like a huge black iceberg. Fire crackers appeared to be darting along the super-structure. I was surprised to see Bob Turner's aircraft appear from under my port wing and swerve across in front of me. His slip-stream pitched us towards the sea. I hauled on the control column and felt the machine shudder. Bob swung to port again. He was going for the same ship. A dotted line of cannon shells were rattling past our nose. I wondered where they were coming from. The ship was right above us now. I jabbed the bomb button and hauled up in a climbing turn to miss the funnel. Bob Turner swung across my nose in a steep turn. I saw him in plan form, large and in detail.

I felt sure he was going to hit the aft derrick. He did. With appal-ling finality the wing sheared off and fell rotating like a sycamore leaf. Distracted for a second, I narrowly missed the bulk of the funnel. As I dived on the far side, out of the corner of my eye I was conscious of his aircraft corkscrewing rapidly around the remain-ing wing. Then came the impact and the vast eruption of smoke and water.

We were on the town now, and I held the aircraft down, skim-ming over the blurred castellated pattern of the roofs and spires. I was too low for the defences to get at me without hitting the buildings. I kept in a turn to the east, and as the development gave way to more open country, tracer and ack-ack puffs started to foul the sky again.

I squirmed and writhed the aircraft as the defences chased us off, staying just inside the coast. As the firing died away, I turned to-wards the sea again and in the turn glimpsed Maxie coming up fast behind me.

Weeky shouted, 'Bandits on the green quarter!' I remember crying out fervently, 'Christ no!'

I wound the aircraft in a turn to starboard to turn into the attack. Tracer scattered past the window like red raindrops. Then I glimpsed the belly of the fighter as it broke off. It was a bi-plane, an Italian CR 42.

'Red quarter!' shrieked Weeky, 'Red quarter! Two bastards coming in!'

I cranked the ailerons hard over in a turn to port and glimpsed over my shoulder Maxie trying to keep station. Good man! Protective formation, that was the thing. In this way, both air gunners could concentrate on the attackers. A continuous stabbing line of tracer raked our path. Weeky's guns were racketing viciously. I dived towards the sea and straightened out as the attack was broken off.

'Green quarter!' shouted Weeky, almost choking in his excitement. I wound the aircraft in a tight turn to starboard, the wingtip almost brushing the sea. 'Christ! They're coming in from both sides!' he called.

With frantic strength, I cranked the ailerons in the other direction. The important thing was to keep near the sea. If the fighters shot past they would probably go in, so it made them break off their attacks earlier. The staccato chatter of Weeky's guns coincided with a double line of tracer but it was wide of the port wing.

I glanced out of the side blister window in time to see the belly of the fighter as it broke off the attack. Weeky's tracer seemed to be curving straight into it. 'Ted Slater's had it!' Weeky shouted. This was double bad news. If they realised that one of the rear gunners were out, they might be encouraged to press home their attacks even closer.

'Where are they now?' I called.

'Red quarter high,' said Weeky. 'They look as if they're turning away! They bloody are! They're turning back!'

'I reckon you got that last one, Weeky,' I said. 'Bloody good shooting.'

'Yes, I reckon I did too,' he replied.

'Is Ted Slater in a bad way?' I asked.

'Oh no, he's not hurt. His turret packed up. It's stuck in the lower port side position. He couldn't get on to those starboard attacks at all.'

'Does it look as if they're coming back?' I asked Weeky anxiously.

'Nope. They've gone right out of sight now.'

I pulled the engine override levers out of the plus-9 position, and the engine note subsided, almost gratefully it seemed. We had been doing around 270 mph during the run-out, and the aircraft had been shaking as if it were about to fall apart.

Benny gave me a course for home and I turned gently on to a northerly heading but stayed close down to the sea.

'Maxie's falling back!' called Weeky. 'His starboard under-carriage leg is hanging down.'

'Yes, well, he's lost his hydraulics, hasn't he?' I suggested. Then, pulling the power back still further, 'Let me know when he starts catching up again.'

I had to reduce the speed progressively to 160 mph before he reclaimed the distance between us, and eventually we settled down to cruise together at 180.

My spirits rose as our distance from the African coast increased. The gloom of the previous twenty-four hours dissolved. At one stage I felt almost elated; then the mood changed swiftly when I remembered that we had left Bob Turner and his crew at the bottom of Tripoli Harbour.

Incredibly we were on our way back unscathed from our final trip. I had never dared to hope that things would end this way.

The glossy sea and unmarked sky seemed to have lost their menace, and with the sun through the cockpit window warm on my neck, I felt a glow of youthful optimism returning. It was as if a heavy yoke had been lifted from me and my life could move on again now after being held in suspension. My mind wandered back over the events of the past few weeks, and I remembered the faces and the voices of those who would never be heard or seen again. I looked out over the plain of that infinite ocean knowing that it concealed so many secrets and held so many unmarked graves. I found myself wondering somewhat morbidly what it must be like. I imagined aircraft that I had seen engulfed, trapped at some crazy angle on the ocean bed with weed already taking possession of the twisted metal, and fish perhaps, pausing to peer at the occupants who would be sitting, and waiting, for their inevitable disintegration. And the ever cheerful and boyish Bob Turner had just gone, barely an hour ago, to join them; what could it have been like in those final few seconds, knowing that control had been wrested from him, to be shown with sudden clarity the inevitability of his own death?

Benny's voice announcing that the Island was in sight brought me back to my senses. It was like waking from a nightmare. I had been reprieved, and with the prospect of seeing little Magda again, I found myself looking forward with pleasure.

Maxie peeled off as we approached the airfield and dived past the control tower to indicate with his dangling undercarriage leg that he had a problem.

He would have to carry out a belly landing, so I decided to get in first before the runway became blocked.

As we turned off the runway and on to the taxi track, I became conscious for the first time that all the dispersals were full of aircraft. The relief squadron had surely arrived.

We watched as Maxie made a very good job of his belly landing, the machine sliding along in its own dust cloud pursued by a motley collection of fire engines and ambulances, then slung our flying gear into the back of the dispersal truck and climbed aboard.

The noise of many voices raised in conversation met us even before we got to the crew-room, and we paused in the doorway at the unaccustomed sight of so many faces.

Quite a few of them were known to us and there were many pleasant reunions. They had landed less than an hour before, and we were struck by their cheerfulness and high morale. However when inquiries about other members of our squadron met with the inevitable reply, the mood began to change visibly. Slowly the message went home, and finally in total silence, one of them said, 'Do you mean to tell me that you and the other crew who have just belly-flopped out there are all that's left?' I nodded, 'Apart from Ivor Broom of course.'

There were murmurs of incredulity. In the silence that followed, I excused myself and led my crew to the de-briefing-room.

Weeky thought we had got the ship, and so did Ted Slater, when he finally arrived none the worse from having the hydraulic lines shot away from under his seat and then being dumped on the runway without the cushioning effect of wheels.

The Wing Commander seemed a changed man. He was delighted with everything we told him and congratulated us on the attack, and the way we had made the run-out and dealt with the fighter opposition. I had never seen him in such good spirits.

'Well,' he said finally, 'is your aircraft all right?'

'I think so, sir,' I replied, 'apart from a few small holes and a three-foot dent in the leading edge of the port wing where we hit some water thrown up by a big brick.'

'Good,' he said. 'Then you can take your aircraft in the morning, load on Sergeant Maxwell and his crew as passengers and head for Cairo.'

'Cairo?'

'Yep. There's no point in taking it to Gib. H.Q. Middle East can do with it, and they'll arrange for your passage around the horseshoe-route back home.'

The engineering officer had been listening, 'I can't get it serviceable by the morning, sir,' he said.

'Why not?' demanded the CO.

The man shuffled impatiently: 'We've got the eleven new aircraft to get out of ferry trim and into operational readiness.'

'They're stood-down tomorrow,' said the Wing Commander, impatience creeping into his voice. 'That gives you another twenty-four hours; so you have these chaps' aircraft on the line by O-eight-hundred hours in the morning or I'll want to know why!'

I was astonished at the new status we seemed to have acquired and mumbled my thanks. The Wing Commander looked embarrassed and then said, 'I want to see you and Sergeant Maxwell in my office.'

This seems more like it, I thought to myself as we followed him down the corridor.

His office was small and rather tattily furnished. He waved us to sit down, and seating himself behind a desk littered with copies of signals and standing orders, he removed his cap and smoothed back his hair before speaking.

'I want you chaps to know, and I want you to tell your crews, how much I have appreciated what you've done in this tour. I've had no illusions how you felt. You must have thought me a complete bastard, but believe me, the hardest thing is to have to give orders that you hate giving, and to be kept on the ground while you send others out to do your dirty work. I only hope that neither of you ever find yourself in my position.' He stood up walked slowly round the desk and offered his hand.

'Goodbye,' he said, and his voice was slightly husky. 'Good luck, and thank you for all you've done.' I was strangely moved as I shook his hand. I no longer felt expendable.

Back in the crew-room, all was confusion as kit was being sorted out and transport arrangements made to Marsa. The clock on the wall caught my eye; it was 1.40. I had to move!

I cornered Benny, 'Benny, I've got to nip down town. I'll see you later. OK?' But Weeky had overheard.

'Where are you off to then?'

'I've got to meet somebody.'

'You sly old sod. Have you got a date?'

'Yep. I'll see you later.'

'Hang on a minute!' he called. 'You can't just push off on our last night on the Island. Where will you be?'

'The WO's and Joe's Club,' I said, making for the door.

I knew it was a mistake to let him know that I was going to the Senior NCOs' Club in the Castille, but I couldn't very well ditch my crew on the last night. I should just have to tell Magda to take no notice of him if he started pulling her leg.

I hurried to the guardroom. I felt exalted, and my luck held, for a ration wagon was just leaving for the grain store at Floriana. I scrambled up into the back as it started off down the hill.

CHAPTER TWENTY-ONE

Goodbye to Malta

FOR SOME REASON, Jerry had failed to put in his usual lunchtime appearance and I got the impression that the locals were going about their business in a cheerful mood; or perhaps it was my own good humour that coloured my view.

The truck dropped me off near the granary and I made my way up the slope that led to the fine baroque structure of the Castille. I arrived with five minutes to spare and hurried inside to the cloakroom to freshen up. As the slow chime of a near-by clock announced that it was two in the afternoon, I took up my position at the top of the steps outside the massive doors, and waited with growing excitement.

The afternoon dances in the club were popular affairs and a continuous stream of servicemen came clattering up the stone steps, while the local girls arrived in pairs or groups usually in charge of an older chaperone, for although the average Maltese family were certainly not averse to their daughters marrying British Servicemen, their outlook was still quite Victorian. There was no hanky-panky allowed; 'marrying' was the operative word.

I found myself wondering if Magda would come alone. I certainly hoped so, but even if there were somebody else, I felt that we would still enjoy a feeling of intimacy together.

On several occasions my heart surged when I thought I saw her lovely young face in an approaching group, for most of the Maltese girls were small and dark and well-rounded. It must have appeared as if I was on the lookout for a partner, for some of them glanced sideways and giggled as they passed me.

By 2.15, I felt sure that having shown a reasonable restraint by not arriving too punctually, she would be appearing at any time, and I stood in the sunlight with warm expectation.

By half past two, the numbers arriving had thinned out markedly and I began to feel a twinge of anxiety. I couldn't possibly have missed her in my strategic position right beside the door. I was sure that I had said 2 o'clock, and I had been on parade spot on time. Any time now, surely, I must see her approaching.

By 2.45, I had to admit to myself that the prospects were dwindling and I found myself wondering what on earth could have happened. I was convinced at the hospital that she had meant what she said, and it gave me a pang when I remembered that brief but sweet encounter. If she didn't make it today, then there must be a good reason; but how would I get in touch with her? I didn't know where she lived, she wouldn't be at the hospital today, and in the morning – and the thought hit me with some surprise – I would be leaving the Island altogether. My mind sought around for ways and means of establishing contact. I could take a garry down to Lija; it was a small village and it shouldn't be difficult to contact her family. But in my mood of settling depression, the unpleasant thought was coming to me that perhaps they wouldn't be pleased to see me, and if she were there, perhaps I would find a change in her too.

My attention had been wandering as I turned over possible courses of action in my mind, but now it was attracted to a group of airmen who were about to cross the wide road that ran to the foot of the steps. There was something familiar about them. In the group were Weeky and Benny. They were too far away to have seen me yet. I slipped through the doors and into the cool dimness of the interior.

The massive bar was packed with servicemen, and I began to burrow my way towards the counter. It took me some time to get to the front rank and I was still trying to attract the attention of a harassed barman, when Weeky's voice hailed me. There were several men between us, but he leaned in front and shouted above the din, 'Where's this bird then?'

'What bird?'

'The one you had a date with.' He was grinning hugely.

'I never said I had a date with a bird,' I said doggedly.

'Oh come off it! You scampered away like a scalded cat.'

I tried again to catch the barman's eye, but Weeky persisted. 'Did she stand you up then?'

I was mouthing a foul word at him when the barman asked for my order.

Inevitably, I met up with the group as I manoeuvred my way out of the press of bodies, and came in for further ribbing from my air gunner, but Benny did his best to head him off.

There were four members of the relief squadron in the party and they were clearly envious that we were leaving in the morning. Understandably, Benny, Weeky, Maxie and Ted Slater along with Arthur Madden were in an exuberant mood, but my own feelings were very mixed. I found my attention wandering as I searched the room in the slender hope of seeing that dark and lovely face perhaps looking for me.

After a while, I put my drink surreptitiously on a window sill and slipped out into the corridor, making my way to the front of the building. The forecourt was bright with sunlight but bare of people. I stood there for some time with a growing feeling of loneliness. The chimes of a near-by clock echoed dully three times across the square. I couldn't hope that she would come now.

I turned and walked back into the building, making my way to the noisy and crowded bar. Benny had bought me a large Scotch. The smell of the stuff made me shudder, but I shot it straight back. I didn't feel like joining in the conversation for my mind was a turmoil of confused and conflicting thoughts, though it just was not possible to stay detached for long in such company.

The warming effect of the alcohol and the general atmosphere brought with them a slow resurgence of optimism. I couldn't get Magda out of my mind, but now I began to feel that the failure to keep our tryst must be due to circumstances beyond her control. Maybe her day off had been switched, or perhaps she had trouble at home. I knew, positively and instinctively that she had intended keeping the date, but the galling thing was that I had no immediate means of getting in touch with her.

It just wouldn't be possible to get on to the military hospital through the normal civilian telephone system, and if I did, I would probably get short shrift from the administrative staff there. However, there was a way. In the morning, at the airfield, before briefing I would ask the orderly-room sergeant who was a very decent guy, to make an 'official' call to Imtafa. I had to speak to her, if only for the briefest moment, to reassure her and to get an address where I could write to her.

Slowly I realised that I was the object of chaff from my comrades. 'Come back, Gillie, all is forgiven!' said Maxie with a grin. Having made my decision, I gave myself up to the holiday atmosphere of the celebration.

The party rapidly got out of control, and after the Senior NCOs' Club closed, we went on the town, an ever-increasing crowd of airmen that gathered speed as it romped from bar to bar. It brought back brilliant flashes of the first bender I had been on in the 'Gut', but so much had happened since then. Miraculously we had stayed the course. Tragically, most of the others had not. Joyously, we were leaving the Island tomorrow. But I still had to get in touch with the small dark-haired girl with the lovely and expressive eyes.

I remembered little of the tail-end of the evening, except that at one stage we were clip-clopping along a country road in a horse-drawn garry, and above me was a velvet night and a canopy of stars. I must have slept again, for the next thing I knew was being hustled up the path towards the barrack block.

I awoke as the first early light touched in the details around me. My head was throbbing and my body felt full of acid. Gentle night noises were still issuing from some of the other occupants. All the beds were inhabited now. Only two nights ago there had been but nine huddled together at one end of the hut. Now all the other barrack blocks were full as well, full of bright and noisy young men just out of their teens.

I eased myself painfully out of my bed and quietly told my crew and Maxie's that the day was about to begin. We went about the business of packing up our belongings in total silence, and crept out without rousing the other men. The farewells were best left unsaid.

On the drive up to the airfield, I thought that the Island had never looked so good. The sun was rising in a burnished sky and the sandstone of the walls and the houses had taken on a golden look. Things would get better from now on, and when the whole thing was over, I would come back of my own free will to a joyous meeting. During briefing, I was waiting my chance to slip away to the orderly room to try and make that call, when I became slowly conscious of the conversation of two airmen who were sitting on a table to one side of the room. They were sharing a copy of the

Malta Times. I came on to frequency as one was saying, 'When was that, then?'

'The night before last,' replied his companion.

'Lija, that's the village just the other side of Luqa, isn't it?'

His companion nodded and noisily turned over a page.

I walked across the room, a feeling of cold dread rising inside me.

'What was that about Lija?'

The airman looked up in surprise. 'It caught a packet, Sarge, the night before last. Five families completely wiped out.'

He turned the paper over again and handed it to me. Under the headlines was a rather blurred picture of a few people standing on the edge of a pile of rubble.

I stared at it, bitterness rising in my throat. Not wanting to believe it was possible, but slowly choking with the knowledge that it must be true. An inert pile of rubble with a handful of people just looking at it.

'You all right, Sarge?' I handed back the paper in silence and turned away.

Benny was calling me, 'Hey, Skipperrr! You ha' to toss up to see who's driving.' Maxie produced a coin and tossed it. I called and won. It didn't matter to me whether I was pilot or passenger.

In the truck that drove us out to dispersals, I stood apart and ignored the banter, my eyes stinging with tears. Someone suggested that I was too hungover to do the flying, but I just smirked and shrugged my shoulders. The aircraft was loaded in boisterous good spirits, kitbags being thrown up to a man on the wing who dropped them through the gunner's hatch. The weight of three extra crew and all the kit might not equal that of a bombload, but the tanks were full of fuel for the long haul to Cairo, and the aircraft was just about up to maximum weight.

The corporal fitter brought me the Form 700 to sign.

'It's nice for some people!' he said bitterly as I checked each column. 'How long you been here, Sarge?'

'About eight weeks.'

He sucked his teeth, 'We've been here eight bleedin' months and likely to be for another eight.'

'Must be nice to be aircrew!' was his parting shot as he walked away.

I went through the pre-flight checks automatically, ignoring the comments of the spare crew who were trying to get themselves comfortable in the confines of the bomb-well. I had never thought it would be like this, leaving Malta. Many times during the past few weeks I had prayed to be able to leave the Island and make a new start with brighter prospects. Now it was like the end; not the beginning.

The engines started readily enough, and I sat waiting dully for them to warm up before doing a power check. I hoped that there would not be a snag. I couldn't face staying on the Island now. Fortunately, they were OK on power check, and throttling back I signalled for chocks away and called the tower for taxi clearance.

We were the only aircraft moving on the airfield, and the machine felt heavy as it lumbered over the rough ground. The occupants had fallen silent in anticipation of the take-off. I felt anxious too as I turned the aircraft into wind and went through the pre-take-off drills.

The tower gave us clearance. I squirmed round in my seat and peered through the tunnel at the faces of the transit crew. 'OK?'

Maxie winked and put up a thumb.

I ran to almost full power before releasing the brakes and we began to move forward very slowly it seemed. Certainly, the acceleration was noticeably less than what we had got used to with smaller fuel loads of the past few weeks.

We were half-way along the runway before I got the tail up and the aircraft felt as if it were on the 'step'. We were bouncing sluggishly and the airspeed was rising with uncertain slowness. The boundary wall was coming to meet us. I watched with a feeling of detachment.

At a late stage I hauled back on the control column almost casually, the nose came up, the wheels bumped lightly a few more times, then came the transition into smooth flight.

I groped for the undercarriage lever, and then, without a conscious decision, instead of setting course straight for the southern tip of the Island, I rolled the aircraft slowly into a climbing turn to port.

We passed low over Safi Strip where the day's activities were just beginning, and circled the village of Luqa dominated by its huge church. The streets were sparsely peopled by moving dots and a few vehicles dragged themselves along leaving tails of dust behind them.

I rolled out on a westerly heading, still climbing slowly. To the right was the smoky area of the dockyard and Valleta. The village of Hamrun slid underneath, and up ahead I could see Balzan, and beyond it – Lija.

In my heart, I knew that it was the wrong thing to do, but the compulsion was too strong. I flew on until details of the village could be seen. It seemed undamaged and a wild surge of hope fluttered in my mind, but then, at the far end, I saw it, a carpet of rubble, looking pathetically small, like a molehill of tiny stones.

There were few people in the vicinity. None of them looked up as I circled. It seemed inert and almost deserted. I continued to circle, looking down past the shimmering disc of the propeller and beyond the wingtip which described a slow arc over the land-scape.

A feeling of hopelessness welled up within me and I rolled out of the turn with a suddenness that must have startled the others in the aircraft.

'What's up, Skipperrr?' asked Benny on the intercom. 'Ha' we got a snag?'

'No, it's all right, Benny. What was that first course again?'

'One-two-eight.'

It took us to the south-eastern tip of the Island, over the bay of Marsaxlokk in fact and it was possible to pick out the barrack blocks that we had left that morning and the mess building where our successors, all thirty-three of them, were enjoying a noisy breakfast no doubt, like we had when the squadron had been at full strength. I felt appalled for them.

The last bit of the Island was now slipping under the nose, Delimara Point like a knuckled yellow finger pointing out to sea. I didn't try to look back. Ahead, there was only the sea. There would be nearly a thousand miles of it to cross before we got to Cairo, and with each mile, the little sandstone island would slip farther and farther behind us, dwindling into the distance. I found myself hoping fervently that with the passing of time, its image would also fade into the dark recesses of my mind.

Epilogue

BENNY, my navigator, was killed shortly after we returned to England when acting as an instructor in a training aircraft.

Ron Weeks, after a period on rest, flew another tour of operations in Italy. He was commissioned and completed a distinguished career without a scratch apart from a scar on his nose which he attributed to one of my lesser landings! He is now a manager in a London bank.

Ivor Broom went on to win great honours as a brilliant operational pilot. He stayed in the Royal Air Force, his character and ability carrying him up to the rank of Air Marshal.

By the end of 107 Squadron's detachment in Malta, 26 enemy ships had been sunk totalling 100,000 tons. In the total concept of war, one might consider that such a result justified the drastic loss of young lives.

The squadron was reformed during the early part of 1942 at Great Massingham in Norfolk, and equipped with American Boston medium bombers. With this equipment, many low-level and high-level raids were carried out over northern Europe as part of the softening up process prior to the Normandy landings. In 1944 the new British medium bomber, the Mosquito, arrived and the squadron was thenceforward based on the Continent as part of the 2nd Tactical Air Force until the end of the war.

Wyndham Books are obtainable from many booksellers and newsagents. If you have any difficulty please send purchase price plus postage on the scale below to:

Wyndham Cash Sales,
PO Box 11,
Falmouth,
Cornwall.

OR

Star Book Service,
G.P.O. Box 29,
Douglas,
Isle of Man,
British Isles.

While every effort is made to keep prices low, it is sometimes necessary to increase prices at short notice. Wyndham Books reserve the right to show new retail prices on covers which may differ from those advertised in the text or elsewhere.

Postage and Packing Rate
U.K.
One book 22p plus 10p per copy for each additional book ordered to a maximum charge of 82p.

B.F.P.O. & Eire
One book 22p plus 10p per copy for the next 6 books, and thereafter 4p per book.

Overseas
One book 30p plus 10p per copy for each additional book.

These charges are subject to Post Office charge fluctuations